YOUR CHANGE
BLUEPRINT
HOW TO DESIGN & DELIVER
AN AI SUMMIT

MICHELLE MCQUAID & DR. DAVID COOPERRIDER

Your Change Blueprint: How to Design & Deliver An AI Summit

Authors: Michelle McQuaid and David Cooperrider

PO Box 230 Albert Park, VIC, 3206 Australia

ABN: 88094250503

www.michellemcquaid.com

Email: chelle@michellemcquaid.com

Design: Michelle Pirovich www.thesqueezebox.com.au

Typesetting: Michelle Pirovich www.thesqueezebox.com.au

Editing: Marian Black, Debbie Hindle, & Claudia Young

ISBN: 978-0-9872714-5-7

For the dreamers, the change makers and those of us willing to do whatever we can to make this world a better place. We hope this book helps to light a path forward to a future where we can individually and collectively flourish.

Contents

CHAPTER 1

In The Beginning …

"The flourishing enterprise isn't a destination.
It's a journey and it's a roadmap."
JULIE REITER, CLARKE SUMMIT

If Michelle hadn't seen it with her own eyes she would never have believed it was possible.

Her normally very serious, quiet and reserved – some might even say dour — chief financial officer was bouncing up and down on his chair, arm waving eagerly in the air like an excited child desperate for the teacher to call on him so that he could share his discovery. And he wasn't alone.

As Michelle turned to look around the Grand Hyatt ballroom where 400 of her company's most senior leaders had gathered alongside their clients, employees and business partners, she could see people's hands shooting up all around the room. There was suddenly a palpable sense of excitement, possibility and energy radiating across this group of usually staunchly pessimistic accountants.

What was happening?

As the brand director for PricewaterhouseCoopers, one of the world's largest accounting and professional services firms, Michelle had persuaded the leadership team to invest in an Appreciative Inquiry (AI) Summit to conduct their annual strategic planning session. Usually a closed-door affair just for the partners of the firm, with David's help she'd convinced them to open the doors and invite their whole system – clients, employees and partners — into a cooperative and systematic search to discover the best of what is, in order to dream of what might be, so that they could fuse their strengths together and design what should be, and ensure collective ownership and commitment to deploy what will be. It was a radically different approach from anything the firm had ever done before, and as the day of the AI Summit approached the leadership team's nerves had been fraught.

On Michelle's way to the Grand Hyatt that morning, she'd received several panicked telephone calls from leaders fearing she was about to embarrass them in front of their clients. Then she arrived to find a roomful of nervous employees wondering why on Earth their leaders would want to hear their ideas. This was not the way most meetings ran in their workplace. When she finally went backstage to prepare, she found David, who had flown in to help facilitate the event, sitting in the wings nervously jiggling his legs and telling her he just wanted to live quietly in the woods and write books.

And then they started. Within minutes, the dull old ballroom was transformed as people began moving to the edge of their chairs, drawn into unusually human conversations by the questions they were being prompted to ask each other. Job titles, stereotypes and preconceived ideas about each other dropped away as they started to see the incredible mix of strengths, hopes and experiences they each brought to their work. As they discovered that their worlds were more similar than different, within a matter of hours the deeply ingrained silos and "not my responsibility" mindsets that usually divided the firm started breaking down as people generously offered to share resources and provide support to realize opportunities that would help the organization be of better service to its clients and employees. By the end of the day even the most challenging cynics had become committed supporters of the process.

Twelve months later, for the first time in the history of the firm, an independent study found that they had finally managed to achieve brand differentiation from their competitors. In a market crowded with technical experts who promised to fix an organization's greatest fears, PricewaterhouseCoopers had become recognized as the people who helped organizations realize their greatest hopes.

What Led To This Moment?

As a passionate advocate of creating positive changes in living systems, by 2007 Michelle had spent more than a decade in large organizations around the world as a senior brand leader trying to encourage and enable people to live the organizational values. After partnering with sixty diverse leadership teams with varied challenges, cultures and resources, she noticed again and again how the deficit-based, mechanistic approaches that were frequently used in change processes could sometimes secure short-term compliance, but rarely ever resulted in a long-term commitment to the desired behaviors.

The problem was that as soon as leaders considered the problem "solved" and moved on, most people went back to behaving as they had before the change effort commenced. Of course, these observations were not unique to Michelle or to the organizations with whom she was working, but a reflection of the long-standing management misunderstanding that people were somehow like machines whose behavior could be controlled.

As Michelle desperately tried to figure out why her best efforts were failing, she stumbled across the emerging science of positive psychology – the evidence-based exploration of human flourishing — and enrolled in the Masters of Applied Positive Psychology program at the University of Pennsylvania. As she immersed herself in the literature, it dawned on her that by always looking for what wasn't working, relying on anxiety and fear as motivators, and manipulating people into action with extrinsic rewards and threats, that psychologically, neurologically, socially and systemically organizations had spent decades undermining their own change investments.

It wasn't until she sat in David's Positive Organizations class, however, that she came to understand:

- The potential power of inquiry over advocacy.

- The importance of generative images.

- How intrinsic motivation and commitment can be gained when every voice across a system is given the opportunity to be heard and to self-organize around a shared sense of purpose and hope.

It was as though having been brought up to believe that the Earth was flat, she'd just discovered it was actually round. Similarly, change in living systems wasn't mechanical or linear as she'd previously been taught, it was complex and adaptive and needed methodologies and interventions that harnessed this natural energy and ways of working.

David agreed to be Michelle's capstone supervisor, and months later we implemented the AI Summit. Despite all the studying she had done, Michelle found that she was still wholly unprepared for what unfolded. Although she'd previously witnessed highly engaging and energizing workshops and conferences in her organization, she had never seen hope, connection, wisdom, generosity or commitment created so quickly, for so many people, as she did during the AI Summit. It was a level of human and systemic flourishing that was unprecedented in the organization and she became committed to understanding how it could be replicated.

Can A Conversation Change Anything?

Around the time of the AI Summit, Michelle had the good fortune to sit down over dinner with David and Professor Martin Seligman, one of the founders of the field of positive psychology. Martin had been invited by Michelle's company to deliver a series of lectures for their clients to share his new PERMA theory of wellbeing, which proposed that in order for humans to flourish, we need:

P: The right balance of heartfelt positive emotions.

E: Opportunities to be engaged in what we're doing.

R: Positive relationships.

M: A sense of meaning and purpose.

A: The ability to accomplish what matters most to us.

Upon accepting, however, he pointed out that while his research specialized in the necessary conditions for individual flourishing, he didn't study group or systems flourishing. His suggestion was that David also be invited so that each could play to his strengths.

As they presented their duet of insights to hundreds of business leaders, David noted that in each of the examples he shared of a system flourishing after an AI Summit, he was also able to observe and track the remarkable rise in each of the dimensions of PERMA.

"As soon as people come together to accomplish 'doing good' out there – by concentrating and connecting their strengths in the service of building a better organization, or world – they begin to activate the PERMA mechanisms for their own and others' flourishing."

DAVID COOPERRIDER

David concluded that this mirror-flourishing effect happens when we actively engage in or witness acts that help others to flourish, our systems to flourish, and the world as a whole to flourish. This is because there is an intimacy of relations between entities to the point where there is no outside and inside, only the creative unfolding on an entire field of connections.

As David, Martin and Michelle pondered these possible connections and what it might mean for interventions to improve individual and systemic flourishing, they first heard the calling for this book, which started as Michelle's doctoral thesis. Thus, using a grounded theory research approach, this book explores the question: *How do AI Summits create a positive disruption that supports systemic flourishing?*

What Enables Systemic Flourishing?

Researchers define a flourishing state as the optimal ranges of functioning associated with high levels of wellbeing and/or vigorous growth that may manifest itself in a variety of ways, including becoming more virtuous, creative, resourceful, resilient, and highly effective. Or like us, you might prefer Professor Felicia Huppert's simpler definition of a flourishing state as: "The combination of feeling good and functioning effectively."

It is important to be clear that flourishing is not a static state but an emergent property of change that enables vitality to be sustained. Just as our individual wellbeing and performance experiences a steady decline when we fail to prioritize and invest in consistent daily actions to maintain our physical, mental and social health, a system needs to keep identifying, organizing and elevating its strengths in an ongoing set of interactions and narratives that help to maintain its energy, and perceive and enhance its full potential.

It's also worth noting, however, that for the last three centuries this is not how we have generally approached systemic flourishing. In a world that often appears chaotic, our hunger for certainty has led us to eagerly embrace the research of Sir Isaac Newton and generally prioritize reason and the search for cause and effect at all costs. As a result, too often we have come to see our world and the systems within it as machines in which every piece knows its place, where individual components can be figured out and controlled, and where numbers hold the answers to all questions. A rational, ordered, predictable world that flourishes when a system runs like clockwork and avoids wearing itself out.

Except that researchers have discovered that we can't unwind or rewind where we are by breaking down the parts of a system that aren't working, try to fix them, and then expect these efforts to make the broken system whole again. Instead, we need to understand that living systems – like organizations or communities — are not closed machines at risk of entropy when their energy is not conserved. Living systems are open, complex and adaptive because they participate in a continuous exchange of energy with their environment by self-organizing into networks of relationships that allow them to change, grow and emerge more resilient over time. Thus, it turns out that living systems flourish as a result of emergence, not through reductionist thinking or behaviors.

For example, Nobel Prize winner Ilya Prigogine found that living systems of any kind are guided by simple rules that allow them to engage in complex behavior as they continuously fluctuate between equilibrium, near equilibrium, and far equilibrium. Rather than predicting the death of a system, disruptions or "bifurcation points" (as he named them) cause the system to either fall apart into a more or less fragmented state or reorganize into a more complex adaptive state.

As a result, Margaret Wheatley, author of the widely acclaimed *Leadership and the New Science,* proposes that living systems flourish when they are engaged in a dance of chaos and order that fluctuates between the states of change and stability. In order to successfully participate in this dance, she suggests that we need to:

- Become more open and curious so that we can learn to live with instability, chaos, change, and surprise that are healthy features of system growth and to let go of the myths that prediction and control are possible.

- Practice seeing the web of interconnections that weave living systems together and accept that nothing exists independently of its relationships.

- Embrace life's dependence on participation and its hunger for the need to self-determine.

- Facilitate processes that allow us to connect to new information, create meaning, and support self-organization.

- Improve our ability to listen, converse, and respect one another's uniqueness because these skills are essential for the strong relationships on which any living system depends.

Looking at this list, it seems reasonable to ask that when it comes to an organization's ability to flourish: Which is the most important influence on behavior, the system or the individual?

"There are no either/ors. There is no need to decide between two things, pretending they are separate. What is critical is the relationship created between two or more elements. Systems influence individuals, and individuals call forth systems. It is the relationship that evokes the present reality."

MARGARET WHEATLEY

Professor Kim Cameron — one of the founders of the field of positive organizational scholarship — and his colleagues echo this observation, and in 2001 established the field of positive organizational scholarship to focus attention on the generative dynamics in organizations that lead to the development of human strength, foster resiliency in employees, enable healing and restoration, and cultivate extraordinary individual and organizational performance. Likewise, Dr. Michael Cavanagh, a coaching and clinical psychologist at the University of Sydney, and his colleagues have been exploring the implications of complex adaptive systems to inform future coaching practices. And Dr. Peggy Kern — one of the founders of systems informed by positive psychology — and her colleagues have also subscribed to this symbiotic relationship of individual and systemic flourishing and have established the new research field of "systems informed positive psychology" to explore these dynamics.

This growing body of research has led researchers to conclude that for a system to flourish it must:

- Encourage and enable caring for the wellbeing of individuals whether they are employees, customers, suppliers, or external business partners.

- Synergistically generate economic, societal, and environmental value through engaged teams that operate in a culture of effectiveness and integrity.

- Be resilient and able to thrive in a complex and volatile world.

Clearly researchers in the fields of positive psychology, positive organizational scholarship and complexity science have uncovered a wealth of intriguing insights and practices to enable individual, team, organizational and systemic flourishing, but how might an AI Summit trigger any of these mechanisms?

Why Might AI Summits Support Systemic Flourishing?

Originally designed as an action research methodology, since its inception in 1985 at the Weatherhead School of Management at Case Western Reserve University in Ohio, appreciative inquiry has been taught to hundreds of organizations and thousands of people around the world. While it is a non-prescriptive discipline in which experimentation and innovation are encouraged, it has evolved into a philosophy and methodology for creating strengths-led changes. In the late 1990s, a 4-D cycle emerged to guide interventions and has subsequently been taught as the foundation of appreciative inquiry approaches.

Focused on a strategically selected affirmative topic, the 4-D cycle unfolds as follows:

- **Discovery** – The strengths of the system are uncovered by asking stakeholders and "best-in-class" benchmark examples appreciative questions about the "best of what is and what has been". These extensive, purposefully affirmative and generative conversations are designed to enhance people's knowledge and collective wisdom across the system and enable the mapping of its positive core of strengths to build upon.

- **Dream** – The positive core is amplified and the system's purpose elevated by asking generative questions that surface people's shared hopes from across the system as they anticipate what positive progress, achievements, breakthroughs and end results could look like at some pivotal point in the future. Big, bold, creative images of the future are explored through an energizing alignment of "what might be" to find not just common ground, but higher ground and generative images that unite people across the system.

- **Design** – The system moves from dialogue to action as stakeholders brainstorm, prioritize and build pathways toward their shared future around crucial change levers in the system, such as strategies, structures, culture, policies, processes, partnerships and offerings. As a result, new collaborations emerge across the system as knowledge, networks and resources are generously shared to realize the collective purpose and "what should be."

- **Deploy/Destiny** – People across the system are empowered to self-organize and mobilize the pathways they have designed to realize "what will be" for the system's future. Small-group initiatives are agreed upon and supported by teams of volunteers who self-organize to ensure the momentum is sustained and the desired results achieved.

To guide effective applications of the 4-D cycle, David and his colleague, Diana Whitney, later identified five core principles of appreciative inquiry, which are now consistently taught to practitioners. They include:

- **The constructionist principle** – This principle reminds us that reality as we know it is a subjective, rather than an objective state. We don't describe the world as we see it, but create distinctions that shape the way we think, feel and act, and thus determine our future. Practically, this means that change is created by the words we use, the conversations we share and the knowledge that we generate through our social interactions.

This is why AI Summits create spaces for people across a system to engage in a conversation where every voice can be heard and everyone is invited to shape shared generative images of the future.

- **The simultaneity principle** – This principle states that every action we take is preceded by a question. This means that the moment inquiry begins, change starts to occur. Therapists have long recognized this pattern and have noted the profound ability of a question to spark and direct our attention, perception, hope, energy, and effort toward growth and action. This is why AI Summits are guided by a series of questions designed to ignite inquiry in a direction that builds confidence, evokes hope and creates generative possibilities for positive system growth.

- **The poetic principle** – This principle points out that living systems are more like an open book than a machine, and thus contain endless sources of learning, inspiration, and interpretation. What is focused on in these stories – employee turnover or employee loyalty, lost baggage or exceptional arrival experiences, lack of diversity or exceptional inclusivity – is up to each of us and fatally shapes what follows. For example, questions about customer complaints elicit stories of how customers have been let down and focuses our efforts on fixing these problems. Whereas, questions about delighted customers uncover stories of how customers have been well served and concentrates our efforts on building on these successes. In either case, like the words chosen by a poet to evoke sentiments and understanding, the choice of words to guide a system reverberates through the stories it tells and the actions that are taken. This is why AI Summits are carefully anchored at the outset to an affirmative topic of inquiry and generative metaphors for organizing that can move a system toward the highest ideals and values of its stakeholders.

- **The anticipatory principle** – Given the complex, dynamic and therefore uncertain nature of any human system, this principle reminds us that it is imagined images of the future that guide our present-day actions. For example, fear-based images – like the Wall Street crash – can incite widespread panic. While, hope-based images – like Martin Luther King's dream of respect, equality, and justice for all in America – can mobilize us to surpass all prior achievements. Often found within the stories people tell about the system, images of the future have been found to advance us and move us forward. This is why AI Summits try to disrupt images of the status quo and stretch the system's collective imagination toward vivid, hope-fueled, generative images of its future potential.

- **The positive principle** – This principle points out that social systemic change requires large amounts of positive affect – hope, excitement and joy — and social bonding if momentum is to be sustained. By asking positive, generative questions that allow the strengths of a system to be discovered and built upon, people's enthusiasm, motivation and commitment to change can be elicited. Just as plants grow toward the light, this heliotropic effect means that social systems naturally evolve toward the prevailing affirmative image. This is why AI Summits continuously seek to unearth generative, life-giving opportunities for growth and intentionally look for ways to nourish, energize and inspire people to self-organize toward realizing the true, the good, and the possible.

To date, researchers have identified eight known applications of these appreciative inquiry practices, including:

- Whole-System 4-D Dialogues, which can take place over multiple locations and an extended period of time.

- Mass-Mobilized Inquiries that gather hundreds or thousands of interviews.

- Core Group Inquiries where a small group of people select a topic and conduct interviews.

- Positive Change Networks where members of an organization are trained in appreciative inquiry and given the resources to initiate projects.

- Positive Change Consortiums where multiple organizations collaboratively engage in the 4-D cycle.

- AI Learning Teams where a small group of people with a specific project engage in the 4-D process.

- Progressive AI Meetings during which an organization, small group or team goes through the 4-D cycle over the course of multiple meetings.

- The AI Summit that brings a whole system of 100 to 1,000 or more internal and external stakeholders together to participate simultaneously in the 4-D cycle.

First proposed by David and later developed by his colleagues around the world, an AI Summit is a large group-planning, designing, and implementation meeting whose function is to discover what gives "life" to a living system when it is at its most effective, alive, and capable in economic, ecological, and human terms.

Underpinned by the social constructionist premise that human systems move in the direction of what they most deeply, rigorously and persistently ask questions about, and by the strengths-management philosophy that people learn little about excellence by studying failure, an AI Summit is a generative process that unites a whole system in a macro-management approach. By enabling surprising configurations and connections of people's hopes and strengths, AI Summits ignite self-organization to deliver agreed actions with speed, dexterity and collaboration rarely seen in most systems.

At first glance, it's impossible to appreciate the power this simple approach can have until you sit in a room and watch it unfold. For example, the level of positive energy, trust, hope, excitement, commitment and accountability an AI Summit builds has enabled:

- The growth of the United Nations Global Compact for sustainability from 1,500 to 8,000 of the world's largest corporations – a 433 percen growth rate.

- Energy improvements across the state of Massachusetts that have resulted in nearly $9 billion worth of benefits for residents and businesses.

- The improbable collaboration of the world's religious leaders to unite more than 7 million people of different faiths to help build a better world.

- Transformational business outcomes, such as those experienced by Nutrimental Foods where within one year absenteeism decreased 300 percent, sales increased 27 percent, and productivity increased 23 percent.

In a review of twenty cases of the use of appreciative inquiry, Gervase Bushe — a professor of leadership and organizational development — and his colleagues found that of the cases that followed the 4-D cycle and the five principles, over 90 percent were successful change efforts. This is a big number when contrasted with research by Professor John Kotter at Harvard University who has concluded that in other kinds of change efforts - not guided by AI - there is a failure rate of nearly 75 percent.

As the use of the AI Summit methodology continues to grow in large corporations including: Hewlett Packard, Fairmont Santrol and British Airways; in government agencies including the U.S. Navy and the Environmental Protection Agency; in industry-wide initiatives including the National Dairy Council; in health-care institutions including Lovelace Health Care Systems and the Alice Peck Day Health Care System; in community-wide initiatives including The City of Cleveland and Imagine Chicago; in school systems including the Canadian Metropolitan School District and St. Peter's College in Australia; in non-profit organizations including The Red Cross and World Vision; and in worldwide initiatives including the United Nations and United Religions Initiative it is critical that we continue to understand if the application of the 4-D cycle and adherence to the five core principles are enough to positively disrupt and support living systems to flourish.

For example, Gervase's review of the twenty appreciative inquiry cases, found that that most (sixty-five percent) of the successful change efforts were single loop changes that realized normal business or performance goals like improved operations, higher growth rates, improved quality, etc. However, in the cases that showed transformational, double-loop changes (thirty-five percent) that created significant shifts in identity, corporate purpose, and deep values, there was a consistent pattern that comprised:

- 100 percent creation of new knowledge, not just new processes
- 100 percent creation of a generative metaphor that guided participants
- 100 percent penetration of grounded organizational beliefs
- 83 percent usage of an improvisational approach in the destiny phase

What made these cases unique was their ability to:

1. Change how people think instead of what people do.
2. Support the self-organizing change processes that flow from new ideas.

Consequently, just as David suggested in his original dissertation, Gervase has argued on numerous occasions that merely focusing on the positive, without focusing on the generative, is unlikely to produce transformational change in living systems.

"AI leads to transformational change when it addresses or creates enough disruption to evoke self-organizing processes that are focused on what is widely desired. Self-organizing processes are channeled in useful ways by, amongst other things, increasing the richness of social networks so that like-minded and motivated people find each other and are encouraged to 'make something happen.' Leaders and stakeholders pay attention to the ensuing experiments, resourcing and extending those they believe are worth supporting."

GERVASE BUSHE

In addition, other studies have suggested that transformational AI Summits are able to:

- Engage large numbers of stakeholders
- Address a problem, issue or concern that is widely shared
- Create a shared appreciative vocabulary
- Encourage equality among participants regardless of roles
- Engender affective and emotional connections to the change process
- Generate and communicate quality insights during the discovery phase
- Secure widespread support for design statements
- Inspire passionate and committed leadership from people with credibility in the system

David has recently built upon these observations, agreeing that in order for systems to excel, AI Summits need to be macro-management applications that embrace top-down and bottom-up approaches simultaneously by focusing on configurations and chemistries of strengths that reach beyond silos, fiefdoms, and specialties. He has proposed that this requires five generativity success factors that include:

1. Preparing systemic change leaders to think strengths.
2. Pre-framing a powerful task with a purpose bigger than the system.
3. Embracing whole configurations that combine constellations of systemic strengths.
4. Creating a system where innovation can emerge from design-inspired collaboration.
5. Making the concentration effect of strengths a vital management skill for creating cultures of open innovation, systemically accelerating and scaling up solutions.

Researchers also caution that when planning an AI Summit, it is essential to consider that:

- AI Summits appear to deliver the most robust returns when focused on creating bold solutions rather than just addressing underlying symptoms of the problem.

- The current position of the organization along the continuum from negative deviance to positive deviance will impact the momentum for change.

- The level of support, openness, and commitment of leadership to full-voice participation, co-creation with stakeholders, and the resourcing of ongoing change and purposeful transformation.

- The extent to which appreciation, discussion of ideals, and a focus on strengths already exist within the system and how problems of real concern can be addressed within an appreciative dialogue rather than denied or suppressed.

- Systems in the pre-identity stage (in which the majority of members do not identify with the system) are generally best served by an inquiry into the ideal given the group's responsibilities, goals, and environment. Those in the post-identity stage (in which the majority of members do identify with the system) are generally best served by a more focused inquiry around increasing the system's competence and capacity.

- There remains the most confusion and least consensus about what happens in the deploy/destiny phase of the 4-D cycle where implementation can be very spotty.

- It is not an "event" but rather a long-term process punctuated by a series of events.

As our awareness of mixed AI Summit results has increased over the last decade there has been a growing call for studies that explore the mechanisms, moderators, and contingencies of successful AI Summits. It is our hope that this book helps to amplify and build upon our understanding of what makes an AI Summit work well and how it can provide a positive disruption that supports living systems to become more adaptive, creative and resilient.

How Did Michelle Conduct The Research For This Book?

Due to the complex, adaptive and relational nature of living systems, Michelle took a grounded theory approach to the research on which this book is based. It was clear from the emerging body of research we have just reviewed that some systems had identified AI Summits as providing a positive disruption that supported their ability to flourish, and so Michelle set out with the following research objectives:

- Identifying what took place in AI Summits where the system was identified as flourishing for a consistent period of time (at least 12 months or more) after the disruption.

- Testing if AI Summits did indeed activate Professor Martin Seligman's PERMA mechanisms for individual flourishing and what, if any, impact this may have had on systemic flourishing.

- Understanding how AI Summits unite, motivate and support people to make positive changes across a system possible.

- Assessing how replicable AI Summits were that created a positive disruption for systemic flourishing in other systems.

Michelle conducted twenty-one interviews with sponsors, participants and facilitators of AI Summits, identified as aiding systemic flourishing. She then conducted a literature review of another ten AI Summits for which in-depth case notes were available. A summary of the AI Summits can be found in Appendix A.

Her analysis surfaced a universal underlying need for systems that invest in an AI Summit to create a positive disruption that supports individual and systemic flourishing. That need was for "creating generative connections."

At a time when the reported rates of loneliness, workplace disengagement, and community disenchantment increasingly inhibit the likelihood of individual or collective flourishing, the challenge for most social systems is to transform the isolation and disconnection within our communities into connectedness and caring for the whole. The key is to identify how this transformation of generative connection occurs.

"Social systems are the external manifestations of cultural thinking patterns and of profound human needs, emotions, strengths, and weaknesses. Changing them is not as simple as saying 'now all change' or of trusting that he who knows the good shall do the good."

DONELLA MEADOWS

Instead, Donella Meadows, one of the pioneers of systems thinking, concludes that living successfully in a world of systems requires more than our ability to calculate or plan, it requires our full humanity: our vision and our morality, our rationality and our intuition, our interconnection and our self-organization, our willingness to participate flat-out and our courage to respond to feedback, and our growth and our resilience.

You see, despite our illusions of control when it comes to trying to change a system, what we have learned is that the future can't be predicted, but it can be envisioned and brought lovingly into being. This is because there is a natural gap between understanding and implementation, and while systems thinking and complex adaptive systems theory can lead us to the edge of what analysis can do and point beyond to the possibilities, in the end, it is the human spirit that will determine what is done. This means letting go of the need to control, and instead, strategically, profoundly, madly letting go and learning to dance with the system.

The rest of this book lays out how we might use AI Summits to create the kind of positive disruptions that can teach us to dance together by answering the following questions:

- **Chapter 2 – How Do You Positively Disrupt A System?** — Discover how the U.S. Dairy Industry got a cow to jump over the moon about sustainability by understanding the basic drivers of any system and how an AI Summit can support these.

- **Chapter 3 – How Do You Support Individual Flourishing?** — Why Dutch technology company, Schuberg Philis, decided that love was the bottom-line when it came to individuals flourishing at work and how self-determination theory and the PERMA mechanisms helped their AI Summit to meet these needs.

- **Chapter 4 – Are You Ready For An AI Summit?** — How Fairmount Santrol evolved from being seen as "dune-rapers" to being recognized as one of the top corporate citizen in the USA while doubling their earnings by first ensuring that their organization met the three criteria for systemic readiness for an AI Summit.

- **Chapter 5 – How Do The Best AI Summits Work?** — What Clarke, a global environmental products and services company learned from running multiple AI Summits and why they needed a 6-D cycle and 12 steps to capitalize on the mirror-flourishing effect.

- **Chapter 7 – How Can We Continue Improving AI Summits?** — How we'll be designing and delivering AI Summits in the future based on the findings of the research and what we still need to learn.

We humbly offer these following chapters with the acknowledgment that while we continue to discover a tremendous amount about how the world works, it is not nearly enough to fully comprehend all that is unfolding. Our knowledge is impressive; our ignorance is even more so. It is our heartfelt hope that these findings provide another step toward improving our understanding of human and systemic flourishing so that we can learn to dance together.

CHAPTER 2

How Do You Positively Disrupt A System?

"It got us to believe in the power of convening the whole value chain and its stakeholders toward a common end."

ERIN FITZGERALD, U.S. DAIRY INDUSTRY SUMMIT

It wasn't your typical conference group. As 250 people began taking their allocated seats around a room filled with round tables, they were a little surprised to look around their small groups and find humble dairy farmers, corporate suits from the milk retailers, tenacious truck drivers, cautious public servants, enthusiastic industry consultants, committed environmental activists, data-driven academics and excited students. It seemed that anyone who touched milk, from the cow to the table, had been seated together.

Never in the history of the U.S. dairy industry had such a conversation been held – in fact, most of the participants had never even been in a room with people whose interests, agendas and experiences felt so obviously different from their own. For example, one farmer, who lived just over a mile from the milk processor's headquarters, had never spoken to anyone there even though they were practically neighbors because they saw each other as opponents in a zero-sum game.

But the notions of sustainability, and the industry's need to deal with its negative environmental footprint in terms of carbon, methane, water toxins and transport requirements was a looming threat that no one knew how to solve. And so rather than leave their future in the hands of environmentalists, lobbyists and bureaucrats, the farmers had warily agreed to come together with representatives from every part of the dairy supply chain to try and create a sustainable dairy future together.

As the AI Summit began, and the participants began to metaphorically "walk in each other's muddy boots," they quickly discovered a genuine sense of respect, appreciation and pride for the roles people around the room played in caring for their land and people's wellbeing. As trust, hope and confidence grew quickly across the group they also began to dream of the real difference they could make as an industry and how they could lead on sustainability practices around the world that would ensure that their land was maintained for generations to come. With tears in his eyes, one student farmer told the group: "I've been worried that I could never make enough money to come back and work on the farm, that there would be no real point no matter how much I loved the idea. But what I'm hearing here is that I can make a difference in this world and I need to try."

Reconnected and reignited by their purpose and passion to be stewards of the land for future generations, all 250 participants agreed to a constitution that captured their shared vision and mission for building a sustainable dairy industry by finding ways to spark sustainability innovations that would strengthen farm businesses, reduce GHG emissions for fluid milk by 25 percent, and increase business value. This set the stage for them to roll up their sleeves and start designing solutions together and in a matter of hours more than twenty-eight potential projects were developed and displayed, from research programs (actual research proposals) to redesigned national transportation systems (actual drawings and concept models were built that people could see and touch).

Leaving the Summit feeling full of hope and commitment, volunteers for each idea then went on to develop a rigorous business case that was taken to the industry's executive leadership for review. In the end, ten projects across the industry value chain were selected to take forward, and conservatively, it was estimated that these projects could increase the order of farm business value by US$238 million within two years and reduce the dairy industry's carbon footprint by 11 percent.

Perhaps most importantly though, almost every participant at the AI Summit walked away recognizing and valuing their own leadership role in the industry. They have taken what they learned back into their local communities, businesses and schools and shared their insights, championed the ideas and encouraged others to be stewards of the land and proud of the difference the industry makes together. People became individual change agents within the system and as a result they collectively created a movement.

(You can see this AI Summit in action at www.thechangelabs.com.)

What Do Living Systems Need?

At a time when leading scientists are suggesting that we face the most significant geopolitical, environmental, social, and economic challenges in history, we are in urgent need of more adaptive, creative and resilient ways to enable systemic flourishing. But in a global landscape littered with failed, Newtonian-inspired attempts at creating change that include: combat strategies that have escalated conflicts, prudent fiscal policies that have resulted in the near collapse of well-established economies, carefully reasoned refugee interventions that have caused more than 60 million people leaving their homes with thousands dying in the process, and global sustainability efforts that have failed to slow the pace at which our environment is melting, it is clear that living systems rarely respond like machines that can be controlled and fixed with simple cause-and-effect solutions.

"Our costly attempts at organizational and social change have mostly failed because we made two mistakes. We tried to change individual behaviors, and we used linear approaches of goal setting, measurement, and accountability. Logically, it all made good sense. Individual behaviors caused problems. Complex problems need to be broken into chunks and then designated as tasks to specific individuals or teams. If everyone knew they would be held accountable for results, they'd be motivated to do the work. And change would happen."

MARGARET WHEATLEY

Despite our long-held Newtonian beliefs that we live in a clockwork world where change and disturbances signal trouble, since the 1960s the research of biologists, cosmologists, physicists, sociologists, psychologists, economists and others discovered that living systems constantly seek their own self-renewal and so fluctuation and change are an essential part of the process by which order is created. For example, researchers have found that disorder can actually be an ally that can provoke a living system to let go of its current form so that it can reorganize into a form better suited to the demands of its changing environment. In fact, it turns out that living systems grow as a result of disequilibrium, not balance.

Take a moment to think of your own life and the times you've personally found yourself at the edge of chaos, and you'll notice that by the end you've emerged changed and often grown stronger. But how often have you ever experienced growth during phases of equilibrium?

You see, while equilibrium often wears the disguise of advantage – everything feels calm, stable and in control — the Law of Requisite Variety suggests that prolonged equilibrium dulls a system's senses and coping mechanisms for new challenges. For example, fish that live in an aquarium are excruciatingly sensitive to the slightest perturbations, compared to fish that live in the sea where survival factors heighten wariness and experimentation. Likewise, when leaders strive for equilibrium and stability by imposing control, constricting people's freedom and inhibiting change, they risk creating the very conditions that threaten their organization's survival and certainly diminish its opportunities for flourishing.

Unfortunately, disequilibrium, loss of control and surprise tend to be experiences that most human systems try to avoid or control for fear that change will exhaust people's energy and leave them at risk of entropy. But scientists have discovered that what distinguishes a living system from a mechanical system is its ability to learn. Everything that is alive partners *with* its environment in a continuous exchange of energy and information that enables it to reorganize into different forms and develop new capacities that ultimately make it more resourceful, adaptive and resilient, rather than rigid and stable.

In their ground-breaking book, *Surfing The Edge of Chaos,* on how complexity science can be applied to organizations, Richard Pascale and his colleagues suggest that the sweet spot for productive change is the edge of chaos, rather than the abyss. In this permeable, intermediate state where order and disorder flow, the potential for generativity is maximized because the components of the system are no longer locked into place, yet their level of excitation is not so extreme that the system has dissolved entirely. In fact, they suggest that being at the edge of chaos is the precondition for transformation to take place.

While this process may sound threatening if stability, not growth, is the goal, it's important to remember that living systems change in order to preserve themselves and that being at the edge of chaos is simply a necessary condition to awaken creativity. As Peggy Holman – an award-winning researcher and practitioner on creating "whole systems" change — explains, every system contains the following forces constantly interacting and mutually influencing each other:

- A drive for coherence (i.e. our longing for meaning and purpose).

- Occasional disruptions that disturb the status quo (i.e. new information from our environment, like a vocal cynic or an unexpected opportunity).

- A drive for differentiation (i.e. our hunger for freedom and authenticity).

We can see this playing out in the experience of the U.S. Dairy Industry during their AI Summit. For example:

- The dairy industry remembered that its collective purpose and passion had always been to be stewards of the land, and it found coherence by reconnecting with its identity — who it is, what its strengths are, and what it is trying to accomplish.

- New information about the need for more sustainable practices created a disruption to the status quo that created a need for the industry to show up differently.

- Given a few guiding principles and the freedom to self-organize the projects created at the Summit met people's need for freedom and autonomy so that a new form of order could emerge that benefited the industry and the individuals in it.

It turns out that at the edge of chaos, a system's stability and sense of order comes from its coherence about who it is, what it needs and what is required to survive in its environment so that it can develop in ways of its own choosing, and over time spawn a stronger, self-organized system. Professor Kenneth Gergen — one of the world's leading researchers on social change — notes that in human systems this coherence is achieved amidst the social interactions that shape people's language and experiences, and so ultimately it is words and conversations that shape human worlds.

Thus, systems scientist, Erich Jantsch, urges leaders to a new role of "equilibrium busters" who recognize that order is never imposed from the top down, but emerges as elements of a system share new information and work together to find coherence and differentiation. No longer required to be the guards maintaining control, this gives leaders the opportunity to become compassionate coaches of disruption who consciously nourish and provoke a system's capacity for emergent growth. After all, it is at the edge of chaos where a complex system can be spontaneous, adaptive, and alive.

How Can We Be Compassionate Coaches Of Disruption?

Disrupting compassionately is an aikido strategy that grows our capacity to deal with difference, upheaval and conflict by empowering us with comfort, strength and courage. For example, Nelson Mandela, Mohandas Gandhi, and Dr. Martin Luther King Jr. are powerful examples of what it means to be a leader who is a compassionate coach of disruption. Although the systems they faced were complex and often hostile, their strategies for creating disruption were compassionate, applied with clear intention and commitment. They enabled people to feel safe enough to liberate their voices and speak their truth, they connected people even while differentiating what mattered to each of them, and they opened people up to new facets of what they were facing by helping them to see the system as a whole in all of its complexity so that they could discern meaningful aspects of what needed to change. And they changed their worlds. Such is the power of compassion to positively disrupt a system.

If leaders are to disrupt systems compassionately, however, they must begin by being mindful that while all change begins with disruption, not all change presents the opportunities for emergence. For example, Harvard Professor Ronald Heifetz urges leaders to distinguish between technical problems (those that are rationally definable and responsive to operational fixes with authority, expertise and procedures to address them) and adaptive challenges (those that are complex and confusing and produce different opinions on whether an issue even exists and that require time, experiments, discoveries and adjustments across a network of relationships). And other researchers caution that much of today's system angst comes from treating all disruptions as if they can be managed through a steady state scenario (handled within the existing situation when a minor fix is made or the disruption is ignored or suppressed), or an incremental shift (the status quo is disrupted and a small change is made to integrate the distinguished changes), instead of recognizing that larger forces are at play that are pushing the system toward the edge of chaos and positively embracing this upheaval to enable emergent change.

Leaders must also acknowledge that while a positive disruption can be predicted (like the growing need for sustainable practices in the dairy industry) and the range of possible transformations mapped (like the twenty-eight change projects that came out of the dairy AI Summit), the end point cannot be certain. The truth is, change is more like a random ramble to enable emergence, than a predictable march to enable progression.

"Left to self-organize in what looks like a mess with no apparent order, agents interacting in a system can produce not anarchy, but creative new outcomes that none of them ever dreamed of... The price is an inability to know the final destination or to be in control of the journey."

RALPH STACEY

Thus, researchers suggest that the goal for any system is to create a large plateau of resilience upon which it can safely dance, rather than a small plateau of certainty or static stability that offers little space for movement and ultimately is likely to lead to its demise. To be compassionate coaches of disruption, leaders must not confuse control with order. Instead, they must be willing to replace procedures that are designed to control with visions and values that encourage lively, independent action that benefit both the system and the individuals in it. This allows them to honor and respect the people they are disrupting.

Peggy suggests that once a leader is confident that there is an opportunity for emergence to arise from a disruption and is willing to relinquish control and allow the system to dance with its environment, there are three activities they can invest in to support emergent change:

- Create a safe container for novel information to be appreciatively shared across the whole system so the disturbance can be welcomed.

- Provide opportunities for individual expression and connection, so self-organization can take place around the actions people are passionate about and willing to take responsibility for in order to be of service to others.

- Reflect together by regularly stepping out of the flow of activity to seek feedback, sense the larger patterns that are taking shape, and find meaning and coherence in the system.

How can you create a safe container for a system?

A container is an intangible, yet real space, (like an AI Summit) in which the potential and possibility of a group can unfold. Once a system is at the edge of chaos, biologist Stuart Kauffman notes that in order to self-organize it needs:

- A relatively safe environment
- Higher levels of diversity than its current environment
- Great potential for complexity from interrelationships
- Sparse prior connections
- A drive to better fit with its environment

Harrison Owen, building on his twenty years of experience as the founder of Open Space Technology to help systems adapt to new levels of complexity after a generative disruption, echoes these recommendations, suggesting that containers should:

- Focus on a real business opportunity that people care about.

- Contain high levels of complexity so that no one person or even one group could solve it alone.

- Seek high levels of diversity – ethnicity, gender, profession, life experience, etc. – across sparse prior connections.

- Spark the presence of passion and conflict and the willingness to take responsibility.

Peggy builds on both of these insights when she suggests that a container should create a space for safely surfacing differences that make a difference by asking appreciative, ambitious, possibility-oriented questions that attract diverse people who care about the system. She suggests that these kinds of questions can create a positive disruption by focusing the system on opportunities for something better and more meaningful, and provide a bridge from chaos to creativity that mobilizes the system's energy.

Researchers have found over the last few decades and across varied populations that the number one thing most people want from their jobs – more than additional money, job security, new opportunities or work/life flexibility – is a sense of meaning. Just as a magnet operates as a strange attractor that draws random iron filings together, when there is an opportunity to do meaningful work on behalf of others, people don't have to be coerced into action, they just need to be invited. After all, as Viktor Frankl in his acclaimed book, *Man's Search For Meaning*, wrote, our greatest motivator in life is not to gain pleasure or to avoid pain but to seek meaning.

"Meaningful work reawakens us to what it feels like to be human beings."
MARGARET WHEATLEY

How can you provide opportunities for individual expression and connection?

Once the container has enabled the system to welcome the disturbance, compassionate coaches of disruption need to provide opportunities for individual expression and connection around new information so that self-organization can emerge. The truth is that when humans are being human they are wonderfully talented. When people believe in what they're doing they're internally motivated, they're naturally creative and want to contribute, and they want to belong and feel part of a community. This is why self-organization can work so well: it engages people around a cause and allows their hearts and minds to find ways forward.

Self-organization occurs when a living system exchanges information with its environment and willingly uses that information to adapt to changed conditions. That sounds simple enough, but in human systems our deep drive to belong means that new information can quickly get shut down when it challenges our identity. In addition, as information has become more readily weaponized there is growing evidence of its intentional use to fabricate data, produce half-truths and spread lies to win people over. And perhaps most challenging of all, the ubiquitous presence of technology and the busy pace of modern life means that when new information is not used intelligently, it can be as much a source of disorder as order.

Be in no doubt, however, that a living system is a learning system. Researchers suggest that chaos is the greatest generator of information, and when stewarded by a compassionate coach of disruption who takes a whole system view and gives participants a voice, and helps them to listen and process different interpretations together, new information becomes positively amplified across the system. As a result, the system develops a wiser sense of what is going on and what needs to be done, enabling it to become more intelligent.

"The role of information is revealed in the word itself:
in-formation."

MARGARET WHEATLEY

Compassionate coaches of disruption need to be aware that while this process sounds straightforward, true dialogue is inherently messy. It involves differences, confusions, conflicts and fantasies that generate paradox and creative destruction in order to generate new possibilities. The good news is that when this diverse interplay is characterized by playful give-and-take, in a respectful environment, where there is a genuine feeling of community and trust, conflicted systems do what only they can do — self-organize to new and higher levels of complexity that are more in harmony with each other, their environment, and their own inner needs. This is why creative interactions that enable individual expression and connection are at the heart of fostering emergence, because by expressing and sharing their differences people realize that they are all connected — their hearts start to open to each other and they discover the seeds of what might be.

If this still sounds risky, remember that order will always emerge out of these interactions because at the end of the day nature seeks simplicity. It is a world of independence and interdependence, a unifying spiral dance of creation with processes that resolve so many of the dualisms we create in thought.

"Order is accessible when diverse people facing intractable
challenges uncover and implement ideas that none could have
predicted or accomplished on their own. Emergence can't be
forced—but it can be fostered."

PEGGY HOLMAN

Reflect together to seek feedback and find meaning and coherence.

When people experience themselves as part of a larger system, something profound happens: their behavior changes. Not only are they changed when they experience emergence, but so are their relationships, how they interact with each other, and how they relate to their environment.

The challenge, however, is that while emergent change is how nature takes great discontinuous leaps to create new forms, it can take time to truly assimilate what emerges as people bump up against old assumptions and behaviors and realize they no longer work. This is why feedback — the means by which a system talks to itself — is so important to help a living system notice the shifts it might otherwise miss. For example, researchers suggest that amplifying or positive feedback draws attention to new possibilities for change, while dampening or negative feedback tries to keep a system on track by signaling deviations from an established goal.

Given that a flourishing living system is a learning system, a system's ability to notice these new forms of information, learn from it, and respond is ultimately what determines its level of intelligence. Thus, in order to stay alert to what's going on in their internal and external environment, compassionate coaches of disruption need to support systems in periodically stepping out of the flow of activity and engaging in reflective conversations so that people can notice the larger patterns taking shape among them and enable meaning to coalesce.

Why Might An AI Summit Support Systemic Flourishing?

What unexpectedly emerged from Michelle's research data was a clear picture that shows how AI Summits help compassionate coaches of disruption foster emergence as recommended by the researchers. For example, observations from the research participants repeatedly noted:

The ability for an AI Summit to create a safe container in which new information could be appreciatively shared across the whole system.

As one research participant explained: "A lot of the magic of AI Summits appears in the planning. It really needs to be planned well to have the right people in the room answering the right questions." Another shared: "We put a lot of thought into framing the effort to create compelling, welcoming invitations so people didn't feel under attack." And another observed: "There was a real sense that people were coming together to make a difference and people felt special to have been invited, excited to connect and were getting their first glimpse of the whole system and the power they had."

Michelle's research found that AI Summits are a powerful way to create a safe space that attracts people with complex, diverse relationships and sparse prior connections to come together and ask appreciative, possibility orientated questions. She also discovered that once these people have been brought together, AI Summits often result in the creation of a positive disruption because it focuses the system on opportunities for something better and more meaningful and thus provides a bridge from chaos to creativity that mobilizes the system's energy.

How AI Summits provide opportunities for individual expression and connection so self-organization can take place.

As one research participant told Michelle: "People were connecting with people they'd never worked with before and discovering that they were remarkable human beings and this opened up new possibilities." Another shared that: "A self-regulation capacity emerges, where leadership shifts and roles move as people get clear on who's good at what. It's not top-down or bottom-up, but it's shared." And another reported: "By the end of the design phase we had mobilized an inspired and empowered cadre of change agents."

As suggested by the research outlined earlier, Michelle found that as an AI Summit enables novel information to be exchanged across the system, order starts to emerge through a surprising, respectful and playful give-and-take. As a result, the system starts to self-organize to new and higher levels of complexity around this information that are more in harmony with each other, their environment, and their own inner needs.

The opportunity post-Summit is to ensure opportunities for feedback to notice the larger patterns taking shaping so that meaning and coherence can be found and flourishing sustained.

The research participants repeatedly stated that: "In many respects the AI Summit is the beginning." Another noted: "Continuing to connect and shape the debate as we move forward has been really important." Someone else explained: "We track how we're doing. We measure, we report and we celebrate our success." And another told Michelle: "We found that we got about three full years of traction out of the work of that first Summit."

Michelle found that AI Summits change people's behaviors, relationships and ways of working together, and that the consistent practice of periodically stepping out of the flow of activity to gather feedback and notice the larger patterns taking shape among them was essential to not only recognize and celebrate the progress being made but to enable meaning to coalesce.

What Role Will You Play In Helping Systems Flourish?

Now, more than ever, we need compassionate leaders of disruption to understand that people are best controlled by concepts that invite their participation, not policies and procedures that curtail their contribution. As one of the leaders of the U.S. Dairy Industry Summit explained to Michelle: "In the end we learned that words really do create worlds. The turning point for our industry was not the notion of sustainability, it was when we turned to the group participating in the AI Summit and said: 'You guys believe in stewardship of the land as you purpose, which is the essence of sustainability. It's having the right values and practices to leave this world better and pass it on to the next generation. How do you want to put those values to work?' That one purposeful, possibility focused, appreciative question asked in the presence of the entire system made the whole industry change."

"Asking appreciative questions is the most effective practice I know for disrupting compassionately. It interrupts the status quo so smoothly that even in challenging circumstances, those disrupted can access enthusiasm and creativity. It often finesses the feeling of disruption."

PEGGY HOLMAN

It is not the intention of this book to suggest that AI Summits are the only way to positively disrupt and support systemic flourishing. Nor, as you will see in coming chapters, do we believe that Michelle's research suggests that AI Summits will always enable people to be compassionate coaches of disruption. We do hope, however, that as we explore the evidence gathered throughout this book, together we will all come to better understand why, when and how an AI Summit can help a system to flourish.

CHAPTER 3

How Do You Help Individuals Flourish?

*"The feeling I remember most from our Summit is
the absolute feeling of connectedness."*

PIM BERGER, SCHUBERG PHILIS AI SUMMIT

The empty Amsterdam passenger airline terminal crackled with anticipation and excitement as 200 employees, customers, partners and other stakeholders of Schuberg Philis – a leading IT solutions developer – took their seats for an event unlike any the company had ever held before. Looking around the magically transformed terminal, they found themselves in a creative design studio full of possibility as they were invited to spend the next three days together answering just one question: What next for this thriving organization?

Answering this question wasn't simply about Schuberg Philis making more money, it was about finding better ways to truly care for people. A company already genuinely and publicly "100 percent" committed to its people and customers, Schuberg Philis wanted to explore how it could build on its success to go even further for the betterment of society. Thus, an AI Summit was being held to bring together people from across the Schuberg Philis system to discuss, debate, and design potential solutions to uncover what was really possible for an organization when it goes beyond satisfied customers, happy colleagues and good citizenship.

What emerged took this organization to a place it never would have imagined. You see, while every voice in that airport terminal — whether it was from somebody inside or outside the company – was treated as equal, the most powerful moment of the AI Summit came from the voices of children whose parents worked at the company. As video screens around the room played short clips of the kids describing what their parents did at the company and why they were proud of them, it quickly became very clear that at its core Schuberg Philis was: "A company based on love."

This dream was immediately put to a practical test in the AI Summit as sixteen different design teams explored "how might we" statements that included: configuring strengths-based teams, attracting and developing the right talent, spreading our DNA and bridging generational gaps with storytelling, sharing our brain power, 100 percent open source sharing of all we have, radial resource efficiency for zero waste and our powerful purpose. For example, four engineers took responsibility for ensuring all future technology contracts in the company are open source. Another group led the introduction of an agile method for IT development to help teams work better together and value each other's strengths.

And while these may feel like small business outcomes, in the hearts and minds of the people working at Schuberg Philis, becoming a company based on love has been a significant emotional shift that meant instead of mandating strategies on sustainability or demanding compliance to policies, there is now one question that guides every action of every employee each day: "Is this the right thing to do for the children who depend on me?"

As a result Schuberg Philis has been able to build a no-manager culture where people are given the freedom to take responsibility for the things they are passionate about, teams are chosen for their strengths and chemistry, and game changing collaboration and fearless learning is enabled. And as a company based on love they have agreed that: "We have the desire for each person to flourish. We are all equal and unique. We see the whole human being — as a colleague, as a parent, and as a friend. When we connect at a deep level, wonderful things become possible."

(You can see this AI Summit in action at www.thechangelabs.com.)

What Do Individuals Need To Flourish?

Flourishing is the combination of feeling good and functioning effectively that is enabled by high levels of wellbeing. A growing body of evidence demonstrates that high levels of wellbeing not only has positive outcomes for individuals, but also contributes to systemic flourishing. For example, higher levels of wellbeing have been found to be associated with people having more energy and resilience, and being happier and healthier, more charitable and liked by others, and more productive and successful at work. Researchers have also found that when organizations institute practices that support employee wellbeing they achieve higher performance in profitability, productivity, customer satisfaction and employee engagement. And in a review of the literature on wellbeing at work, the New Economics Foundation concluded that not only does focusing on wellbeing at work benefit individuals and their organizations, but it also plays a central role in creating flourishing societies.

So what enables people to flourish? Different researchers have proposed different models for human flourishing. For example, sociologist and psychologist Professor Corey Keyes defines flourishing as the presence of emotional wellbeing (positive emotions and life satisfaction), social wellbeing (contribution, integration, actualization, acceptance and coherence) and psychological wellbeing (self-acceptance, environmental mastery, positive relations, personal growth, autonomy and purpose). Professor Ed Diener — renowned for his decades of global research on wellbeing and happiness — and his colleagues define flourishing as a person's psychological and social functioning that can be measured by the presence of purpose, positive relationships, engagement in activities, social contribution, feelings of competence, self-respect and optimism. Professor Felicia Huppert and her colleagues suggest that feeling good and functioning effectively requires the presence of competence, emotional stability, engagement, meaning, optimism, positive emotion, positive relationships, resilience, self-esteem and vitality.

One of the most popular current models of human flourishing being used in organizations, schools and cities around the world has been proposed by Professor Martin Seligman who, as noted in Chapter 1, has suggested that in order to flourish, we need the right balance of heartfelt positive (P) emotions, opportunities to be engaged (E) in what we're doing, positive relationships (R), a sense of meaning (M) and purpose, and the ability to accomplish (A) what matters most to us. This is often referred to as the PERMA theory for wellbeing and as we will see below these pillars incorporate many of the elements identified by the other researchers.

"Well-being cannot exist just in your own head. Wellbeing is a combination of feeling good as well as actually having opportunities for engagement, meaning, good relationships and accomplishment."

MARTIN SELIGMAN

What good are positive emotions?

Researchers have found that the experience of heartfelt positive emotions — like joy, gratitude, serenity, interest, hope, pride, amusement, inspiration, awe, and love — can help us to be more optimistic, resilient, open, accepting, and happier and healthier overall. For example, studies conducted by Professor Barbara Fredrickson – one of the world's leading researchers on emotions — and her colleagues have repeatedly demonstrated that positive emotions help to broaden and build the way people's brains respond to opportunities and challenges by: expanding their field of peripheral vision so they can see more of what is happening around them; flooding their brains with the neurotransmitters dopamine and serotonin, which can help them make and sustain more neural connections; and broadening their social responses by helping them feel closer to others, expanding their circles of trust, and overcoming bias.

And like money in the bank for a rainy day, studies have also found that while people's experiences of positive emotions may often feel brief and fleeting, as they accrue they help to build their psychological, social, intellectual, and physical resources, placing them on a positive trajectory of growth. As a result, Barbara concluded that positive emotions help to broaden and build people.

"The latest scientific evidence tells us that positivity doesn't simply reflect success and health, it can also produce success and health."

BARBARA FREDRICKSON

It is also important to note, however, that people who consistently flourish also experience negative emotions. In a world where rejection, failure, self-doubt, hypocrisy, loss, boredom, and annoying and obnoxious people are inevitable, Barbara acknowledges that people can't really be connected and grounded to life without encountering difficulties, challenges, and pain. And while people are often tempted to try and ignore, suppress, distract or control their response to these feelings of fear, anger, or sadness, she points out that these emotions also offer important emotional, mental, and social learning opportunities. Rather than trying to avoid the discomfort these emotions can bring, researchers suggest that people's goal should be to feel robust enough to withstand emotional distress by being able to realize that these emotions are simply signs that something is not going right, to take the required actions, and to let the emotions pass. After all, emotions

49

themselves are neither good nor bad; it's what people choose to do with them that appears to really matter.

That said, Barbara's research has found that people who flourish do experience a higher frequency of heartfelt positive emotions compared to heart-straining negative emotions each day. She suggests thinking of this like the balance of levity and gravity. Too much levity — like too much heartfelt positivity — and people risk being disconnected from reality and floating away. But too many heart-straining negative emotions – like the weight of too much gravity — can put people at risk for being left flat on the floor, and unable to get up. Thus, people's wellbeing and ability to flourish each day depends on them creating or finding opportunities to strike the right balance of positivity and negativity to support their wellbeing.

Why do people need opportunities for engagement?

Professor Mihaly Csikszentmihalyi – one of the founding fathers of positive psychology — describes the state of optimal engagement as "flow." It's the feeling people get when they're fully absorbed in what they're doing and is often described as "being in the zone" or "one with the music." Flow occurs when people have a clear goal that balances their strengths (the things they are good at and enjoy doing) with the complexity of the task at hand, when they feel a sense of autonomy and choice about how they're approaching the task, and when they receive regular feedback on how they're doing. In flow, people's skills are fully utilized, stretched to a manageable limit so they're learning, growing, improving, and advancing.

_____

"Enjoyment appears at the boundary between boredom and anxiety, when the challenges are just balanced with the person's capacity to act."
MIHALY CSIKSZENTMIHALYI

_____

When people experience flow they often lose track of time, feel less self-conscious, find performing effortless, and are left with a deep sense of satisfaction and competence about what they've been able to accomplish. As a result, researchers have found that the experience of flow can help people to: feel more involved in life, rather than isolated from it; enjoy activities more, rather than feeling bored; have a stronger sense of control, rather than feelings of helplessness; and connect with a stronger sense of self, have more self-belief, and a higher level of confidence in what they're actually capable of doing.

How do positive relationships impact people?

Professor Chris Peterson – one of positive psychology's most influential researchers – noted that if you gathered everything researchers have learned to date about improving wellbeing it could be summed up in three words: "Other people matter." Perhaps not surprisingly, given what we learned in Chapters 1 and 2 about the connected dependencies of living systems, studies have found that loneliness, social isolation, and the lack of social support place a person at high risk for psychological distress, physical and mental illness, and early mortality. In contrast, a sense of belonging has been found to correlate with a range of positive outcomes, including higher self-esteem, greater life satisfaction, faster recovery from disease, lower levels of stress, less mental illness, and a longer life.

Professor Jane Dutton – one of the pioneers of the field of positive organizational scholarship — suggests that this is because people have a biological need for social support and each time they joyfully connect with another person, the pleasure-inducing hormone oxytocin is released into their bloodstreams, immediately reducing anxiety, and improving their concentration and focus. In fact, studies suggest that when people experience warm and trusting feelings toward another person, it improves their vagal tone, which helps to naturally calm high heart rates, regulates glucose and cardiovascular health, regulates attention and emotion, and enhances social skills.

More than simply a physical response, however, Jane explains that the positive interactions people experience help them meet the deep psychological needs all human beings share to feel respected, valued, and appreciated. She calls these encounters "high-quality connections" and a growing body of research is finding that these moments contribute to individual flourishing and to team and organizational effectiveness.

"People who have high-quality quality connections experience more energy and more positive emotions such as joy, interest, and love. This state of being increases their capacity to think and act in the moment. In turn, this change builds more capacity and desire to effectively interact with others, generating more opportunities for energy to spread."

JANE DUTTON

For example, Professor Adam Grant – one of the world's leading organizational psychologists and researchers – suggests that when people invest in effective high-quality connections and behave like "givers" – who are willing to help others without expecting anything in return — rather than "takers" – who are only interested in getting what they want — they become more efficient at solving problems, getting things done, and balancing demands to ensure consistent performance. They are also able to build teams that are more cohesive and coordinated and establish environments where other people feel that their needs are a top priority, which helps systems to flourish.

Why does meaning matter?

For decades, people have ranked having a sense of purpose in their work as more important than promotions, income, job security, or even flexible hours. After all, as we saw, Viktor Frankl suggests that people have a universal need to feel that what they do matters, and a growing body of evidence suggests that when people do they are likely to be happier, more motivated, more committed, and more satisfied, which enables them to perform better and improves their wellbeing.

"Those who consistently rank their jobs as meaningful have something in common: they see their jobs as a way to help others."

ADAM GRANT

Professor Adam Grant suggests that the single strongest predictor of meaningfulness is people's belief that their job has a positive impact on others, but that they struggle to find meaning in their jobs when there is a lack of autonomy, variety, challenges, feedback, and the opportunity to see things through from start to finish. The good news is that researchers believe that meaning can be found in any job. For example, in one set of studies with hospital janitors — who were responsible for sweeping the floors, dusting, and emptying wastebaskets — researchers found that they were equally likely to describe their work as a job that paid their bills, a career that would lead them to other opportunities, or a calling that helped people to recover from illnesses by ridding the hospital of dangerous germs. Having observed this pattern in a wide range of professions, they concluded that when it comes to find meaning in our work what matters is not the work that people do each day, but how they think about the work they do each day and their ability to have a positive impact on others.

That said, Professor Robert Vallerand – one of the world's leading researchers on motivational processes — cautions that it's also important that people's passion for making a difference remains harmonious, rather than obsessive. For example, his studies have found that when people's passion starts taking control of them and making it difficult to engage in other things or with other people, their passion has become obsessive. This often leads to their self-esteem and self-worth becoming dependent on the outcomes of their passion, and their inability to "switch off" can damage their relationships, undermine their wellbeing, and eventually lead to burnout. In contrast, when people feel in control of what they love doing they generally have the kind of harmonious passion associated with higher levels of physical health, psychological wellbeing, self-esteem, and work satisfaction that enables them to flourish.

Can people accomplish what counts?

Professor Carol Dweck – another of the world's leading researchers in the field of motivation — suggests that when it comes to accomplishing the things that matter most to people, more important than their abilities is the belief that they can improve their abilities with motivation and effort. This is not to say that talent doesn't matter, but that people's talents, natural abilities, and basic biological makeups define the range of what might be possible for each person, but doesn't guarantee the outcomes they will achieve.

For example, in a study of competitive swimmers the very best performances were not purely a matter of extraordinary talent, but the confluence of dozens of very ordinary skills or activities that had been carefully drilled into habits, then synthesized into a whole. What made these performers extraordinary was the fact that they were able to consistently and correctly complete the required actions at the right time. This and a wealth of other studies on the interplay of talent, motivation and performance have led researchers to conclude that it is people's willingness to exert effort and learn from their successes and failures that ultimately turns talent into achievements.

———

"More important than believing in your abilities, is the belief that you can improve your abilities."
CAROL DWECK

———

Fortunately, Associate Professor Kristen Neff – one of the world's leading researchers on self-compassion – notes that while making mistakes, bumping up against our limitations and falling short of our ideals is part of the human condition, what matters most is what people say to themselves in these moments of failure. Her research has found that although the human brain is wired to attack any source of threat – including ourselves – learning to respond in these moments with self-compassion by acknowledging the fear or pain being felt, and talking to ourselves like a wise and kind friend, helps people to see things in a clearer and more balanced way. As a result, studies have found that self-compassion activates the brain's caregiving and self-awareness systems, making it easier for people to believe that they are capable and worthy, and making them less self-conscious, less likely to compare themselves to others, and less likely to feel insecure. Far from being self-indulgent or "soft," the deliberate use of self-compassionate talk has been found to be an effective means of enhancing people's motivation, their performance, and their resilience so that they can make informed choices about when to persist, when to try a different path, and when to let go and put their energy into something that will serve them better in the long term.

Thus in the end, Professor Angela Duckworth – one of the world's leading researchers of self-control and character — and her colleagues suggest that what sets gritty people apart from others is the deep underlying belief that with effort, practice, and the willingness to learn, they can always improve. Consequently, they focus on controlling what they can, and instead of simply setting performance goals for the outcomes they want, they prioritize learning goals that highlight the knowledge and skills they need to build to have the best chance of producing their desired results. This boosts their confidence to take on new challenges, to learn from criticism and feedback, and to see failure as a teachable moment.

Carol describes this as "a growth mindset." Her studies have found that a growth mindset makes it easier for people to set stretch goals, to ask for help, and to feel motivated to achieve the things that matter to them most.

Sparking hope by helping people to feel like they have nothing to lose and everything to gain if they step outside their comfort zone, growth mindsets move people beyond their present limitations toward realizing their true potential.

Can wellbeing be improved?

Researchers believe that people's wellbeing — much like their body weight — has a genetically determined set-point range that for most of the population is naturally stable and relatively positive. Thus, just as eating well and exercising regularly has been found to help people maintain or even improve their optimal body weight, the same seems to be true when they consistently engage in practices that support their wellbeing. Like any living system however, people's state of flourishing will ebb and flow depending on what's happening in their environments and their openness and flexibility to embrace these changes.

In order to flourish, Martin suggests that people need to cultivate each of the PERMA pillars while being mindful that how much each person needs of any one pillar will vary depending on the type of person they are, the environments they are in, and the outcomes they hope to achieve. And of particular benefit for our efforts to better understand how AI Summits work, the PERMA theory of wellbeing provides us with ways to measure and understand the presence or absence of activities that have been found to support human flourishing and thus shape how AI Summits are designed and delivered.

How Can We Support Individual Flourishing?

To assume that people can simply activate the PERMA pillars and thereby determine their levels of wellbeing, however, would return us to the dangers of Newtonian thinking and ignore all we have learned about living systems and the dynamic dance between an open system and its environment. In order to support individual flourishing, therefore, we must also consider how the environment in which people are operating might impact their wellbeing and ability to flourish.

In attempting to answer this question we are aided by Professors Richard Ryan and Edward Deci's extensive and renowned body research on self-determination theory (SDT), which examines how biological, social, and cultural conditions can either enhance or undermine people's inherent individual human capacities – such as the PERMA pillars — for psychological growth, engagement, and wellness. They explain: "Clearly, it is in our 'natures' (i.e., our evolved capacities and acquired propensities) to attain greater or lesser degrees of healthy psychological, social, and behavioral functioning and to more or less realize our human capacities and talents. We can also see natural experiments everywhere in which promising human potentials are diminished by impoverished or oppressive social conditions. Self-determination theory thus uses both experimental studies and field observations of such natural experiments toward understanding what humans really need from their psychological and social environments to be fully functioning and to thrive."

They posit that an environment that is effectance supportive (versus overly challenging, inconsistent or otherwise discouraging), relationally supportive (versus impersonal or rejecting) and autonomy supportive (versus demanding and controlling) provides the necessary nutrients for people to move toward integrity, wellness and flourishing. In other words, when people are able to satisfy their basic and universal psychological needs for competence, relatedness and autonomy, not only are they more likely to be motivated, energized and willing to act, they are also more likely to flourish in the process.

How can we support people's need for competence?

In the classical view of human development from Aristotle through various philosophical and modern theories in biology and psychology, people are thought to possess a biologically based propensity toward the extension, progressive transformation, and integration of experiences that facilitate their growth and greater wellbeing. In fact, anthropologist Edward Hall has concluded that the drive to learn is the "most basic in the human species."

Robert White, who gave birth to the modern era of motivation research, has argued, however, that while the ultimate goal of learning and gaining competence is undoubtedly the acquisition of the skills on which human survival depends, the more immediate aim is often just the spontaneous feeling of satisfaction and enjoyment that comes from people producing effects on their internal or external environment. For example, researchers point out that when playing children regularly exercise and stretch their competencies simply for the pleasure or satisfaction that the activity provides, rather than for any external rewards the activity may result in.

"Competence is the ability to interact effectively with the environment."
ROBERT WHITE

Robert labeled this tendency "effectance motivation," and has demonstrated that regardless of the extrinsic rewards and material benefits that someone might gain from competent behavior, people have a strong intrinsic need to exercise and extend their capacities. As a psychological need, therefore, feelings of competence are not only functionally important, but are also experientially significant, as they nourish people's sense of self and provide them with the energy and motivation to self-organize.

In order to develop a true sense of competence, however, researchers caution that people's actions must be perceived as self-organized or self-initiated. For example, studies have found that performing well on tasks for which someone doesn't feel a sense of self-initiation and self-regulation will not reliably enhance their perceived competence, intrinsic motivation or vitality. This is because the positive effects that accrue when people's need for competence is met only arise when activities originate from the self and are aligned with their identity, rather than from those that are governed by guilt, disapproval or the threat of punishments or promise of rewards. In other words, to satisfy people's need for competence they must feel genuine ownership of the activities in which they succeed.

How can we support people's need for relatedness?

Researchers agree that it is not possible for people or living systems to flourish without relationships. As we saw in the PERMA pillars, this need for connection is not simply due to the fact that human survival depends on others, but also highlights the consistent finding by researchers that one of the primary goals of all behavior is the feeling of belonging and of being significant or mattering in the eyes of others.

In fact, William James, the father of modern psychology, suggested that the deepest principle in human nature is the need to be appreciated. And other researchers have found that people have a basic need to feel responded to, respected and important to others, and conversely to avoid rejection, insignificance and disconnection, that shapes a great deal of behavior. For example, many hygiene habits, social rituals, and preoccupations with image, status and achievement are all driven by people's need for relatedness. As are people's tendencies, for better or worse, to internalize the values and behaviors from the environments they move within and are drawn toward.

In order to satisfy the psychological need for relatedness, however, it is not enough for people to simply behave in ways that they think others would like in order to feel connected with them. High-quality connections may be enjoyable in the moment, but researchers note that it is not merely being admired that counts. Unless people feel that others care for them unconditionally and that they are accepted for who they genuinely are, then their hunger for belonging will remain unmet and their energy and wellness risks being undermined.

> *"Social pain and pleasure make use of the same neural machinery as physical pain and pleasure, creating a powerful motivational drive to maximize our positive social experiences and minimize our negative ones."*
>
> **MATTHEW LIEBERMAN**

This is why relationally supportive environments allow people to autonomously and authentically care for others and to feel willingly and genuinely cared about. In the most satisfying interactions, no matter how well someone knows the other person or how long or frequent their encounters, it is in the experiences where people are present and accepting and supportive of each other that they feely truly connected. In contrast, when people feel ignored, ostracized or excluded, social cognitive neuroscientists have found that this "social pain" triggers some of the same neural activation patterns as physical pain, and is directly and almost universally related to psychological distress and ill-being.

How can we support people's need for autonomy?

As noted in Chapter 2, enabling diversity, variability, experimentation and self-organization so that living systems can self-evolve requires letting go of control, which can be a frightening prospect. The good news is that, contrary to many worldviews, social psychology researchers have found that when given opportunities to regulate their lives in self-determined ways people are more likely to be motivated, efficacious, creative and concerned for others.

Autonomy is shaped by the extent to which people feel their behaviors are volitional and congruent with their interests and values, rather than feeling coerced, compelled or seduced by forces that are external to them. This gives people the freedom to act authentically, and enables them to participate wholeheartedly so that they willingly engage their talents, abilities, and energies in ways that leave them feeling energized and satisfied.

"The course of human history has always moved in the direction of greater freedom. And there's a reason for that— because it's in our nature to push for it."

RICHARD RYAN

Although providing people with autonomy can be feared for its potential to result in impulsiveness, defiance or rebellion as people push toward independence, researchers have found that autonomy actually relies on people's connections with others. As we learned earlier, living systems exist in a world of independence and interdependence and are wired to change in order to preserve both their identity and their coherence. Thus, rather than autonomy leading people into a descent of destructive disorder, it has been found to be the nutrient that supports self-organization and enables order to emerge in a system. This process is evidenced in examples around the world of organizations who have found that by supporting autonomy rather than enforcing control, they have been able to not only help their employees flourish but have also improved their bottom-line.

While Richard and Edward hypothesize that environments that help people to meet all three psychological needs are essential to individual flourishing and are completely interdependent, they have concluded that autonomy in particular helps people to: "gravitate toward, make choices in relation to, and employ optimizing strategies for satisfying each basic need." That said, they recommend that metaphorically we think of supporting our wellbeing like a three-legged stool — pull out any one of the needs and the stool will fall.

How does our environment impact our ability to flourish?

The truth is that in accordance with our understanding of human nature, most people want to contribute; they want to experience competence in what they do, and they want to feel like a meaningful part of a collaborative system. When their environment thwarts the satisfaction of these basic and universal needs for competence, relatedness and autonomy, however, Richard and Edward have found that the dark side of human nature often emerges and people have a tendency to engage in aggressive, greedy and malevolent behaviors as they struggle to manage the effects of ill-being. Thus, it is not enough for someone to simply understand or know how to leverage the pillars of PERMA and expect them to be able to flourish. Instead, people must be motivated, energized, willing and able to consistently invest in actions that build the PERMA pillars, and this requires an environment that provides the nutrients to meet their psychological needs of competence, relatedness and autonomy.

Why Might An AI Summit Enable Individual Flourishing?

As noted in Chapter 1, David's hypothesis of the ability for an AI Summit to enable the PERMA pillars and create a state of mirror flourishing was one of the reasons Michelle undertook her research. Without ever being directly prompted to confirm this hypothesis when the research participants reflected on their experience of AI Summits and what they saw unfolding, they repeatedly described experiences that the researchers in this chapter have found help to improve the PERMA pillars. In itself, this finding was not really surprising, but has provided confirmation of David's hypothesis and a more nuanced understanding of how the PERMA pillars can be more consistently leveraged throughout an AI Summit to support individual and systemic flourishing.

It wasn't until later in the coding process that it started to become clear that it wasn't just experiences that improved the PERMA pillars that were enabling people to flourish, the AI Summits were also providing a safe place that supported people's needs for competence, relatedness and autonomy. The discovery of an AI Summit's ability to be effectance supportive, relationally supportive and autonomy supportive was somewhat surprising, as although references from emerging researchers have tentatively linked appreciative inquiry and self-determination theory, none of the seminal researchers in either field have explored this connection to date.

Thus, Michelle's analysis of what happens in an AI Summit that might heighten the ability for individual participants to flourish found a clear activation of the PERMA pillars inseparably interwoven with the necessary nutrients for self-determination as people engaged, interpreted and acted within their complex dynamic systems (see Figure 1).

| | AI Summit | | | | | |
	Pre	Discovery	Dream	Design	Destiny	Post
PERMA						
Positive Emotion	Medium	High	High	Medium	Medium	Medium
Engagement	Medium	High	High	High	High	High
Relationships	Medium	High	High	High	Medium	Medium
Meaning	Medium	Medium	High	High	High	High
Accomplishment	Medium	High	Medium	High	Medium	Medium
Self-Determination						
Relatedness	Medium	High	High	High	Medium	Medium
Competency	Medium	High	Medium	High	Medium	Medium
Autonomy	Medium	Medium	Medium	High	High	Medium

Figure 1: AI Summit Presence of PERMA Pillars and Self-Determination Nutrients

As a result, Michelle found that AI Summits can:

Enhance efficacy and spark an appetite for learning and growth.

The research participants reported a notable shift in their feelings of confidence and sense of competence throughout the AI Summits that opened them to further learning. This is particularly apparent at the end of the discovery phase when people had been immersed in reflecting on their individual and collective strengths, and at the end of the design phase when they could tangibly touch the pathways they were creating to carry them toward realizing their dreams. For example, one participant noted: "There was a sense of uplift in the room. People started realizing they'd always had these great strengths to draw upon. There was definitely a heightened awareness of their ability." Another reported: "There was a buzz of joy and excitement. There was a real feeling of pride and awe." And another observed: "There was a sense of passion, promise, hope and pride about what we could achieve."

AI Summits provide an environment that is effectance supportive and as a result enables participants to heighten their experience of some of the PERMA pillars – in particular the positive emotions of interest, awe, joy and hope, and a sense of accomplishment that is savored and celebrated as they reflect on their strengths and how these could be built upon to create a better future. It is important to also note, however, that people's sense of accomplishment and feelings of effectance support do go up and down during different stages of the AI Summit process. Following the stages of divergence (in the dream and destiny phases as people try to fuse their diverse hopes and ways of working together) and convergence (at the end of the discovery and design phases as people fuse their strengths and then later select and build a prototype to find ways forward together) these two very different thinking processes can feel uncomfortable and messy unless people have been encouraged to practice the skills of a growth mindset, self-compassion and the courage to have kind conversations with each other (i.e., respecting and valuing the person in front of you enough to let them know when you disagree).

Create a deep sense of belonging around a shared generative purpose.

The research participants repeatedly spoke about their heightened sense of connection to each other as a shared generative purpose started to emerge through the AI Summit process. This is particularly apparent at the end of the dream phase by which time the nutrients for relatedness have been deeply sown, but it is also still noticeable post-Summit in the most transformational examples. For example, one participant reported: "Once they went through the discovery interviews those boundaries, those walls we have, came down and people were just part of one big team." Another shared: "There was a real feeling of kindness that started to appear in the room. The feeling they were connecting to each other as human beings rather than being biased by snap judgements." And another explained: "There's a sense of shared meaning and purpose. We're on a shared quest now."

AI Summits provide repeated opportunities for participants to experience high-quality connections, to act with kindness and generosity toward each other, and to create a shared sense of meaning and purpose about the individual and systemic difference people want to make for others. Interestingly, Michelle found that the systems that experienced fewer long-term transformational changes post-Summit often struggled to sustain the heightened relationally supportive environment created during the Summit, thus to ensure people continue to flourish beyond the AI Summit event it's essential to consider how a relationally supportive environment can be maintained through the destiny phase and beyond.

Fuel the power, energy and commitment for people to self-organize and make a positive difference.

Given it's often thought that people are reluctant to embrace changes in their system, the research participants were often surprised at the AI Summit's capacity to fuel a sense of power, energy and commitment to the degree that people willingly self-organized to start making a more positive difference. Michelle found that this was particularly notable as people emerged from the dream phase and were given the permission and tools in the design and destiny phases to make their shared hopes a reality. For example, one participant observed: "When you give people permission to help create the future, that's the real turning point." Another noted: "People felt empowered to make things happen. They didn't have to wait for management." And another shared: "I don't know anyone who has time to spare so it was amazing to see people lining up to put their name on paper and commit their time to post-Summit actions."

AI Summits provide an autonomy supportive environment that boosts people's sense of engagement, it creates opportunities for them to use their strengths in the service of others and invites them to take responsibility and action for the things they care about. However, Michelle also found that this can pose a challenge in systems where people are not used to this kind of freedom as they struggle to imagine what their role will be post-Summit and what is being asked of them. As one participant noted: "Reality set in. There was a feeling of ownership by this point of their ideas and now they started to wonder what was really going to happen. Were they empowered to do this?" Thus, in order to be compassionate coaches of disruption in systems that have previously relied more on methods of control than self-organization, it's important to be aware that people can become anxious during the destiny phase unless explicit permission and some clear guiding principles are provided so that the emerging teams feel supported and safe as they begin to explore the boundaries of self-organization together.

What Role Will You Play In Helping People Flourish?

Unfortunately, most people lack the knowledge, tools and support to intentionally and consistently invest in experiences that enable the PERMA pillars to support their wellbeing. Thus, AI Summits provide a wonderful – but often missed opportunity – to empower people with a deeper level of understanding about why and how the "magic" of an AI Summit often enables them to feel better and function more effectively than they do most days at work. After all, for many participants it is the desire for more of this "magic" that also attracts them to volunteering for post-Summit activities.

But we need to be mindful that it is not enough to simply teach people about the PERMA pillars, while ignoring the impact of the environment they are operating within. As Richard and Edward's research has repeatedly demonstrated, a system directly impacts people's levels of motivation, learning, performance, creativity, health and humanity by either supporting or thwarting their basic psychological needs for competence, relatedness and autonomy. Thus, while an AI Summit is likely to provide a safe and effective container in which to meet these needs, careful consideration should also be given to the environment participants will return to and how the post-Summit process can help to create a more effectance supportive (versus overly challenging, inconsistent or otherwise discouraging), relationally supportive (versus impersonal or rejecting) and autonomy supportive (versus demanding and controlling) space in which people can flourish.

To guide you, we recommend taking inspiration from Schuberg Philis' post-Summit decision that being a company based on love means that: "We have the desire for each person to flourish. We are all equal and unique. We see the whole human being — as a colleague, as a parent, and as a friend. When we connect at a deep level, wonderful things become possible."

CHAPTER 4

Are You Ready For An AI Summit?

"It was the high point moment of my career.
This is how I want us to be all the time."
CHUCK FOWLER, FAIRMOUNT SANTROL SUMMIT

Fairmount Santrol's customers were taken by surprise. First an unexpected invitation arrived from the industrial sand company's CFO to join 350 people for a three-day planning Summit. Now they found themselves seated at one of fifty tables alongside the company's executive team, sand load operators, operations managers, product designers, suppliers and environmentalists from around the world, and being invited to roll up their sleeves and participate in a real-time strategy session to shape the company's future by harnessing the innovation capacity of sustainability. This from a company environmental protesters had once referred to as "dune-rapers." It was not what people expected.

Within thirty minutes however, the ballroom was buzzing as every single person dove into an appreciative interview with someone they didn't know – for example, the CEO was talking to a sand load operator for the first time — they started uncovering the strategic strengths, the hidden opportunities, and the game-changing possibilities that existed within this surprising organization. The call was for disruptive innovation and as every voice – regardless of job title — was treated with the same respect and value the room became alive with a sense of freedom and possibility.

As they moved into the design phase of the AI Summit, the energy of the group was further heightened as a new multimillion-dollar business opportunity emerged from one of the tables. A chemist shared how spent sand, when placed on farmland, has been shown to help grow higher yields of biomass. One of his table-mates observed that the company's sand mines were located in rural locations near many farms. And as lightbulbs started going off around the table the team began to ask: "How might we create a business from spent sand?" Before the Summit was complete they had outlined a new partnership with rural farmers where sand-assisted biomass growth could become the basis for lower costs and green biofuels to power fleets of heavier trucks.

Within two years, this single innovation coupled with a dozen other sustainability breakthroughs from the AI Summit — such as a low-cost, sand water filter to purify and clean putrid water in areas where families have no access to clean health water — resulted in Fairmount Santrol being recognized as the top corporate citizen in the United States, while increasing their per year earning growth by 40 percent in each of the years following the Summit. But Chuck Fowler – the company's CEO at the time – explained that the greatest value was people took the appreciative inquiry approach back to their workplaces, their communities and their families and as a result it helped them to flourish as they worked, played and lived together.

Following this AI Summit, Fairmount Santrol made a commitment to bring the whole system together every three years to advance new sustainability visions and strategies. One of the early changes to emerge from these Summits was the company's commitment to its Three P's: People, Planet and Prosperity. As a result, Fairmount Santrol now record and report every dollar spent on their appreciative inquiry practices and have found that although they have spent six to seven million dollars to date over the last decade, this commitment has yielded well over twelve million dollars of benefits for the company.

(You can see this AI Summit in action at www.thechangelabs.com.)

Can You Create A Positive Disruption?

Buzzing. Bumpy. Astonished. Tension. Passion. Propel. Electric. Suspicion. Freedom. Urgency. Hope. Mobilized. On fire. Tumultuous. Alive. Out of control. Nervousness. Generosity. Action. Ownership. Progress. Game changing. Ablaze. As you can see below (Figure 2), these are just some of the words research participants used when talking about their experiences of AI Summits.

Figure 2: Summary Words Used To Describe An AI Summit By Participants

There are many highly desirable words reported in this image that attract people to an AI Summit. After all, there aren't many human systems who don't want their people to be more connected, excited and energized as they use their strengths to take ownership and make a difference to others. But if you look at Figure 2 carefully you'll also see some less obvious words appearing – for example, bumpy, tension, tumultuous — that remind us that moving a system to the edge of chaos is not for the fainthearted and that even a positive disruption needs to be enacted with compassion.

Chilean biologist, philosopher and neuroscientist Francisco Varela notes: "You can never direct a living system, you can only disturb it." As we saw in Chapter 2, the most we can do is nudge a system toward the edge of chaos by:

- Creating a safe container that invites a diverse mix of people into a conversation.
- Introducing new information that challenges old assumptions.
- Providing the freedom for self-organization to emerge.

In our minds, these are the essential ingredients for enabling a positive disturbance.

"Very great change starts from very small conversations, held among people who care."
MARGARET WHEATLEY

Researchers caution, however, that while living systems can be positively disturbed with a reasonable expectation of progress, this seldom conforms to the straight path that we might wish. While self-organization and emergence do tend toward order rather than randomness, they do so in their own unique ways and are incredibly sensitive to the system's initial conditions. As the Sufis warn us: "You think that because you understand 'one' that you must, therefore, understand that one and one make two. But you forget that you must also understand 'and.'"

Edward Lorenz, a meteorologist, first drew attention to the sensitive dependence in which a small change in conditions can lead to large differences downstream when he famously coined the term the: "butterfly effect." Describing how the theoretical example of a butterfly flapping its wings in Tokyo can generate a storm in New York a month later, he pointed out that a system's sensitive dependence on initial conditions was an inescapable consequence of our interconnected world.

Although the details of the AI Summits Michelle studied varied considerably — from their purpose, the planning approach, the number of participants, the duration, the activities used to execute the 4-D cycle, and follow-through — all of the research participants interviewed were confident that the AI Summit methodology could be used to create a positive disruption to support systemic flourishing in other systems. Given numerous participants had participated in multiple AI Summits — either in various systems or repeated iterations over time in one system — we believe it is reasonable to be cautiously optimistic about the replicability of using AI Summits to help other systems flourish. However, to assume that an AI Summit will create a positive disruption merely because it follows the 4-D cycle and the five core principles, while ignoring the initial conditions in which the system finds itself, is to risk missing the 'and' on which every living system depends.

Appreciative inquiry researcher and practitioner, Frank Barrett suggests that an AI Summit is best suited for situations where organizations have any of the following intentions to: accelerate planning, decision-making, and innovation; radically shift, inspire, or generate new visions for future organizational action; forge mergers, alliances, and partnerships across entire systems; or design or build momentum for a new organization or a new initiative. While these guidelines are helpful, when Michelle mapped her initial sample of thirteen AI Summits against the AI Summit recommendations of previous researchers as outlined in Chapter 1, what emerged were three clear system dependencies likely to impact the ability of an AI Summit to positively disrupt a system and enable flourishing. These were the:

- Current state of the system
- Openness to generative conversations, ideas and actions
- Support for self-organization

What Is The System's Current State?

What happens in living systems is a dynamic dance between change and stability as it grows and adapts to its environment. In order to be compassionate coaches of disruption, before we try to tip a system toward the edge of chaos and change the tempo of this dance, we must first assess its current state. Is it currently at equilibrium, near equilibrium or far equilibrium? Will this disruption tip it toward the edge of chaos or is there a risk that we may push it into the abyss?

Positive organizational researcher David Bright proposes that one way to understand this dance is as a continuum of organizational states and forces related to change (see Figure 3).

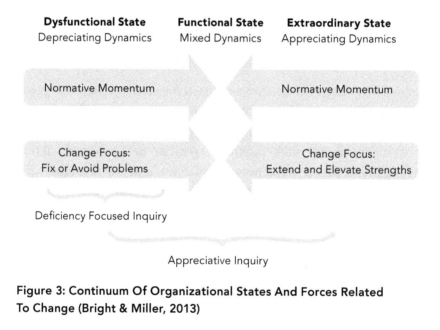

Figure 3: Continuum Of Organizational States And Forces Related To Change (Bright & Miller, 2013)

At the extreme left end of the continuum is the dysfunctional state – a condition of negative deviance, depreciating dynamics and spiralling entropy – and at the extreme right end of the continuum is the extraordinary state – a condition of positive deviance, appreciating dynamics and consistent flourishing. Of course in reality it is rare for any organization to function at either extreme as the force of "normative momentum" or adaptation acts to reduce variance or deviance and return the system to the middle of the continuum and the ordinary state – a condition in which acceptable norms rule and conformity is reinforced.

While researchers have suggested that a living system can be lured by strange attractors and feedback modifiers toward the edge of chaos so that it can redesign itself into a new and more sophisticated form, when presented with an opportunity to create a positive disruption we should ask one fundamental question: Is the change intended to repair and fix a dysfunctional aspect of the system, or is it intended to extend or elevate its strengths? While both intentions have merit, the methods for accomplishing them may need to be quite different depending on the forces shaping the system's momentum for change, and thus determine the suitability of an AI Summit.

Is system in a dysfunctional state?

For example, in a system struggling with the forces of depreciating dynamics people are likely to feel less engaged, less connected and lack the presence of psychological safety, making them more defensive and focused on self-protection and self-preservation. At the far end of this continuum, introducing an AI Summit is likely to be met with great suspicion and skepticism, and when asked to answer unconditionally positive questions, people could feel disingenuous. Without context for the introduction of a positive disruption and groundwork to begin building a genuine culture of appreciation and psychological safety, the use of an AI Summit risks creating a negative disruption because it is seen as a diversionary tactic by management or as a means to silence criticism.

However, when a system is in a dysfunctional state but moving toward a more functional state — although there often remains an absence of appreciation or focus on developing strengths — there is usually some degree of psychological safety that enables an AI Summit to be plausibly positioned as an inquiry into the system's "shadow." By creating a safe container for the system to explore everything people refuse to acknowledge about themselves and the untapped, trapped potential that lies within, an AI Summit can unleash renewed energy and creativity as it helps the system to appreciate and build upon its shared strengths. In fact, researchers suggest that the discovery phase of an AI Summit for a system at this stage of dysfunction is likely to have a more significant impact than for a system at the extraordinary end of the continuum because people will find the experience surprising, positive and exciting in contrast to their normal world.

It's also important to point out that for systems struggling in a dysfunctional state the strengths-focused nature of AI Summits shouldn't preclude a concern with problems. Instead it should empower the system to deal with the problems differently, by flipping "deficit discourses" into more "generative inquiries" of possibilities. For example, when British Airways was struggling to address their problem of "lost baggage," their AI Summit provided an opportunity to flip this deficit discourse into a generative inquiry of "exceptional customer arrival experiences." Stimulating this kind of generative change doesn't simply harness the system's normative momentum to solve the problem and return to equilibrium, but can create enough positive momentum to shift its fundamental assumptions about what it means to function at a higher level and push it toward the extraordinary side of the continuum.

Is the system in an extraordinary state?

At the extraordinary end of the continuum where the forces of an appreciative dynamic are present, people are more likely to feel safe, connected and engaged, making them more open and equally concerned about both their own and other people's interests and wellbeing. As a result, the effects of an AI Summit are often less dramatic because there is an existing general awareness of the system's strengths and potential, and generative conversations are often a cultural norm. Thus, researchers suggest that the goal of an AI Summit for a system in this state should be to positively disrupt the normative pressure every system experiences to be ordinary, and create a safe container for the simultaneous development and acceleration of human and social capital to enable the creation and implementation of generative ideas that push the system far beyond its everyday experiences.

It is also worth noting that in a highly functional system, the appreciative dynamics that exist make it possible to harness the potential energy found in negative forces. For example, the affirming and nonjudgmental approach and opportunity-finding nature of appreciative inquiry can provide the safe space for people to talk openly and honestly about the pain, uncertainty or difficulties they may be facing, while working proactively to envision a more positive future. When treated as a positive disruption into a system's shadow an AI Summit can liberate the collective energy of a system by respectfully and generatively exploring its: concerns and reservations, the stories behind its doubts and reluctance, and the topics that are most challenging to discuss openly. By choosing to recognize and honor a system's capacities, frailties and vulnerabilities, an AI Summit can allow people to reclaim parts of themselves that bring them into wholeness.

Finally, when a system is consistently functioning in an extraordinary state and is vibrant and full of life due to people's extensive and expansive connections and daily participation in generative conversations, it is important to consider whether an AI Summit will really add any benefit. Researchers note that any process that promotes transformation in an organization has to be counter-cultural to the organization in which it is used, so when an appreciating dynamic is already well established it is likely that an AI Summit will create less of a positive disruption. For example, anecdotal evidence has suggested that appreciative inquiry approaches may lose their potency in systems that have used it successfully for a period of time.

Is the system ready for an AI Summit?

It appears that an AI Summit is less likely to create a positive disruption when a system is at either end of this continuum, but can be an effective and powerful way to create a safe container when a system is able to benefit from the new connections, appreciative feedback and opportunity to establish, extend or elevate norms that help people to flourish as they work together. Consequently, we recommend that before any commitment is made to invest in an AI Summit, compassionate coaches of disruption ask: What is the current state of the system? Can an appreciating dynamic be built or is it already present? Are generative conversations already the norm in this system?

Is The System Open To Generativity?

In Chapter 2 we also learned that new and novel information that disturbs the status quo is what triggers disruptions and creates chaos in living systems. In fact, without novel information, researchers suggest that living systems cannot give birth to anything new. Thus, rather than trying to explain the past, appreciative inquiry is designed to be a method for the generative creation of new ideas, perceptions, metaphors, images and theories that offer better alternatives for action within a system.

Of course, the need to generate new information and connections within a system doesn't mean that an AI Summit is the right container to create the positive disruption. If you recall in Chapter 2 we learned that it is most likely to suit complex and adaptive challenges – rather than technical cause-and-effect problems – that unit people with limited existing connections around an issue or opportunity they truly care about. Consequently, Professor Gervase Bushe suggests three ways the generative potential of an AI Summit can be assessed:

1. The opportunity for a generative topic.

2. The willingness to ask generative questions.

3. The courage to hold generative conversations.

---

*"Generativity is the processes and capacities that
help people see old things in new ways."*
GERVASE BUSHE

The most generative images influence people's feelings and motivations, thereby changing the way they think and the decisions and actions that they take, so that over time a new normative order arises based on these shared assumptions that changes a system's culture. Gervase notes that these images don't have to be new to the world or even to the system, they just need to be ones that have not been widely considered and allow people to identify new options, formulate new strategies, and even reform their identity.

Is there the opportunity for a generative topic?

While all topics can be generative to the extent they guide how people see things in new ways, a generative topic in an AI Summit is often a powerful juxtaposition of words that open up new avenues for thinking and acting. They put life back into a system that has become conceptually frozen and overly simplified. They overcome resistance by addressing difficult topics indirectly. And they provide positive and compelling new images of possibility.

Gervase suggests that for a topic to be generative it has to have two qualities:

- It has to allow people to look at problems in a new way and see new opportunities for action.
- It has to be compelling enough that people want to act on the new ideas the image generates.

He recommends that for a generative topic to work it should:

- Capture the core issue those sponsoring the change are interested in.
- Match the identity state of the group in which it is being used (i.e. pre-

identity groups need to focus on creating a stronger sense of identity and membership in the group, while post-identity groups need to focus not on who we are but on what we do and how we do it).

- Frame the focus of inquiry in a way few people have considered before by focusing the system's attention away from the issues themselves and toward the exploration of images that are novel, meaningful and kindle hope for what it wants to grow in the future.

- Draw on the explicit or conceptual metaphors used by people to describe what is happening in the system.

- Challenge polarities, paradoxes and either/or thinking that seem to be keeping the system stuck (i.e. sustainable development).

- Ensure the chosen words touch people's hearts and spirits so that topics capture the interest and energy of those people who need to be engaged in the change.

- Capture the interest and energy of those people who need to be engaged in the change.

For example, when the city of Cleveland, one of the most polluted cities in America, decided to try and create a greener economy, their first AI Summit topic was: "Creating an economic engine to empower a green city on a blue lake."

Is there the willingness to ask generative questions?

Gervase suggests that while most people planning an AI Summit begin by having people focus on each person's peak experiences, a "best of" example, this alone is not enough to create generativity. For example, he shares that once while encouraging a group of forty-five construction managers to share their best experiences of leadership it became clear that they never thought much about leadership and had little in the way of personal stories of inspiring leadership stories to tell, resulting in nothing generative emerging from their conversation and a very long and painful workshop!

Instead of simply drawing out positive experiences, Gervase has found that generative questions have four qualities:

1. They are surprising because they create space for people to reflect and think about things they haven't generally considered before.
2. They prompt people to talk about things they feel emotionally engaged about.
3. They engender conversations that invite people to be more open, vulnerable and connected with each other.
4. They invite people to look at reality differently by disrupting people's current beliefs.

He also recommends that for pre-identity groups (in which the majority of members do not identify with the system), questions that identify what is most valued by members and dreams for the group will be most generative, whereas for post-identity groups (in which the majority of members do identify with the system) questions in support of the group's efficacy in achieving its purpose will be more powerful.

Is there the courage to hold generative conversations?

Gervase notes that who, when, where and how people answer these questions can increase or decrease the generativity of the discovery phase of an AI Summit. When more people are involved in interviewing as well as being interviewed, he has found that it generates a lot more interest, engagement, excitement, relationship building and ongoing conversations. In particular, the stories of marginalized members of a system often surface new ideas and ways of thinking that have been overlooked or undervalued in the past. He concludes that the more widespread the engagement with generative questions is across a system, the larger the potential for positive disruptions to take place.

It is also imperative that these generative questions are not used as a means of repressing negative conversations in a system. This doesn't mean that AI Summits should become bogged down in conversations about what's not working and why, but it does give people permission to talk honestly and openly about what's missing, what they want more of and what's creating the gaps between their hopes and reality. If this is the conversation a system needs to have, an AI Summit can provide the space for an incredibly safe, authentic, and generative discussion that surfaces new ideas and images and points a system toward a better collective future provided it has the courage to have this conversation.

Finally, Gervase urges systems not to shy away from opportunities for differentiation and divergence throughout an AI Summit. For example, he suggests that the purpose of the dream phase is not to simply illustrate the similarities in people's dreams – although surfacing shared hopes can be useful and necessary – but to surface the values and aspirations that enliven the system by giving people the opportunity to share what they really feel and want. A generative dream phase should encourage people to stand for what they value and encourage them to openly explore the differences and diversity of their hopes. A system needs to have the courage to get a little messy in the service of generating new ideas.

Is the system open to being generative?

AI Summits help to enable transformational change when they create a positive disruption that evokes generative images, questions and conversations about shared opportunities, and challenges that mobilize people's passion and willingness to take responsibility for agreed, generative actions across a system. As appealing as this may sound, it is important to note that as we saw in Figure 2, generativity can be surprising, messy, bumpy and create tensions. Being open to generativity requires a system to get comfortably uncomfortable as it embraces uncertainty, surrenders its quest for predictability and embarks on a journey of iteration that dances between order and chaos.

We recommend that before any commitment is made to investing in an AI Summit, compassionate coaches of disruption ask: Can you identify a generative topic for inquiry? Are leaders happy for people to ask generative questions? Will people have the courage to embrace generative conversations, even when it means getting messy or uncomfortable?

Will The System Support Self-Organization?

In Chapter 2 we learned that at the edge of chaos a system's stability and sense of order comes from its coherence about who it is, what it needs and what is required to survive in its environment so that it can develop in ways of its own choosing and over time spawn a stronger, self-organized system. For example, Gervase's analysis of twenty appreciative inquiry cases described in Chapter 1 found that post-Summit six of the seven transformational cases adopted an "improvisational approach" that allowed people to self-organize, rather than top-down management approaches. Thus, before we intentionally introduce a positive disruption we must also assess the system's ability to self-organize so that order will surface.

Why might this be essential for a positive disruption to support systemic flourishing? Recall that research suggests that unlike a clockwork machine that is static, stable and can be controlled, living systems are adaptive, resilient and flourish through growth. Wired for preservation, when a system is faced with increasing levels of disturbance it possesses an innate ability to reorganize as it deals with the new information to ensure its growth and resilience. This innate ability for order and form are made possible not by complex controls or constricting people's freedom, but by the combination of a few guiding principles that express the system's overall identity and provide high levels of autonomy for people within that system.

The reality is that a living system maintains itself and grows stronger only as it encourages greater amounts of individual freedom. While this can be a frightening proposition for leaders who have grown up believing that they can control and predict a system — despite all the evidence to the contrary

— as we learned in Chapter 3, rather than autonomy leading a system into a descent of self-centered disorder, people's drive for coherence and belonging mean that in this densely interconnected world order emerges without the need for control.

"If we believe that there is no order to human activity except that imposed by the leader, that there is no self-regulation except that dictated by policies, if we believe that responsible leaders must have their hands into everything, controlling every decision, person, and moment, then we cannot hope for anything except what we already have—a treadmill of frantic efforts that end up destroying our individual and collective vitality."

MARGARET WHEATLEY

Trying to control a living system by imposing rigid structures to solve complex challenges is a fool's errand. Instead, Harrison Owen suggests that the power of authentic leadership occurs when: "people's passion and responsibility for a cause inspire others to make it a common cause. Not by domination and control, but through invitation and appreciation." He goes on to note that for order to emerge people must be given the chance to voluntarily respond to such an invitation so that those who care enough connect, not because they were ordered or commanded to do so, but because they are willing to take responsibility for what is happening. It is around this strange attractor, that Harrison describes as "a nexus for caring," that people choose to self-organize and order begins to arise.

Is there leadership support for self-organization?

Gervase suggests that from the outset a system needs to accept that the purpose of the AI Summit is to have a large number of motivated people acting on strategic, self-generated "probes" – small, fail-safe experiments – rather than a list of winning ideas to be project managed. David Snowden and Mary Boone's award-winning paper on *A Leader's Framework For Decision Making* supports this recommendation, suggesting that when working with complex challenges where the answers are unpredictable, an emergent change process is needed. For example, studies of organizations that thrived in complexity found that the most successful companies invested in "firing bullets" — low cost, low risk, low distraction experiments — to empirically validate what works, and then concentrated their resources to "fire a cannonball" at the opportunity and kept marching to capitalize on their success.

Thus, Gervase recommends that:

- Prior to the AI Summit, leaders need to imagine, prepare and budget for the kind of resources and support (i.e. money, meeting space, equipment, time, communication channels) likely to be needed by these small, self-organized groups post-Summit. They also need to put tools in place to help teams share, track and celebrate their progress and maintain their momentum so that the system can continue reorganizing at higher levels of complexity.

- During the destiny phase people are invited to publicly volunteer to help advance a design proposal or take some form of personal action toward the shared dreams. People need to believe that they have permission to take these actions, and that it is up to them to take responsibility and self-organize around the ideas about which they are most passionate. It is important to be clear that other than providing the boundaries of vision and purpose, and some guiding principles for working, leaders will not be doing this for them.

- Post-Summit leaders need to be willing and able to "track" (look for the appearance of what you want more of) and "fan" (add oxygen to heighten the blaze) rather than plan and control the emergent changes. While it is essential that self-organized groups are encouraged to put effort into trying what they have proposed, it is also important that the outcomes are held lightly and that the opportunities for adaptive learning and growth are celebrated and disseminated. Ideas that show promise will need to be cultivated and integrated into the organization. The leaders' role post-Summit is less about decision-making and more one of compassionate and wise coach.

This is why Peggy Holman urges us as compassionate coaches of disruption to embrace the complexity, disruption and messiness that emergent processes entail as simply "nature's way of change." She suggests that instead of trying to avoid disturbance, we should harness its momentum for a creative dance with chaos and order. Instead of holding outcomes so tightly, we should focus on intentions and finding the best ways of working together. And instead of demanding action, we should invite people to take responsibility for the things they feel passionate enough to follow through on, and learn from their energy. After all, as Erich Jantsch observed, in the end the more freedom we provide for self-organization, the more order emerges.

Is the system able to support self-organization?

The self-organizing potential of a living system is enhanced by:

- Increasing the number of people being invited to help shape the system.

- Enriching the quality of connections between people to build new networks based on a wider understanding of their shared hopes for the system.

- Fueling these networks with generative information and the freedom to spark further evolution.

They also caution, however, that for self-organization to flourish, a system requires clear boundaries provided by a shared purpose and vision, and simple rules that encourage the desired values and behaviors, otherwise self-organizing masses risk veering wildly off course. Additionally, if self-organization is sought but then throttled back with excessive control because leaders really "know the answers" and just wanted superficial buy-in from people, they risk poisoning the system.

An AI Summit can be a great way to support self-organization, but in order to be a compassionate coach of disruption we must first assess the existing levels of autonomy and the system's willingness and ability to support this way of working post-Summit. For example, Gervase notes that encouraging self-organization in a system used to a command-and-control approach could result in people feeling anxious and pushing back because they feel ill-equipped and unsupported to work together in this way.

Thus, we recommend that before any commitment is made to invest in an AI Summit, compassionate coaches of disruption ask: To what degree does the system already encourage self-organization? Is the system willing to actively allow opportunities for self-organization after the AI Summit? What support might leaders and teams need to ensure order emerges from self-organized, generative actions after the AI Summit?

How Can We Apply These Ideas Practically?

In an effort to better understand the suitability of an AI Summit to create the kind of positive disruption that might help a system to flourish, Michelle went back to her data and started looking for ways to:

- Decipher a system's readiness for an AI Summit.
- Determine a system's willingness to support self-organization.
- Discover a system's openness for generativity.

To do this she experimented with the following scale:

Never -5					Sometimes 0				Consistently +5
O	O	O	O	O	O	O	O	O	

What is the current state of the system?

1. Do people interact with each other in appreciative ways?

2. Do people feel psychologically safe to take risks and challenge each other?

3. Is this system having a positive impact on the people it serves?

Is the system open to generativity?

4. Is there the willingness to invest in generative topics and generative questions?

5. Is there the courage to have generative conversations across the system?

6. Are leaders willing to support and resource generative actions post-Summit?

Will the system support self-organization?

7. Is there a clear vision and agreed values to guide people's choices?

8. Are self-organized teams already encouraged and supported in this system?

9. Is this system willing to explicitly support self-organized teams post-Summit?

FIGURE 4: System Suitability For An AI Summit

Based on the data Michelle gathered from the initial thirteen in-depth interviews, she explored the potential likelihood of an AI Summit creating the kind of positive disruption that might help a system to flourish. Here is what she found:

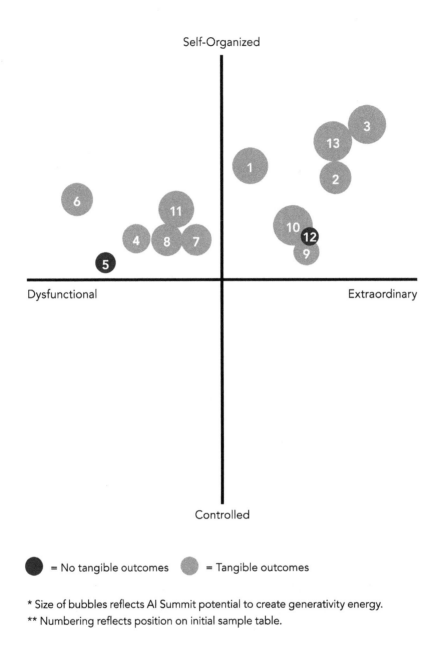

Figure 5: AI Summit System Suitability For Initial Sample

As the AI Summits Michelle sampled were chosen because there was evidence they had helped to create a positive disruption that enabled systemic flourishing, when assessed against David Bright's continuum of organizational states, it is not surprising that these systems are neither extremely dysfunctional nor extraordinary. For example:

- The system for which Summit 3 was held – which was assessed as the closest toward an extraordinary state — while experiencing tangible outcomes, reported fewer overall changes than the other Summits in the sample, supporting David Bright's cautions for working against a system's normative momentum.

- The systems for which Summits 4, 6, 7, 8, and 11 were held – which were assessed slightly more toward a dysfunctional state – experienced tangible outcomes that reached much further across their systems and in many of these cases resulted in the transformational change of entire industries or communities. Again, this supports his suggestion that systems at this stage of dysfunction may experience a more dramatic and positive impact from AI Summit because participants will find the encounter surprising, positive and exciting in contrast to their normal world. It also reinforces his reassertion that when a generative approach is taken to addressing the problems these systems may face, an AI Summit will not simply harness the system's normative momentum to solve the problem and return to equilibrium, but can create enough positive momentum that it shifts a system's fundamental assumptions about what it means to function at a higher level and pushes it toward the extraordinary side of the continuum.

- The systems for which Summits 1, 2, 9, 10 and 13 were held – which were assessed slightly more toward an extraordinary state – experienced tangible outcomes that created considerable transformational change across their system, but relied more heavily on the generative nature of the AI Summit – particularly the creation of new relationships — to offset the system's normative momentum and create positive energy to move the system closer toward extraordinary.

Thus, Michelle's analysis concurs with the suggestion that an AI Summit is likely to create the most positive disruption when the system's current state can benefit most from an appreciative dynamic being elevated or extended.

Gervase notes that AI Summits lead to transformational change when self-organizing processes are channeled in useful ways by increasing the richness of social networks, so that like-minded and motivated people find each other and are encouraged to «make something happen." In Michelle's analysis we can see that:

- Summits 1, 2, 3, and 13 were assessed as being implemented in systems that strongly supported self-organizing processes. For Summits 1, 2, and 13 this was because previous Summits had been run in these systems and laid the groundwork for self-organization practices to continue. For Summit 13, this was because the system had already intentionally embraced self-organization as a means for people working together. In all cases, the design and destiny phases for these Summits were much less "bumpy," "anxious" and "tumultuous" than in other systems. Post-Summit groups had a better understanding of what was required of them, leaders were able to better support the groups and there was acceptance that some ideas would flourish, while others would wither, but that the point was to keep learning and creating new connections in the way they worked together.

- Summits 6 and 11 were assessed as being implemented in systems that did not yet have strong support for self-organization processes but had leaders that were very strongly committed post-Summit to establishing this as a way of working for the teams that emerged. This support was crucial in ensuring that transformational change was created.

- The remaining Summits were assessed as being implemented in systems with less support for self-organizing processes and less understanding of the need for leadership commitment post-Summit to establish this support. As a result, there was a heightened sense of anxiety, uncertainty and nervousness about their roles and the ability to realize their shared dreams during the destiny phase of the Summit. Systems often scrambled to provide enough support post-Summit, and in the cases of Summits 5 and 12 the inability to support self-organization was a key contributor to tangible outcomes not being achieved.

Thus, Michelle's analysis concurs with Gervase's recommendation that an AI Summit is likely to create the kind of positive disruption that supports systemic flourishing when the system already has or is willing to invest in post-Summit self-organizing processes that increase the richness of social networks, so that like-minded and motivated people can find each other and are encouraged to work together to "make something happen."

As noted earlier, Gervase has also argued that opportunities for generativity – the processes and capacities to help people see things in new ways – are essential if an AI Summit is to influence how people think and the decisions and actions they might take over time to transform the system's culture. In Michelle's analysis she found that:

- The generative nature of Summits 1, 2, 3, 9, 10 and 13 was essential to creating a positive disruption in these systems because the new information and new relationships they created provided renewed energy and momentum for transformational change.

- The generative nature of Summits 4, 6, 7, 8 and 11 also helped to create enough energy and momentum that they were able to not just solve the challenges they were facing, but to shift the systems' fundamental assumptions about what it means to function at a higher level and thus support their ability to flourish post-Summit.

- Summits 5 and 12 struggled because leaders were not willing to support generative actions for these systems post-Summit. As a result, even though the topic, questions and conversations in the Summits were experienced as generative, there was not the momentum required to support the system to deliver tangible outcomes and flourish.

Thus, Michelle would strongly endorse Gervase's recommendation for generative opportunities to help people see things in new ways and see new opportunities for action. And in his five generativity success factors for AI Summits mentioned in Chapter 1, David also urges systems to make the concentration effect of strengths a vital management skill for creating cultures of open innovation that systemically accelerate and scale up solutions.

The ability to assess the potential suitability of an AI Summit to positively disrupt a system and support its ability to flourish is not a tool leaders or practitioners have previously been able to access. As noted throughout this chapter, while other researchers have previously explored these dimensions, they have not yet been presented as a means for assessing and mapping a system's environment and how this may help us to be compassionate coaches of disruption, and thus as the Sufi story urged us: better understand the dimensions of 'and.'

CHAPTER 5

How Does An AI Summit Work?

"The flourishing enterprise isn't a destination.
It's a journey and it's a roadmap."
JULIE REITER, CLARKE SUMMIT

"If you don't do something different, you're going to end up where you're headed," said the poster Lyell Clarke III took from a seminar room in 2008. As the CEO of Clarke, a mosquito control products and services company that had been established 1946, and that in his view had become stale, slow to change, and conservatively "old school," Lyell was ready to do something different.

He wanted to inspire a change. Although the company enjoyed a significant share of the mosquito control pesticide and service market, Lyell longed to hand the next generation a company that was a flagship for environmental sustainability. As Lyell himself points out though: "Transforming the business from our roots as a mosquito control service and pesticide distribution company to one with a broader vision of sustainability focused environmental products and services, couldn't be done with a company memo or by simply calling people into a room and announcing a new direction. That approach just wasn't going to work."

After exploring different large-group planning approaches to start setting sustainability goals and establishing its initial sustainability working committees, Lyell decided that if he really wanted to ingrain sustainability into the mindset and practices across the company, then an AI Summit might be what was needed. So even though Clarke's chief financial officer had cautioned Lyell that he couldn't afford an AI Summit right now, as his company was slowly emerging from the effects of the 2012 economic recession, Lyell welcomed 200 people from across Clarke's system to the "Accelerating Sustainability Summit."

"It was scary. It was a risk. It was also the right thing to do," said Lyell.

You can imagine Lyell's relief three days later when despite the uncertainty of participants going into the AI Summit, his biggest challenge had become enabling people to deliver on the phenomenal excitement, positivity, and innovations they had created to realize Clarke's dream of accelerating sustainability. Turning to his Head of Human Resources, Julie Reiter, Lyell asked: "What's next?" To which Julie bluntly replied: "I have no idea. But I'm going to figure it out."

Within weeks, Julie had set up a twelve-month post-Summit plan to guide the development of initiatives and innovations arising from the AI Summit and to support the leaders and working teams in their areas of opportunity. Using an iterative planning process, priorities and budgets were agreed, conversations continued evolving and ideas were turned into realities to the point that sustainability has now become part of Clarke's daily practices.

"I'm always cautious about any bold statements about Clarke being sustainable or flourishing," explained Julie. "I would definitely say though, with that caveat, that post-Summit we are embracing the concepts of striving to be a more flourishing organization to invite the whole employee, the whole self to work, to celebrate the whole self, to engage the whole self, and to pay attention to our employees in our community and our environment in a holistic fashion."

As a result Julie notes that Clarke's culture has changed, with people now significantly more engaged in the greater purpose their work could have, the opportunity to be aspirational and seek out new opportunities, and the willingness to take a positive orientation to their interactions with each other. In fact, the AI Summit delivered such valuable and widespread results that four years later Clarke decided to do it all again in their second Summit. This time to continue advancing their hopes for flourishing people, a flourishing company and a flourishing world.

(You can see this AI Summit in action at www.thechangelabs.com.)

What Does It Take To Run An AI Summit?

As noted since the late 1990s, a 4-D cycle has consistently been taught as the foundation of appreciative inquiry approaches, and an AI Summit is no exception. In the early stages of Michelle's research it became clear, however, that while she never primed or intentionally asked the participants, there was a 6-D cycle consistently required to make the AI Summits she was studying work. As shown in Figure 6, the 6-D AI Summit cycle includes: define, discovery, dream, design, destiny and what we have termed "drum."

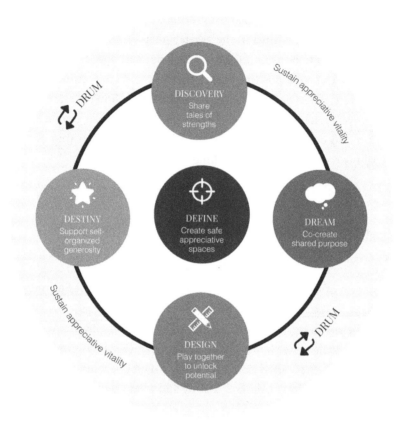

Figure 6: 6-D AI Summit Cycle

This finding was not entirely surprising. The Clergy Leadership Institute in the U.S. has previously suggested "define" as the first step to identify the affirmative topic for any appreciative inquiry effort and as a result some AI models have referred in the past to a 5-D model. Widely used AI Summit practitioner guides have also emphasized the importance of the pre-Summit steps of planning and designing for what will unfold during the 4-D cycle, and the post-Summit steps of communicating outcomes, supporting innovation teams and embedding appreciative intelligence in the system.

What was surprising was how resolute the research participants were about the importance of these additional steps to the model in an AI Summit. "The pre-Summit experience is something we learned is absolutely critical," said one participant. "The magic of an AI Summit happens in the planning," emphasized another participant. "It's what happens after the Summit that really makes the difference," cautioned someone else. "Make a solid commitment to the post-planning process," urged another.

In fact, it became clear over the course of the interviews that these steps were not simply pre and post preparations for executing the 4-D cycle, they were a fundamental part of the process and without them the ability to create a positive disruption that might support systemic flourishing would be severely limited. Given the diversity, variability, experimentation and self-organization we've seen that is required for a system to flourish, it makes sense that when the 4-D cycle is applied across an entire system in an AI Summit format, an extended 6-D cycle is required to support the emergence of a generative purpose, connections and practices.

What Makes The Best AI Summits Work?

As the research participants described what was unfolding throughout their AI Summit experiences, consistent psychological, neurological, social, and systemic mechanisms emerged during each of the 6-D phases. When Michelle laid these observations against the insights we have gained in the previous chapters about what enables systems and humans to flourish, 12 magic mechanisms emerged (see Figure 7) that explain the best practices of the research sample.

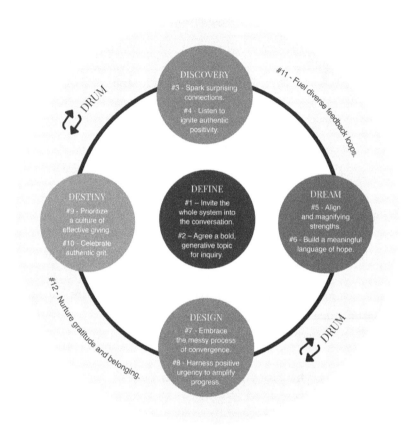

Figure 7: The 12 Magic Mechanisms Of The AI Summit 6-D Cycle

During the define phase the research participants create safe appreciative spaces by:

• Inviting the whole system into the conversation.

• Agreeing to a bold, generative topic for inquiry.

During the discovery phase they share tales of strengths by:

• Sparking surprising connections.

• Listening to ignite authentic positivity.

During the dream phase, they co-create a shared purpose by:

- Aligning and magnifying strengths.
- Building a meaningful language of hope.

During the design phase they play together to unlock potential by:

- Embracing the messy process of convergence.
- Harnessing positive urgency to amplify progress.

During the destiny phase they support self-organized generosity by:

- Prioritizing a culture of effective giving.
- Celebrating authentic grit.

Finally, during the drum phase they sustain appreciative vitality by:

- Fueling diverse feedback loops.
- Nurturing gratitude and belonging.

This rich tapestry of practices at times intentionally applied, but often instinctively used, draws upon multiple fields of research about what enables individuals, groups and complex adaptive systems to flourish. For example, the presence of the PERMA pillars and the satisfaction of people's individual needs for self-determination underpin each phase. Team based practices from positive organization scholarship and design thinking are woven throughout. And finally, the insights of social constructionism, social cognitive neuroscience, dialogic organizational development and complex adaptive systems reflect our emerging understanding of how living systems self-organize as their environments change to enable growth, resilience and flourishing.

What Does This Look Like Practically?

In the rest of this chapter we'll walk you through the 6-D cycle, detail what happens during each phase and explain how to apply the relevant 12 best practice steps to leverage the psychological, neurological, social, and systemic mechanisms Michelle found were used in the AI Summits within her research. With the kind permission from the generous team at Clarke, we'll also share their 2016 AI Summit planning materials, workbooks and outputs to provide a real-world example of these practices. Of course, Clarke didn't intentionally set out to follow the 6-D cycle or to leverage the 12 mechanisms that Michelle's research surfaced, but it is reassuring that when reviewing their materials throughout their examples you'll find consistent alignment with Michelle's findings.

As we dive into the detail, it is important to note that every AI Summit looks different depending on the needs of the system. What we're sharing are the best practices that Michelle's research found, but we should remain mindful that even the best research on human and systems behavior only tells us what works for some of the people and some of the system, some of the time, and thus these suggestions should be intelligently applied to suit the context of each system and the people within it. Our hope is that the research insights will accelerate your understanding of how the best AI Summits work, inspire ideas for potential applications and give you the confidence to pull these approaches apart and find what best serves the systems and people you want to help to flourish.

Define: Create Safe Appreciative Spaces

Figure 8: Summary Of Words Used To Describe Define Phase By Research Participants

Researchers suggest that in order to relinquish control and allow a system to dance with its environment and support emergent change, we need to begin by creating a safe container for novel information to be appreciatively shared across the whole system so that the disturbance can be welcomed. Thus, the goal of this phase of an AI Summit is to create a safe, appreciative space to enable a positive disruption to take place.

David and his colleagues have explained in the past that to appreciate is to value and recognize the best in people or the system around us. By affirming past, present and potential strengths, and understanding what gives life – health, vitality and excellence – to a living system, appreciation enables us to increase the value of what works well.

The good news is that in order to exist every system already works to some degree, so instead of fueling a downward spiral of fear, blame and shame that can often be sparked by organizational inquiries, appreciative spaces enable an upward spiral of confidence, curiosity and hope that is grounded in the reality of the strengths the system has to build upon. Appreciative spaces disrupt, but they do so by bringing together diverse people who care and focus them on opportunities for something better and more meaningful. And they create a welcoming environment that opens the way to discover what wants to emerge, even when the starting place may be: "Given all that has happened, what is possible now?"

As a result, Michelle found that appreciative spaces provided the psychological safety for people to share their truth, to honor their dreams, and to ask for the support that they needed. And they created a sanctuary so that when people stepped into disruption, uncertainty or upheaval, they were able to face the unknown together and find answers that supported the system's growth, resilience and ability to flourish.

How do AI Summits create safe, appreciative spaces?

In order to create a safe, appreciative space, Clarke and other research participants began by:

- Selecting a champion who is passionate about the initiative, influential with decision makers, driven to get things done and able to provide post-Summit support.

- Establishing sponsors from the leadership team who have the authority to make key decisions in relation to the AI Summit, provide financial and other resources, give visible and enthusiastic support to the process and outcomes and use their influence to ensure its success.

The champion and sponsors worked together (and often drew on the expertise on an external consultant) to gain a good understanding of:

- The AI Summit process and the importance of the whole system participating.

- The generative, task focused nature of what will unfold.
- The goal of finding common ground around shared passions for which people are willing to take responsibility.
- The need to support people to self-organize and take action.

It is worth noting, that as we have explored in previous chapters, this is not typically the way most systems currently work. Thus, these teams also found it is important to assess the suitability of an AI Summit to create a positive disruption in the system's current environment at this stage.

"The sobering question that has to be asked and honestly answered is: 'Are we truly committed to and invested in soliciting this feedback and engaging our stakeholders in the future of our organization, whatever that is? Are we committed to engaging their energy, ideas, passion and souls?'"

JULIE REITER

If an AI Summit was deemed to be a good fit for the system, the sponsors and champion then agreed on a clear, strategic focus for the AI Summit that clarified the desired change agenda by answering questions such as:

- What do we really want from this Summit?
- What are the ultimate hopes and aspirations for our stakeholders?
- What will success look like?

For example, the U.S. Dairy Industry agreed on building a sustainable dairy industry. Schuberg Philis agreed on extending partnerships with all stakeholders. And Fairmount Santrol agreed on harnessing the innovation capacity of sustainability.

Once the strategic focus was agreed, an AI Summit steering committee or planning team who were representative of stakeholders across the system who care and "ARE IN" – those with authority, resources, expertise, information and need – were invited to take part in a series of appreciative conversations to:

- Learn about appreciative inquiry and how an AI Summit works, clarify the context and purpose of the Summit, and agree on a Summit topic (or topics) and objectives which became the "North Star" that influenced all decisions about how the Summit will unfold (see more below for selecting the topics). In addition, some AI Summits were given their own brand name, logo and tagline to capture people's imagination and create excitement where this was considered necessary or appropriate.

- Identify who and how many people from across the system will attend based on those who care and "ARE IN" (typically AI Summit events ranged from fifty people to 1000 people or more with 70-80 percent of these people being internal stakeholders and the other 20-30 percent external stakeholders), issue invitations, track who would be attending, create a mix-max seating plan with tables of six to twelve people so a representation of the system is at each table (often making use of the power of improbable pairs by seating people next to each other who represent opposite extremes), and creating name tags to make it easy for people to meet each other.

- Determine the AI Summit format and the number of days over which the event itself would be held and draft an agenda. Typically AI Summits were two to three days in length but this varied from one day to four days depending on how many people were involved (i.e. the more people present, the more time was needed for sharing and reporting back in activities), the topic being undertaken (i.e. the newer or more complex the Summit topic, the more helpful it was to add speakers to create a common understanding the group could build upon), and how far self-organized teams needed to progress while already gathered (i.e. the more established these teams needed to be before they left the Summit, the more time they needed for the destiny phase together). If it was impossible to pull the system together for this length of time, multiple mini-Summits spread over weeks or months also seemed to work, or a pre-work and/or a post-work sequence was another effective way to break up the 6-D cycle.

- Create the AI Summit design by agreeing on the flow of speakers (in some systems this was a great opportunity for subject matter experts or representatives from other organizations with an important message to share to be present, provided it didn't overboard and turn a working session into a presentation) and the activities that would guide participants in an engaging, energizing and effective experience to enable them to build diverse and authentic connections. Careful consideration was given to the mix of individual, small-group and plenary activities and how people's brains perform at their best (i.e. most people's energy moves in a wave of ninety minute to two-hour cycles). Once agreed, the design details were captured and printed in a workbook for each person attending and any supporting presentation materials that were required were prepared. Decisions were also made on how to document the AI Summit proceedings and whether a graphic recorder or videographer would be used, or if the artifacts produced (i.e. written stories, the positive core, images of dreams, lists of priorities, photos of prototypes, and written aspiration statements and volunteer names) would simply be gathered for the final report. Then all of these design timings and instructions were typically added to an AI Summit agenda to create a more detailed, moment-by-moment guide to make managing the actual event easier.

- Map a communication plan up to and beyond the AI Summit event to ensure people across the system – both those attending and those unable to attend — remained curious, confident, and committed about what was unfolding and their invitation to be part of the change happening. This included emails, newsletters, media articles, meetings, events, videos, websites, intranets or online internal chat tools, posters, postcards, SMS messages, and any other vehicles the system could leverage. For example, at Hunter Douglas the organizing team decided to wear buttons that said: "Ask Me About Focus 2000" (which was the name of their AI Summit).

- Arrange the logistics for the AI Summit like any warm and welcoming host would by: selecting a venue people could easily reach and would create a life-enhancing opportunity for conversations (i.e. a room that people would want to spend a lot of time in, could easily play in, and would feel safe for them), ordering catering that would make it easy for people's brains and bodies to flourish (i.e. sugary and fried foods were kept to a minimum), setting up staging and audio-visual requirements that made it easy for anyone to engage (i.e. thought was given to hearing, visual or physically challenged people attending), creating a registration area to welcome people and answer any queries they had, and considering any other supplies that would be required (i.e. most AI Summits had printed workbooks for participants, creative materials for the dream phase and building kits and boards for the design phase).

- Put in place plans, resources and support for the generative actions of post-Summit teams and ensure leaders were ready to take on the role of compassionate coaches. Generally, this was ready to implement within days of the AI Summit event's completion.

Depending on the expertise and previous experience of the people involved and the size of the AI Summit being planned, this process took anywhere from three to twelve months. Generally, the larger the Summit, the larger the steering committee and the more time for planning was needed for this phase.

As Julie explained: "The pre-Summit experience is something we learned is absolutely critical." And other research participants agreed, emphasizing over and over how important the define phase is to a successful AI Summit.

(Visit www.thechangelabs.com for examples of Clarke's AI Summit materials.)

Why invite the whole system into a conversation?

Inviting the whole system into an appreciative conversation is a decision that many of the research participants observed made leaders nervous. For example, Lyell noted that: "It gets a little scary when you're opening up your business to the world." The research participants consistently reported, however, that inviting the whole system was a critical success factor for creating a positive disruption that supported their system's ability to flourish. One urged: "Work very hard to bring together as many people as you can and listen to them." Another shared: "It was important to have the whole system in the room." And another explained: "When you put every part of the ecosystem in the room and give them a voice, there's nothing like it."

Quantum physicist David Bohm suggests that wholeness is in fact essential to a well-lived life. He points out that the word "health" in English is based on an Anglo-Saxon word "hale" meaning "whole": thus to be healthy is to be whole. Diana Whitney and Amanda Trosten-Bloom, in their acclaimed book *The Power of Appreciative Inquiry,* suggest that the experience of wholeness comes about when people are able to hear, witness, and make sense of each other's differing views, perspectives, and interpretations of shared events. They note that this sense of understanding the whole story — with all its differences and distinctions — brings with it a kind of contentment that does not require agreement but enables people to safely focus on issues of higher purpose and the greater good for everybody.

———

"In life, the issue is not control, but dynamic connectedness."
ERICH JANTSCH

———

While leaders often worry about the system's ability to find any common ground with so many different voices present in an AI Summit, surprisingly, researchers have found that similar ideas surface over and over when people with different perspectives creatively interact. This is because no matter where people come from, what is most personally meaningful is universal and as they experience this for themselves they shift from thinking of "I" to wanting to be part of "we" and this allows a shared identity and sense of community to emerge. When people have the opportunity to discover they are the system, everything changes as their commitment and confidence to act in support of each other is strengthened. In this moment their differences cease to be obstacles, and instead become creative pathways to unexpected innovations and growth that contain what is vital and energizing to each and all of us.

Bringing the whole system together, particularly when there are sparse prior connections, is one of the key mechanisms for creating a positive disruption that supports systemic flourishing. The most successful AI Summits in Michelle's research invited those who cared and "ARE IN" – those with authority, resources, expertise, information and need – across different stakeholder groups (i.e. customers, vendors, non-profit organizations, researchers, neighbors, industry partners and associations, regulators and government bodies, media, etc.) and levels of seniority to stimulate new knowledge and new connections. This included inviting the cynics and detractors who cared and "ARE IN" to ensure that the doubts people have are given a voice. With a shared intention and more eyes, ears, hearts, minds and hands involved, researchers have found that there is more of a chance of emergent change occurring.

Magic Mechanism Tip

Invite those who care (even the cynics) and "ARE IN" – those with authority, resources, expertise, information and need – across different stakeholder groups and levels of seniority to stimulate new knowledge and new connections to be part of the steering committee and participants in the AI Summit.

Why agree a bold, generative topic?

Bold, generative topics and questions bridge chaos and creativity. By definition generativity is about shifting people's way of seeing the world in a direction that is deemed desirable and creates an image that is compelling enough that people want to act on the new ideas it generates. While David has previously pointed out that several decades of research — from the placebo effect to the Pygmalion effect, self-fulfilling prophecies and biofeedback — consistently support the observation that "positive images lead to "positive action," researchers caution that it is not simply the positive nature of these images that pull us forward but the fact that they are meaningful to people that ensures they are generative.

As we learned in Chapter 4, defining a generative Summit topic is central to successful appreciative inquiry efforts. Based on Michelle's research we believe that this is because bold, generative topics work like strange attractors that draw people together by providing a sense of coherence and guidelines around the kind of meaningful work they can do together, while giving them the freedom for self-organization so that new configurations and a shape of wholeness can emerge from the actions each person cares enough to take responsibility for. For example, one research participant explained: ""When the steering committee decides on what they're going to call the Summit and why, people light up and are committed in a way we rarely see in workplaces." Another shared: "People felt connected and passionate about the task." And another observed: "There was a feeling we were working on something of importance together."

Researchers suggest that strange attractors are never milled from new material. Instead, they materialize when what is already within the system is expressed in ways that provide meaningful shape and substance and foster breakthroughs and outcomes that were previously unforeseen and unimaginable. In order to honestly address the shadow sides or problems that a system may be facing, this may require surfacing conflicting ways of framing the issues. For example, in one study where a municipal healthcare department first felt the need to inquire into "absenteeism" and why 5 to 10 percent of their nursing workforce was missing on any given day and how they could fix this problem, it wasn't until this framing was flipped to inquire into why 90 to 95 percent of the workforce was reliably coming to work and how people's commitment could be supported that they secured a drop of 27 percent in absenteeism over a period of six months. As Donald Schön – one of the key contributors to the theory of organizational learning — notes, it is not that advocates of different approaches often disagree about the facts, but that they attend to and emphasize different facts.

In an effort to surface these different facts with an appreciative eye, Michelle found that the most successful AI Summits agreed a bold and generative topic by having the steering committee members use versions of the following two questions to interview each other (the more diverse their partners' experience the better) and then share their findings and note the generative themes emerging:

- What factors give life to this organization when it is and has been most alive, successful, and effective?

- What possibilities, expressed and latent, provide opportunities for more vital, successful, and effective (vision-and-values congruent) forms of organization around the strategic focus for this Summit?

_____

"People do not resist change, per se. People resist loss."
RONALD HEIFETZ

_____

To guarantee the best lift-off for an AI Summit, David and his colleague Lindsey Godwin – as part of their new P.O.S.I.T.I.V.E. change platform — also suggest that the steering committee ensure the topic represents an epic opportunity inspired by urgent optimism by reviewing the generative themes emerging from their interviews, and asking:

- What do we most want to create around the strategic focus?

- What has our rich history prepared us for, and what is the world calling for — customers, communities and our world?

- What is a situated opportunity so compelling and strategically significant that the call feels epic, filled with meaning, value and significance, and hence urgent optimism?

At Clarke this was done by bringing together a steering committee that was representative of the stakeholders across their system and inviting them to read The Flourishing Enterprise: *The New Spirit of Business* by Chris Lazlo and his colleagues. Influenced by the ideas of evolving beyond sustainability and the limits of simply having less negative impact, to having a more positive, regenerative impact, when the Clarke team came together for the pre-Summit workshops the group quickly moved from discovering Clarke's strengths to exploring bold, generative topics that could shape their AI Summit. As words like "heart," "love" and "euphoria" started spontaneously emerging in the reflections, it was clear that any past reluctance to bring more spiritual concepts into the workplace had dissipated. Before long — without any overt moves by leadership — the committee had agreed the bold, generative topic of: "Clarke. Bigger, Braver, Bolder: Igniting our passion and imagination to realize a prosperous and flourishing world." The idea of "flourishing" had given them the permission to think bigger than they had ever done before and to be brave in that process.

As words have been found to create worlds, it is reasonable to expect considerable dialogue and deliberation over particular words or phrases being chosen for topics. After all, topic choice is fateful and sets in motion the disruption that follows because human systems have been found to move in the direction of what they most frequently and deeply ask questions about.

Magic Mechanism Tip

What has the system's rich history prepared it for? What are the people this system serves calling for? What difference does the system want to make for others that feels so compelling and strategically important that the call feels filled with meaning, value and urgent optimism? Within the answers to these questions lies a bold, generative topic that can shift the way people see the world and want to act upon these possibilities.

Discovery: Share Tales Of Strengths

Figure 9: Summary Of Words Used To Describe Discovery Phase By Research Participants

New and novel information that is freely generated and exchanged from diverse sources is one of the greatest generators of chaos because it enables more meaning, order, and growth to arise in new structures. Once the define phase is complete, the whole system begins to gather for the discovery phase of the AI Summit to share their tales of strengths and uncover the system's positive core.

Stories — the written or verbal accounts that link a set of ideas or a series of events into a meaningful storyline – are what enable people to make sense of what is happening in a system. They are at the heart of a human system's identity – both personally and collectively – and are the vehicle through which cultural expectations are made meaningful. Thus, creating a positive disruption in a system that will support its ability to flourish requires compassionate coaches to amplify the generative stories told about its past and fan the emergence of strength-focused narratives that create a catalyst for change around the AI Summit topic(s).

"Organizational change occurs through language, storytelling and communication."
DIANA WHITNEY

As noted in Chapter 1, researchers have found that a system learns little about excellence by studying failure. However, by enabling the exploration of the consistent life-giving factors that every system possesses – even in its most challenging moments – the positive core of its strengths and the essence of the system at its best emerges, enabling people's confidence in the system and themselves to grow, and feelings of competence and capacity to become enriched. Rather than allowing the past to be romanticized, eulogized or a static set of events, the exploration of people's stories about the system "at its best," opens up positive possibilities through which the positive disruption can be met. David and Lindsey describe this experience of discovering the resources available across a system's strengths spectrum — outside and inside, including social and cultural assets, technical and economic ones, psychological and spiritual strengths, ecological strengths of nature, and the strengths of moral models, positive deviations and collaborative creativity – as the strengths density of the change initiative or "wholepower."

How do AI Summits share tales of strengths?

In all the AI Summits Michelle studied, the discovery phase began with an appreciative interviewing process where people were invited to share their tales of strengths by answering a set of predetermined, generative questions about their best experiences in the system, what they valued about their work and the system, exploration of the chosen Summit topic(s), and their hopes for the system's future. Intended to be a "holographic beginning" – in which the scope of the entire AI Summit process and topics were explored – the discovery phase questions were designed to elicit stories, stimulate reflection and learning and surface the system's strengths people are performing at their best.

Some of the systems Michelle studied chose to conduct pre-event discovery interviews to begin seeding the positive disruption and creating connections, energy and excitement prior to gathering in a physical space. For some this involved interviewing a sample of the system or everyone in it. Others used the steering committee to conduct the interviews or trained a team of interviewers from across the system – although researchers have noted that the more people involved in interviewing, as well as being interviewed, the better. In all cases where discovery interviews were conducted the data was processed and summarized ahead of the AI Summit event. For example, Hunter Douglas Windows Fashion Division conducted interviews with 600 employees and 100 customers, vendors and community members, synthesized and summarized this data and provided it to all participants invited to their AI Summit.

Other systems in Michelle's sample simply conducted the discovery interviews as the first activity when everybody had physically gathered in the room. People were asked to interview someone at their table who they didn't know or didn't know well, by using the questions provided in their workbook for about forty-five minutes, and then their partner interviewed them. They were encouraged to really listen to their partner's story with the kind of curiosity and wonder a child would use, to draw them out with additional who, what, when, why and how questions if needed, and to really discover what mattered most to their partner around the chosen topics. They were told to write down as many notes as they needed, as they would be asked later to share their partner's tale of strengths with the rest of the table.

Regardless of whether the discovery phase questions were asked pre-Summit or during the Summit, it is important to understand that they are fateful and profoundly affect the success or failure of the disruption. The AI Summits Michelle studied typically asked three types of questions during the discovery phase:

1. Opening questions that were the things people value most about themselves, the nature of their work and the system.

2. Questions centered on the AI Summit topic(s).

3. Closing questions to surface the system's strengths and their hopes for its future.

The questions were generally written with a positive preface (part A) that planted the seed of what people were being asked to study and bridged the system's needs with their own emotional needs, and then the question itself (part B). They were stated affirmatively and designed to value the best of "what is," phrased in a way to build rapport and encourage people to use storytelling and not reporting of data, and ambiguous enough for individual interpretations and hopes to surface. Researchers suggest that the best generative questions are surprising, touch people's hearts and spirits, help people to build genuine connections, and to see reality a little differently.

For example, the first question asked of the Clarke AI Summit participants was:

Q1. What do you think makes people most light up and come alive — in their work and in their life?

Times of highest happiness or even feelings of euphoria often happen when we are part of something greater than ourselves — when we are part of a special team doing great work; when we are building better lives for our children, communities or workplaces; when we are helping our customers or co-workers to succeed; or when we are doing something positive to help nurture our planet to thrive, for example, advancing new green products or ways of living and doing business, or cleaning up our soil and lakes and air for future generations, etc.

Reflect on a time from your life — here at Clarke for those who work with Clarke, or in your own organization or life for those outside of Clarke.

A. What are the things that light you up and engage you more than anything else in your organization, your work, and your life?

B. Think of an example or experience that stands out — one we might learn from. If you could choose any story from your work or life where you and others came together to "make a difference," what is one experience that for you is most memorable and made you feel great? Tell the story. What happened? When? Who?

C. The dictionary defines the word euphoria with words like excitement, joy, inspiration and passion. How might you define euphoria in the context of an organization? When are people in your organization or team most engaged and inspired? If you were leading the organization, what is one thing you would do to make sure it happened more often?

(Visit www.thechangelabs.com for all of Clarke's discovery questions and the holographic beginning they created for their AI Summit).

It is hard to adequately describe the level of energy that the research participants reported emerging from these interviews. "Excited," "elevated," "surprised," "buzzing," "joy," and "ablaze" are all words we can see appearing in Figure 9 from their descriptions of what was happening in the room. In fact, many of the research participants described this paired interview process during the discovery phase as the "magic moment" they would never skip or rush in an AI Summit. Lyell noted: "It's incredible how quickly they get engaged in talking about something they are proud of. It might be the first time someone's asked them."

After these interviews, as people gathered once again on their diverse mix-maxed tables, some of the research participants noted that a powerful moment could be created here by asking people to notice what they observed about the process of sharing an appreciative conversation, how it left them feeling and the impact it had on their relationship with the other person. This reflection not only seems to help the system to unite around its shared experiences in the room, but to help people understand the power of appreciative conversations and how they could be used in any part of their work or their life.

People were then consistently invited to introduce their partner's tale of strengths to the rest of their table group. As is the case in all the AI Summits Michelle reviewed, Clarke invited the table groups to self-manage their required tasks and assign group leadership roles (for example: a discussion leader to keep the group on track, a recorder to capture what is being learned, a timekeeper to manage the time available and a reporter to share the group's knowledge back to the whole system). This began to sow the seeds for the self-organization opportunities that would follow.

In the Clarke Summit each person in the group was asked to first introduce their partner to the table team by sharing a couple of highlights from the "opening" and "closing" sections of their interview about their best experiences, what they value and their future hopes for the system. This was an opportunity to discover the resources of the system as people came to see and appreciate the experiences, strengths, connections and aspirations of others around the table. People were encouraged to listen to the "aha moments" as these stories were told, and the recorder made two lists on a piece of flip chart paper:

1. Key insights or patterns from system stories.

2. Emerging images of the future.

The table groups were then asked to go deeper into one of the middle questions that focused on the Summit topic(s) from their interview. For example, tables 1-10 focused on what makes people light up and come alive, tables 11-20 focused on proudest greater purpose and progress moments, and tables 21-30 focused on images of the future. Again, each person shared their partner's story as the strengths, assets, capacities, values, traditions and practices and other factors that drive the success of the system were uncovered. The recorder captured the examples and insights from these stories on designated worksheets (see example at www.thechangelab.com) and prepared a flip chart to summarize the responses ready for the reporter to share back to the full system in a three-minute report that included one or two of the most powerful stories or examples that came from their group.

With so many tables to report back, the facilitator made it clear that while not every table's reporter would have the opportunity to present their findings to the room, every flip chart would be gathered and collated into the final report so no table's insights or stories were lost. Then moving through the three allocated questions, reporters volunteered to share their discoveries for the rest of the system to hear. To be clear, this was not a controlled process with a pre-planned outcome. Instead, researchers suggest thinking of it as a journey off the beaten track that often starts to disrupt and change the system as people talk. They also caution that while the temptation may be to eliminate or remove the disclosing of views that might dislodge treasured certainties in the system, the gift of co-inquiry is the elevation that it creates so people can see the new vistas that are enabled by their shared connections. For this reason, Clarke worked hard in their de-brief to ensure that no particular history or story was considered more significant than another.

Thus, as the reporters shared their tables' stories the goal in Clarke's Summit was not to find common ground, but higher ground as stories that departed from the norm served to make the exceptional seem plausible. It was an opportunity for shared meaning making, or "sense making" as organizational theorist Karl Weick describes it, as the whole system engaged in a deeper level of dialogue, learning and exploration that started to open doors to short-term and long-term possibilities.

Finally, the discovery phase was completed during the Clarke Summit with people moving to table teams that were representative of just their stakeholder group. Again, they were invited to self-manage their required tasks and assign group leadership roles as desired using a provided template (see example at www.thechangelab.com). On a flip chart they made a list of all that their stakeholder group was doing or had done that they were most proud of and/or the greatest strengths that their group brought to the objectives of this AI Summit. Together they selected the group's top three "proudest prouds" or "strongest strengths," identified one story to share that illustrated these in action, and as a group shared their biggest hope for the AI Summit. All of which the team's reporter was asked to be ready to share in a three-minute report for the rest of the system to hear.

Again, with so many tables to report back, the facilitator made it clear that while not every table's reporter would have the opportunity to present their findings to the room, every flip chart would be gathered and collated into the final report so no tables' insights or stories were lost. As the top three lists were gathered these were used to visually map the positive core of Clarke's system in the Heart of Clarke activity, and the patterns, themes, highlights and surprises that emerged from these lists across the system became visible — like the images used throughout this chapter — so that everyone could now see the positive possibilities through which the disruption could be met and the system able to flourish.

Why spark surprising connections?

Although the discovery phase may sound like it is all about gathering novel information and data from across the system to nudge it toward the edge of chaos, it would be a gross mistake to underestimate the power of the dynamic connections that are facilitated through this process. For example, Lyell was amazed by how many times around the room he could hear people saying: "I didn't know you were part of that. You were the one who did that?" Another research participant noted: "It's really the first interview that created the magic and the special heart space and connectedness that made the Summit work." Another shared: "As the conversations progressed people were leaning forward toward each other. Even though they were from different faiths there was this sense of: I'm so glad I'm sitting here with you." And another observed: "People were dumbstruck to discover the people they worked alongside of weren't just stereotypes but real people with lots of talents and interests they had no idea about."

In the earlier chapters, we learned that people have a deep drive to belong and yearn to feel respected and important in the eyes of others. It is clear from Michelle's research, and it has been argued elsewhere, that the act of sharing tales of strengths in an AI Summit creates a rich environment that expands people's feelings of relatedness to each other and can lead to profound transformations. This is because good generative questions aren't simply interested in surfacing data, but are focused on experiences that touch people's hearts, thus requiring them to reveal something important about them to others. The sense of vulnerability that arises from these conversations increases people's open-mindedness, and as a result allows them to feel safe and affirmed with each other even when their stories are quite different.

"The deepest principle in human nature is the craving to be appreciated."

WILLIAM JAMES

For example, one research participant shared that: "During the reflections a dockworker stood up and said: 'I've been working here for fifteen years, and the whole time I thought that managers were out to get us, make us work as hard as they could make us work, and pay us the least amount. And I didn't really care a whole lot about the customers, they didn't really matter to me. I just came and put in my time and went home. But now I see things differently.' And then a supervisor stood up and said: 'I used to think that the dockworkers were the biggest pain in the ass that I had to live with, but

I realize now that we're not enemies, we're allies. We're trying to survive in a highly competitive environment, and right now, our competitors are beating us at the front door. So we need to work together, and I make a vow that I'm going to do the best I can by the company, by the men who work on my shift, and for my other supervisors here.' We heard these kinds of reflections again and again across the many AI Summits we ran across the system and some people would almost be in tears they would be so moved when they were talking, or moved by what they heard."

Building on the emerging work of neuroscientists, Professor Barbara Fredrickson suggests that when people share the kind of heartfelt positive emotions that arise from telling tales of strengths and really listening to each other they experience a moment of "positivity resonance." In these moments studies suggest that people's brains begin to synchronize with one another's, they start to mirror the positivity in each other's emotional state and feelings of mutual concern and care flow forth unimpeded as they move from a state of "me" to a state of "we." This led her to conclude that in a moment of positivity resonance, to some extent, people become a reflection and extension of the other person helping them feel safe, connected and united. Consequently, as people discovered kindred spirits among the diverse mix of strangers in the AI Summits Michelle studied, lasting connections formed, a sense of community grew and their confidence to act was heightened as they discovered they were not alone.

Moments of positivity resonance were created during the AI Summits through the diverse pairing of partners, the asking of generative questions and heightening people's willingness to listen through the responsibility of publicly introducing each other's stories. These small, but important, design choices built psychological safety incredibly quickly between strangers, by creating a learning mindset, recognizing the contributions of others, helping people to show each other mutual respect, and ensuring boundaries that existed within and between groups became spanned by reaching across barriers of all kinds. As one research participant noted: "There was a feeling of collective safety in the room."

Consciously leveraging the opportunities of improbable pairs, mix-matched groups and stakeholder groups during this phase created a powerful opportunity for creating new knowledge and strengthening connections across a system. Likewise, the creation of generative questions that were surprising, touched people's hearts and spirits, enabled people to build genuine connections, and to see reality a little differently shaped the kind of conversations that unfolded. In and of themselves, these conversations became mini-positive disruptions that sparked surprising connections and opportunities to support flourishing that created momentum and energy for change that rippled not just across the AI Summit event, but in many cases across the system for weeks, months and sometimes years to come.

Magic Mechanism Tip

Create a seating plan that ensures mix-maxed groups with representatives of stakeholders across your system seated at the tables together from the outset of the AI Summit. Like planning a wedding, this takes some work but is worth the investment, as the opportunity to meet other people across the system and to hear their stories of strengths and hope creates significant change in itself. Encourage improbable pairs as people commence their appreciative interviews and equip them with generative questions that help them to connect with each other about the things they truly care.

Why listen to ignite authentic positivity?

Generative stories are powerful because they grab people's attention, they are memorable, they move people's heads and hearts, and they challenge how people see and understand the world and open them up to action. But people have to be willing to listen. Listening is what cultivates people's sense of the whole by surfacing a system's differences, connections and shared meaning making.

Researchers suggest that when people listen with sincerity, generosity and compassion others feel heard and a bond of trust emerges in the relationships. This style of deep listening requires people to listen not simply with their ears, but with their eyes, their hearts and the nonjudgmental parts of their minds. As a result, the quality of their listening changes the conversation, as meaning is found in places they would never have experienced alone. It opens unexpected doors to elevation, creativity, belonging and self-control.

Professor Jonathan Haidt — one of the world's leading researchers on awe — notes that elevation occurs when people are exposed to cases in which another person displayed talent, perseverance, generosity, kindness or other skills and virtues. Left feeling "surprised, stunned, and emotionally moved" by seeing or experiencing these unexpected acts of goodness, people encounter a distinct feeling of warmth and expansion that is accompanied by the motivation to open up and be kind toward others. It makes people feel uplifted and optimistic about the system and the people in it, and to want to create or strengthen their relationships.

Jonathan has found that elevation is a calming, rather than an energizing emotion, because it releases oxytocin, which has a sedative and stress-reducing effect. For example, one research participant noted: "People were discovering each other and all the things they have in common. It was very moving." Another reported: "You see the emergence of generosity as people listen to each other." And another shared: "As soon as the interviews began the energy shifted. There was a sense of camaraderie in the room that they were in this together, to trust the process and then the possibilities began to unfold."

During the discovery phase however, Lyell reported witnessing more than just elevation in the room. He noted: "I couldn't believe how engaged people were. It was so loud. People were buzzing." Another research participant observed: "There was a lot of excitement that we were coming together to do something." And another commented that: "By the time they finished interviewing each other the room was ablaze and emotions were incredibly heightened."

Previously, researchers have proposed that by engaging in appreciative reflections of the past and beginning to imagine desired images of the future during this phase, a surge of positivity and creative energy can be fostered within the system to support the change process and systemic flourishing. As we learned in Chapter 3, Barbara's research has found that the experience of heartfelt positive emotions can help to broaden people's sense of possibilities, their ability to think quickly and creatively, and their feelings of connection with each other, while also building their physical, psychological, intellectual and social resources.

As neurological research continues to evolve, however, studies suggest that it is not simply the presence of positive emotions that impacts people's levels of creativity (which is vital during the dream and design phases of the AI Summit), but the intensity of the emotions they are experiencing. For example, the experiences of positive emotions that occur after a goal has been accomplished (e.g. the happiness, gratitude or pride people feel as they share their peak experiences of the past during the discovery questions), often appears to have a lower level of motivational intensity for people, which broadens their cognitive scope and helps them to see more possibilities around them. In contrast, the experiences of positive emotions that occur before a goal has been accomplished (e.g. the desire, enthusiasm or excitement people feel as they share their hopes for the system's future during the discovery questions) often appears to have a higher level of motivational intensity for people, which narrows their cognitive scope so they can focus on making things happen to fill these urges. Researchers believe that creativity requires both of these states. Thus, people need to be given opportunities to share stories that generate both low and high intensity positive emotions during this phase of the AI Summit.

It is also important to note that while the frequency was significantly lower, many research participants also observed the presence of negative emotions during this phase of the AI Summit, especially at the outset. As one participant explained: "There was a lot of anxiety and uncertainty as people walked in." And another shared: "There was always some suspicion of what it was all about."

In an interesting neurological twist, Scott Barry Kaufman – one of the world's leading researchers on creativity – points out that just as the intensity of positive emotions can impact people's levels of creativity, the intensity of negative emotions appears to have a similar effect. For example, negative emotions that have a lower motivational intensity (i.e. sadness or skepticism) have been found to broaden people's cognitive scope to open their minds, whereas negative states that have a higher motivational intensity (i.e. disgust and anger) appear to narrow people's cognitive scope. Thus, rather than trying to force people into positive emotional experiences during the discovery phase, we recommend trusting that the safe space created by the AI Summit and the use of the magic mechanisms can hold the full breadth and depth of emotions that open people up to creative exploration.

"Openness to experience speaks to our desire and motivation to engage with ideas and emotions—to seek truth and beauty, newness and novelty—and the act of exploring often provides the raw material for great artistic and scientific innovations."

SCOTT BARRY KAUFMAN

Finally, it is worth remembering that researchers have found that people rarely experience purely positive emotions or purely negative emotions, rather they tend to experience mixed emotions or "emotional ambivalence" and this is particularly true during organizational events that are focused on creating change and when people are placed in unusual environments. The good news is that a growing body of research suggests that the experience of ambivalence can help improve people's flexibility and engagement, and provide many benefits for individuals, groups and systems. For example, Karl Weick posits that the attitude of wisdom – how knowledge is held and how it is put to use without excessive confidence or excessive caution – arises from ambivalence and facilitates adaptation and adaptability.

Researchers have also found that ambivalence can help people to positively engage with others in the system by expressing ideas and suggestions in a constructive, beneficial manner to change the status quo and create improvements. For example, David recalls that in the midst of the discovery phase reporting during the AI Summit for the United Religions Initiative there was an exchange of heartfelt fear, pain and frustration among those gathered around the tensions between Islamic, Jewish and Christian theologies of love versus theologies of justice and the actions each group were taking in the name of religion that were causing harm to others. It wasn't until the Dalai Lama used the safe space created by the AI Summit to help the participants re-discover the power of weaving together loving kindness and justice that those gathered were able to not only move forward together, but decided to take the time that evening to walk together and pay their respects at the Jewish Wall, Christ's Tomb and the other important religious monuments for each of the faiths present.

However, as most of us have experienced, emotional ambivalence can have two sides and can lead to less flexibility and disengagement, unless the environment creates psychological safety, reaches across the barriers that exist within and between groups, and is autonomy supportive. David Bright and his colleagues concur and remind us that as compassionate coaches of disruption, although generativity is associated with positive sentiment, this does not equate the exclusion of negative sentiment. Rather, flourishing usually includes a dynamic relationship between positive and negative experiences. Thus, to ensure that every voice feels free to be heard during the discovery phase, the goal should never be to shut down or repress negative sentiments, but rather to focus on the degree to which positive sentiment finds expression relative to negative sentiment. It is also worth remembering that negative sentiments in conversations serve as a cue to the presence, not just of cynicism, frustration or fear, but also of hope.

Michelle's research found that by creating opportunities where every person knows they will have the opportunity to speak about what matters to them and that what they share will be valued and appreciated by the people around them, the AI Summits studied encouraged people to be more generous in how they listened and more willing to open their hearts and their minds to different points of views and experiences. As a result, people's experience of mutual appreciation and surprise eclipsed the human tendency to be self-focused, and resulted in the unexpected deepening of bonds between speakers and listeners as they shared heightened feelings of authenticity and positivity. As David has written in the past of the discovery phase: "It is here, in this synergistic moment of empowering continuity and novelty, that boldness emerges alongside of abandonment, and any sense of resistance evaporates. The result is a combination of courage and surrender, key elements in the study of creators."

Magic Mechanism Tip

At the outset of the appreciative interviews, ask people to listen carefully and take notes about their partner's story so they can share what they learn with the rest of the table. Not only does this help people to open their hearts and their minds to different points of views, it also ensures that every voice feels heard, respected and valued. Trust the safe, appreciative space you have created to hold the full breadth and depth of emotions that may arise during the interviews, knowing that the opportunity to authentically share how they feel heightens people's feelings of safety and positivity.

Dream: Co-Create Shared Purpose

Figure 10: Summary Of Words Used To Describe Dream Phase By Research Participants

In order to enable emergence from a disruption, researchers recommend that people need to be given opportunities for individual expression and connection to self-organize around the ideas they feel most passionate about. In fact, they note that creative interactions in which people can fully participate with their heads, hearts, bodies and spirits are at the heart of engaging emergence because it entices them to explore the familiar and unfamiliar with new eyes or a beginner's mind, as the Buddhists might say.

Thus, the goal of the dream phase in an AI Summit is to surface the values and aspirations that enliven the system. It is an invitation to align and amplify its positive core – ensuring that the hopes that emerge are practically grounded on the system's strengths — by pushing the creative edges of positive possibilities, wondering about the system's greatest potential and uncovering opportunities for the system to have a more positive impact on its environment.

> *"When individuals clearly identify what they*
> *truly care about (have passion for), and take personal*
> *responsibility for what is happening, things start to move."*
> **HARRISON OWEN**

Researchers suggest that to maximize generativity during this phase, it's important not to simply surface the similarities in the system's hopes – although this is useful and necessary — but to also encourage people to stand for what they value and to openly explore the differences and diversity of their dreams. Encouraging people to pay attention to what they truly care about challenges them to rise to the best in themselves, and to bring out the best in each other and the system. It is an act of service that supersedes people's egos, enables them to contribute their creative potential and connects them to something more universal that enables win-win outcomes and higher-order coherence to emerge. The reality is that the most creative, energized, committed results occur when people follow their passions while being of service to others in the system. It is how shared purpose is co-created across a system, so that leaders finally see what people are actually intrinsically motivated to do and what "might be" as the system grows. After all, people excel and learn not because they are told to, but because they want to.

How do AI Summits co-create shared purpose?

In most of the AI Summits Michelle studied, the dream phase kicked off the second day of the AI Summit event. As people re-entered the physical space facilitators ensured they were given an opportunity to reconnect to the energy, excitement and hopes that they left with the previous day. For this reason people were generally seated back in their original mix-maxed groups so tables once again were representative of the system, and the surprising connections that were sparked the day before could continue to deepen.

As this phase began, the facilitator often introduced people to the idea that positive and meaningful images of the future tend to pull us into positive actions. For example, Fred Polak, who launched a sweeping study of Western civilization, found that the rise and fall of images of the future predicted the rise and fall of cultures – including the advancement of art, architecture, music, commerce, science, politics, and education – due to the "activation effect" of positive images. This led him to conclude that meaningful, positive images have the capacity to become self-fulfilling, self-propelling engines for change that determine the future of a system. Likewise, when a system holds a clear, meaningful and positive image of where it wants to go, the image "activates" the conversations, choices, commitments and behaviors necessary to get there. David and Lindsey suggest that this is because magnetic images of the future paint pictures of vivid victories, call out to the hero within people and attract the emotional energy and physical resources needed to support change. To make these insights personally relevant, the AI Summit facilitators frequently gave people a chance to reflect on examples in their own lives where positive images have led them to positive actions.

The facilitators then provided three guidelines for this phase. Firstly, people were encouraged to build on the positive core they uncovered during the discovery phase to ensure their dreams were both practical and grounded in the organization's history and strengths. Secondly, people were encouraged to aim higher and to help each other to be bold as they looked for ways to use their passions and resources to be of service to others around the AI Summit topic. Finally, people were encouraged to think like artists and to use the stories and hopes from the discovery phase like a palette of colors that allowed them to paint vivid, compelling, meaningful images of what the future could look like if their best ideas became a reality.

While the rest of the dream phase can be executed in different ways depending on the needs of the system, most of the AI Summits that Michelle studied — including Clarke — used what is called a "creative dreaming" approach that began with table groups once again deciding how they would self-manage their own discussion, data, time and reports and assigning group leadership roles. People then moved into a "dream dialogue," where in Clarke's case, each person imagined themselves waking up in the year 2021 and visualized the Clarke they really wanted — as if it existed now. Given enough time to imagine concretely the bigger, braver, bolder Clarke organization of their dreams, they were asked to share their hopes, dreams and sense of opportunities by answering the following questions:

- How can we take the "heart of Clarke" into our organization of the future and our world's future in ways that are bigger, braver and bolder? How might we do things to make communities more livable, safe and comfortable in ways that were barely imagined in 2016?

- How might we become — on the inside of our organization — an organization that truly empowers a euphorically engaged workforce and human wellbeing?

- How might we bring "the heart of Clarke" into the world in a manner that inspires and transforms others, ultimately helping to leave a legacy of a more prosperous and flourishing world?

- What do we want our customers, partners, industry and communities to be saying about us? How do we go beyond satisfied customers? Beyond good community citizenship? What's next?

As the group listened to each other's dreams, they were asked to look for common and unique elements. What were the bigger, braver, and bolder images? What were the smallest changes that might help Clarke reach something bigger?

Table groups were then asked to choose a creative way to present the envisioned future by preparing a three-minute "portrayal" (i.e. a TV special, drama, a day in the life, a work of art, panel presentation) as if it was happening now and ensure that all group members had a role. They were told that the more playful the portrayals the better, so art supplies, costumes, instruments and other props were provided to help people fire up their imaginations and give the guiding image of their future a gripping appeal, while anchoring their hopes and dreams into their bodies and psyches.

The creation of these presentations was typically one of the most fondly remembered parts of the AI Summit – even in the most traditional systems who "didn't do" creative presentations – because of the levels of energy, excitement and commitment this activity unleashed in the system for the co-creation of a meaningful purpose. People were never forced to do something they didn't want to in this step, instead it was a genuine invitation and opportunity for individual creative expression and each table group self-organized to select the medium and content that felt authentic for them.

In many of the AI Summits studied during the preparation of the presentations the groups recorded were asked to use an opportunity mapping worksheet (see www.thechangelabs.com for Clarke's example) to summarize the core elements of their group's vision. This ensured that the team's hopes were adequately captured for reporting, while their creative interpretation breathed life into the ideas to inspire and motivate the rest of the system.

Typically facilitators then invited groups to the front of the rooms to share their dreams. By the time eight to ten groups had presented, most of the AI Summits reviewed found that the law of diminishing returns often kicked in as people had expended so much emotional energy delivering and watching the presentations that their hearts and minds were full. Common themes often also started being repeated at this point, even though the format of the presentations may have differed. There were some AI Summits, however, where every group wanted to share their dream and to rob them of this opportunity – particularly if it was a live act – risked leaving people feeling disappointed that their hopes would not be heard by the system. Thus depending on the number of groups in the AI Summit the reporting out process was sometimes managed by: breaking into different rooms with simultaneous presentations, splitting presentations over a break period, combining tables (although it was generally suggested that groups were no larger than twelve people), or setting creative tasks that were visual, like a newspaper front page that could be viewed as a gallery of hopes. In all cases, people were encouraged to take notes throughout the presentations of the elements of the visions they found most exciting (what), and the opportunities and possibilities for action (how).

Lyell noted that: "The freedom to dream just sets them free. It gave them permission to say anything and do anything as they created the future together. Now they really start to work as a team and for me, this was the real turning point." Another research participant observed: "A big turning point for a lot of the management team was to see how creative, how innovative, how engaged the drivers and dockworkers, the union employees, really were when they were given the opportunity and they were asked to do something, rather than always being told what and how to do it, and see just the overflow of creativity and engagement that came out at that point." Another shared: "When people's ideas weren't dismissed as silly or we can't do that, but captured and used as springboards for more ideas, the enjoyment for everybody escalates." Another commented: "You realize that a lot of the times you're seeing similar things and you're dreaming similar dreams. And so I think that there's a sense of now it's wow, all these outsiders and we all really have a lot of things in common." And another reflected: "There was a moment where people were just laughing and cheering for each other so much and applauding and had tears in their eyes when they were sharing some of the dreams of the future. Realizing, 'I like the taste of that dream.'"

After the creative presentations had been given, the facilitators once again created space for the system to reflect on the dreams that had been offered. In each AI Summit studied, the goal was not to come to a consensus, as this risked robbing the group of energy, but to surface the guiding images of a meaningful future about which people felt passionate about and were willing to take responsibility for making a reality. At Clarke this was done with each group creating flip chart pages that captured the "what" and "how" elements of the visions that were most meaningful and energizing for them. These summaries were then displayed around the room over lunch for people to absorb the shared hopes and positive images of the system's future.

Why align and magnify strengths?

Peter Drucker – one of the greatest scholars of leadership and management over the last century – suggested that the ageless essence of leadership is to create an alignment of strengths in ways that make a system's weaknesses irrelevant. David agrees, arguing that strengths don't simply allow people to perform, but to transform a system as new combinations and configurations of strengths become activated and elevated.

While this sounds simple enough, researchers have found that the human brain is wired with a negativity bias that means people are more adept at spotting weaknesses and feeling an evolutionary pull to fix them, than they are at being able to identify and build on strengths. As a result, David has pointed out that deficit-based thinking has virtually become synonymous with the idea of any "helping profession" where the draw of the problematic, the broken and deficient leaves 80 percent of people in most organizations focused on fixing what's not working, and only 20 percent focused on building on the available strengths.

Yet every living system works to some degree, and thus has strengths — those things that bring it to life and make it feel strong — that can be built upon when responding to a disruption. In fact, a system cannot excel by simply trying to fix its weaknesses and limiting its failures, it is only by amplifying and magnifying its strengths so that it understands "what is best" and imagines "what is next" that an upward spiral of growth is created. This is why David has repeatedly urged us to see human systems as mysteries and miracles of relatedness that are webs of infinite strengths and limitless human imagination, instead of as machines incessantly in need of repair.

"It takes far less energy to move from first-rate performance to excellence than it does to move from incompetence to mediocrity."

PETER DRUCKER

David and Lindsey suggest that in order for a human system to flourish there are three primary tasks that should shape its response to a positive disruption:

1. The elevation of strengths at the individual or small group level.
2. The alignment and transformational use of the system's positive core.
3. The elevation, magnification and refraction of its highest human strengths outward to the world.

They note that this can be achieved by wrapping a disruption in the richest theater of assets and strategic strengths available – the whole power — during the discovery phase, and then giving people the freedom to align, magnify, and refract the power of every relevant resource from outside and inside the system during the dream phase as they explore the dream dialogues and creatively collaborate on their dream presentations.

For example, as Clarke brought their dreams to life and the real possibilities for the amplification of their strengths took center stage, their sense of shared power and feelings of hope, inspiration, joy and awe at "what might be" created a state of conscious co-elevation and their "whypower" – their sense of purpose — emerged. Lyell observed that during the dream phase: "There was a real sense of respecting each other's dreams and looking for ways to build a future together." Another research participant noted: "There's a concentration effect as people's strengths begin to be connected and a sense of collective awesomeness of the power in the room." Another shared: "People were really opening up to possibilities and seeing opportunities they probably had not ever seen before." And another shared: "Meaning kicks up a lot because of what they've created. It's their dream now and they feel ownership of what's happening."

Nurtured by the appreciative and caring eyes through which people start to see each other and the system during the discovery phase, the dream phase created a space in the AI Summits for the zone of proximal development – the distance between someone's actual development level and their higher level of potential development in collaboration with more capable peers – to occur and strengthen people's learning and capacity. To realize this opportunity, the AI Summits studied asked generative questions that helped people to align and magnify their individual and collective strengths around the AI Summit topic and gave them the freedom and permission to share their passions for serving others during the dream dialogue. Mindful that words create worlds, the questions asked shaped the system's hopes and set changes in motion as the positive images generated began to pull people into action.

The opportunity for the table groups to then reflect on the common themes and generative ideas from their shared hopes, and identify what they truly cared about around the AI Summit topic, enabled breakthrough innovations and inspired performances to happen. By challenging them to package and present their shared hopes in a creative format that breathed life and energy into their ideas, people consistently started taking responsibility and feeling a sense of ownership for their dreams. Being able to physically and emotionally embody and share what might be possible when the system is enlivened by its values and aspirations was one of the most powerful moments that repeatedly emerged across the AI Summits.

It turned out that only by surrounding themselves with other stars were people truly able to shine. For example, one research participant noted: "We literally had people who were transformed. There was a trucking guy at the Summit who became an extraordinarily passionate advocate for the role of transport in the value chain to leverage good practices in the industry. He became a crusader and started working with the Environmental Protection Authority. The mobilization of a single human being into a passionate evangelist was the most important outcome of the Summit."

Magic Mechanism Tip

Having discovered "what is best", use the appreciative space you have created to enable proximal development by inviting people to align and magnify their strengths by imagining "what's next." Help them to look ahead, and visualize what might be possible across this system if everything went as well as it possibly could around the AI Summit topic. Encourage people to bring these dreams to life in a creative and collaborative way to spark a genuine sense of ownership and commitment to the ideas they are proposing, and enliven others with feelings of hope and excitement about the future.

Why build a meaningful language of hope?

David believes that the creation of positive images of the future pulls people forward into new possibilities that fuel them with hope and put them on the road to finding solutions, helping people to realize they have the power to make things happen. How might this work? Studies suggest that the very idea of having the rewards that come from getting something that people are hoping for is enough to kick-start a cascade of dopamine — the brain's reward drug — through key neural pathways in the brain that have the power to move people from intention to action.

For example, for decades the four-minute mile was considered a natural limit for runners. It was unthinkable to go faster. Then English athlete, Roger Bannister, set himself the impossible goal, started training accordingly, and in May 1954, he shattered this barrier on an Oxford track. Within three years, sixteen other runners had also surpassed this "human limit." There was no fundamental leap in human evolution during this period; what had changed was people's ability to imagine what was possible and to talk with each other about how to make this happen.

Charles Snyder – one of the world's leading researchers on hope – notes that hope springs to life when people understand that the future is fundamentally undetermined and open to human influence. Powered by people's imagination, it is a life sustaining force that connects memories of past success with the potential of tomorrow and determines how they live now. Psychologist Verena Kast explains: "By hoping, we walk toward a light that we do not see but sense somewhere in the darkness of the future."

Researchers explain that hope is generated and sustained when people, facing the mystery of the future, share their highest ideals or "ultimate concerns" that provide them with meaning and purpose – that which Plato calls the good, the true, and the beautiful. Thus, hope prospers when people reach beyond the self and place themselves in the service of others and pursue what matters most to them, providing them with a heightened sense of meaning and purpose.

Hope has also been found to be an essential ingredient in systemic flourishing because it acts as a strange attractor that spawns generative conversations and creates a shared vocabulary that offers a potent "life-giving" force for challenging the status quo and mobilizing the moral, social and relational energies a system needs to translate vision into reality and belief into practice. After all, as influential philosopher Ludwig Wittgenstein once explained: "The limits of my language are the limits of my world."

Researchers suggest that a meaningful language of hope – stories, theories, evidence and images — is built when people are given the opportunity to nurture cooperative relationships by:

- Inquiring together into their most deeply held values and highest aspirations.
- Exercise a sense of optimism about their capacity to influence the future.
- Generate positive affect and action.

- In the AI Summits studied, Michelle found that the creative presentations and summaries that accompanied them often surfaced key words, phrases, expressions, images, stories and artifacts that enabled a meaningful language of hope to emerge around the AI Summit topic. Where possible, these words and images were immediately embedded into the rest of the AI Summit experience to help provide a set of compelling values and ideas for generative and systemic action in response to the positive disruption.

For example, Lyell observed that the dream phase: "Becomes a much more collaborative exercise." Another participant shared: "There was a shift in language from doing good to becoming a force for good. This is when the synchronization of meaning occurs and people start talking the same language." Another reported: "You get this sense of shared vision and that we're all in this together." And another noted: "Hope was definitely in the room."

Lyell also noted, however, that for some people there was a sense of fear about the quality of their ideas and their presentations, and whether they had the ability to realize the hopes they were voicing. While the presence of fear during the dream phase was not specifically noted by other research participants, hope researcher Shane Lopez explains that hope walks hand in hand with fear to remind people of realistic limits and alert them when they're straying from the path to a meaningful future. Unfortunately, people's natural fear of loss is often much stronger than their desire for gain, so in order to be a compassionate coach of disruption it's important to try and ensure that uncertainty and doubt doesn't unnecessarily hijack people from their chosen passion to serve others.

"Hope is created moment by moment through our deliberate choices. It happens when we use our thoughts and feelings to temper our aversion to loss and actively pursue what is possible. When we choose hope, we define what matters to us most."

SHANE LOPEZ

This challenge was brought to life in a study of ten organizations simultaneously involved in system-wide change by researcher Linda Robson, who coded more than 52,000 words from interviews, live meetings and written documents and found that high-performing (change-successful) systems had a positively biased imbalance of over 4:1 toward a positive discourse (statements that articulated, "any mention of strengths" or "hope toward the future" or "active effort to include others" or "mention of surprise, curiosity or excitement") versus deficiency discourse ("deficiency in self or others" or articulations of "unfulfilled expectations" or "predictions of a negative future"). Note this was not a 4:0 ratio, suggesting that when people feel connected, safe and heard there is room to talk about their fears and uncertainties.

David calls this the "Robson Ratio" and recommends using it as a North Star and guide for the kind of shared language a flourishing system needs to build. Thus as the dream phase is crafted, we believe it is also important to consider how the generative questions for the dream dialogue will enable the Robson Ratio to be reached. Are they helping the system move toward a positive discourse versus deficiency discourse? Is there compassion and empathy for the potential presence of fear that often walks alongside hope and that people may need to express? If this feels like a big ask, Julie reassured us that during their AI Summit Clarke found that: "The possibilities of approaching something not as a problem but as an opportunity, simply stated, were just endless."

Magic Mechanism Tip

Aim for the Robson Ratio North Star for positive discourse when crafting the generative questions for the dream phase. Try to help people paint clear, vivid, compelling images of the future they most want around the AI Summit topic. Then as the dream dialogues and creative presentations unfold help the system to identify, adopt and embed key words, phrases, expressions, images, stories and artifacts that will enable a meaningful language of hope to grow around the AI Summit topic. Be sure to immediately use these words and images throughout the rest of the AI Summit experience, and include them in post-Summit reports, ongoing communication and workspaces if you want to help the system to become fluent in this new language.

Design: Play Together To Unlock Potential

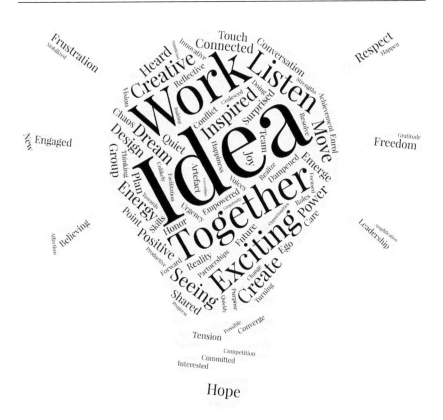

Figure 11: Summary Of Words Used To Describe Design Phase By Research Participants

The National Institute For Play founder Dr. Stuart Brown notes: "We are built to play and built through play." His research suggests that playing together gives people the freedom to see things in a different way, and as a result they stumble upon new behaviors, thoughts, strategies, and ways of working and being. It allows people to create imaginative new cognitive combinations that enable them to discover what works. Found to be critical not only for people's levels of creativity and innovation, play is a catalyst that energizes people, makes them productive, helps to sustain their social relationships and impacts their ability to flourish.

Thus, the goal of the design phase in an AI Summit is to evoke new thinking, new partnerships, and new ways of working together by playing to surface pathways to realize the system's shared hopes. Without the use of an exhausting or paralyzing search for consensus, people are encouraged to converge and self-organize around the hopes about which they feel so passionate they are willing to take responsibility for designing potential ways forward for the system. Then by embracing a generative design thinking process that is open, engaging, adaptive and playful the system's magnified strengths help people to produce a blueprint for execution of the system's shared hopes that is so inspiring and functional they want to begin immediately making it happen.

Playing together in this way relies on improvisation, and that means never really knowing what's going to happen in this phase. Play is a state of mind, rather than a specific activity. It requires people to be curious and willing to let go of their expectations, to be open to serendipity and chance, to include seemingly irrelevant elements in their play, to use their strengths in the service of others and to let go of any feelings of self-consciousness, and embrace the feelings of exploration, absorption and enjoyment that playing affords them. It is the essence of freedom and safety because it is free of expectations — after all, they are just playing.

The good news is that mammals who feel safe, play spontaneously. For example, play theorist, Brian Sutton-Smith has found that lifelong play is central to people's continued wellbeing, adaptation and social cohesiveness because it creates a sense of belonging when we play together. In fact, he argues that it is when people stop playing that their behavior becomes more fixed, they lose interest in new information, and find fewer opportunities to flourish in the world around them.

"The opposite of play... is not work, it is vacillation,
or worse, it is depression."
BRIAN SUTTON-SMITH

In recent years the design phase of AI Summits has undergone significant change as David and his colleagues have introduced the insights of design theory and the practices of design thinking into this phase to help systems flourish. This has been aided by the fact that in an increasingly uncertain and dynamic world, a new level of appreciation for the value of playing together has been emerging as organizations have rediscovered the pragmatism for "abductive reasoning" (logical leaps of the mind from a single deviating data point) and realized that even mistakes offer materials for new possibilities.

Many of the AI Summits in Michelle's research – including Clarke — used this approach (sometimes referred to as an AI Design Summit), and given this is the model increasingly taught to practitioners we felt it was helpful to capture the best practices for this approach. For a more traditional design phase approach that invites participants to create a design possibilities map, select high-impact design elements and craft and enrich provocative propositions, we highly recommend *The Appreciative Inquiry Summit: A Practitioner's Guide for Learning Large-Group Change* by James Ludema and his colleagues.

How do AI Summits enable people to play together to unlock potential?

Typically most of the AI Summits Michelle studied – including Clarke – moved into the design phase on the afternoon of the second day of the AI Summit event. To prepare for these steps over lunch, the facilitator usually sat down with members of the steering committee who had been taking notes during the dream phase and identifying the ideas that seemed to resonate with people and could potentially represent a design opportunity area that would give the system traction to move forward. By comparing their notes and thinking carefully about what they had heard during the dream phase, they tried to answer one question: "What are the tangible opportunity areas that we could impact?"

For example, the Clarke team identified the following opportunities:

- Agent of World Health Benefit
- Culture of Euphoric Engagement
- Exceptional Customer Brand Experience
- Guiding Principles
- The Heart of Clarke
- International Market Opportunity
- Movement of Social Generosity
- National Leader in Aquatic Habitat Management
- Pervasive Innovation
- Voice for Our Industry

While some of these opportunity areas had been identified as potential hopes by the steering committee prior to the AI Summit event, as was typical for many of the systems studied, over 50 percent of them had not been anticipated. It is worth noting that there was no "right" number of opportunity areas for a system to pursue, there was only what was "right" for each system given the number of people in the AI Summit and the number of self-organized teams that could be resourced and supported after the AI Summit event to take the ideas forward.

The groups then framed these opportunity areas as "How might we?" questions. A design thinking tool used to frame a system's shared hopes into opportunities for design, "How might we?" questions give people a powerful frame for innovative thinking by suggesting that an answer is possible and offering people the chance to answer it in multiple ways. Neither too broad, nor too narrow, these questions create a launchpad for people to start brainstorming, but also give them enough breadth to explore wild ideas.

For example, the "How might we?" question Clarke created around the "Heart of Clarke" opportunity area read as follows:

How might we bring the heart of Clarke?

How might we bring "the heart of Clarke" to the world, by continuing to develop, codify and teach the ways in which we intentionally create a flourishing corporate culture? How might we consider sharing this wisdom across generations, through strategic academic partners, and outward to a global audience? How do we capture and tell this story exceptionally, in a way that goes beyond just telling our story, to creating transformation in how the world goes to work, lives sustainably, etc.?

You can see all of the Clarke "How might we?" examples at www.thechangelab.com.

Typically as people returned from lunch, they would find that a series of design studios comprising large foam core boards had appeared throughout the room with the "How might we?" question displayed on the top, piles of sticky notes and sticker dots for voting. The facilitators then usually shared some of the insights and practices that guide design thinking and how to embrace a designer's mindset as people were encouraged to come together and play with ways to make their shared hopes of making a difference for others a reality for their system.

In all of the AI Summits studied, people were given the freedom to vote with their feet and move to the design studio for the opportunity area that they felt passionate enough about to take responsibility for shaping. To enable this voting to occur, the facilitator and steering committee members usually quickly explained each of the opportunity areas, reminding people of what they had heard and seen during the presentations, using the shared language of hope that had emerged from the dreams, and the "How might we?" statements to help people embrace a designer mindset. To ensure no one's dreams were missed the question was also asked: "Are there any other opportunity areas anyone wants to add a design studio?" Sometimes these ideas had been captured in the chosen opportunity areas already but needed further clarification or if someone felt passionate enough and there were others in the room also willing to take responsibility for the opportunity, then this was added as a final design studio so that no one was left feeling that their shared dreams had been hijacked or dismissed.

In the Clarke AI Summit, people were also asked to be clear on their first and second choice opportunity areas, in case places in the group they moved to were already full (again there is no "right" number of participants in a group but it is helpful to be aware that the bigger the group the more likely onlookers, rather than active participants, will emerge in this phase). With their choices clear, people then quickly moved to their chosen design studio and met their new team members.

Once everybody had joined a design studio, facilitators outlined the instructions for a brainstorming exercise to answer their "How might we?" question. Asked to once again self-manage and assign the roles of a timekeeper, a recorder, a brainstorm facilitator and a brainstorm radical (to challenge the group and contribute bold and wild ideas), the groups were asked to imagine that anything was possible to answer their "How might we?" question, and to begin brainstorming their answers by quickly writing their ideas on sticky notes, explaining them to the other participants, and sticking them on the large foam core boards so that as ideas were added they could start to be grouped around common themes and built upon. People were instructed that their goal for this exercise was quantity over quality, ensuring that they were adding radical breakthrough possibilities, building on each other's ideas and avoiding evaluation.

As each of the design studio teams were ready, people were encouraged to stand back, do a quick read of the most promising ideas or combination of ideas that were emerging on their board, and begin to think about the ideas that could be designed into something that was tangible and would add value to the system based on their shared hopes (for example, new structures or services, training manuals, redesigns of a program, new communication programs, tools for efficiency, new process designs, customer programs, etc.). For the sake of enabling their design studio to build at least one prototype, people were asked to narrow and prioritize their brainstormed list and each given five color sticker dots to vote on the items they most wanted (they were able to place all their dots on one item, or could vote for five different items). The recorders then documented the key themes and ideas onto a sheet of paper with clear notes so that no ideas were lost.

Once each design studio had captured their ideas in writing, the facilitators introduced the practices and examples of rapid prototyping to the whole room to enable the design studios to make their ideas tangible, to learn through playing, and to quickly get feedback on their ideas. Intended to convey an idea – not to be perfect – people were shown how to show – rather than tell – by rapidly building a prototype to test their idea.

Each design studio was then given a design kit to build with (usually a large envelope containing paper, scissors, tape, modeling clay, pipe cleaners, wooden sticks, balloons, string, and other building items – see a suggested shopping list at www.thechangelabs.com), and asked to select just one of their most highly voted ideas to prototype and to start building. Larger design studio teams in the AI Summits (some groups had up to thirty or more people in them) were generally encouraged to break up into smaller groups to work on discrete elements of the prototype. For example, the Heart of Clarke opportunity area wanted to prototype their ideas for a Clarke 101 deck that captured the company's history and information for new hires, so some team members worked on building the history components, and others worked on building information on the way Clarke works.

Typically each design studio team then prepared and delivered a three to five minute presentation of the prototype and received feedback. For example, in the Clarke AI Summit teams were asked to share the business case, the innovation case and the sustainability case for the initiative they prototyped and name the discrete design elements and big ideas they chose to include. Then as people watched the presentations they were encouraged to write down their feedback for the teams on sticky notes with "what's best" and "ways to strengthen." When all the presentations were complete, people were given the opportunity to do a gallery walk through the prototypes and provide their feedback.

Depending on the number of design studio teams, this can result in a lot of presentations and it can be challenging for people to stay engaged at this point. David suggests that as an alternative, just the gallery walk is sometimes used with one team member staying with their design studio, and the other team members spreading out to visit prototypes all around the room. Generally a bell is rung to give people ten to fifteen minutes at each design studio so the prototype team member can make the brief presentation, and people can ask questions and give feedback before moving to the next group.

Once everyone had provided feedback, typically the second day of the AI Summit event finished with time for people to share what had resonated with them, what lit them up with hope and excitement for their individual and collective future, and how they were feeling about the AI Summit process. Facilitators also usually explained that their last day together would be to ensure that their dreams and designs could be taken forward into action. Michelle found that this process allowed people to savor what they had accomplished, to continue building their shared language of hope, and to own any feelings of disquiet that they may be experiencing about what is being proposed or how the dreams and designs they have created could ever be realized by the system.

Lyell noted: "Because they voted with their feet, as they're designing they're beginning to take ownership of the strategic initiative and there's passion to make that part better. There's intense concentration in the room, but I would say for the majority of the people there is also real joy and happiness because they're actually designing the future." Another participant observed: "It allowed us to physically see where people's energy went." Another shared: "The energy was more quiet and reflective. They were still on task but it's requiring more thinking. They were engaged and on task but now they had these big visions and weren't sure what they were going to do to realize them." Another explained: "There was very much a sense of let's get to work." And another saw that: "People experience a growth mindset moment where they really see that our transforming of reality is possible."

Why embrace the messy process of convergence?

AI Summits are crafted to deliberately encourage generative and divergent thinking in the dream phase and brainstorming in the design phase, to multiply a system's choices. By testing sometimes competing ideas against each other, design thinking leader and IDEO CEO Tim Brown has found there is an increased likelihood that the outcomes will be bolder, more creatively disruptive and more compelling. He notes that Linus Pauling said it best: "To have a good idea, you must first have lots of ideas"— and he won two Nobel Prizes.

More choice, however, also means more complexity, which can make the system's shared hopes difficult to execute. While generative divergent thinking is the route to ensuring opportunities for a disruption to be positive, convergent thinking enables the system to make choices and eliminate options to support its ability to consistently flourish. It is a practical way of deciding among existing alternatives, and this is why design studio teams are asked to prioritize their ideas and select one prototype to build during this phase.

Researchers caution, however, that inviting people to take responsibility for what they love can be a messy process because most people have not been taught to self-organize and take responsibility for themselves. Fortunately, they note that when invited to do so from a place of caring and wanting to make a meaningful difference for others, people consistently rise to the occasion and discover that both the needs of individuals and the needs of the collective can be served. In fact, this discovery quickly becomes the measure of success as higher-order coherence emerges and people's uniqueness turns into creative contributions for the whole system.

For example, one research participant observed: "There were feelings of excitement, chaos, competition, frustration and conflicts of ideas as we tried to make our dream a reality." Another noted: "There was a little frustration because now they're trying to converge and pull their dream into a plan." Another shared: "There was a lot of conversation to try and resolve different positions of faith and honor our common purpose." And another explained: "Leadership skills were really important at this stage to help us find a common path."

Researchers have found that while people often fear that collaboration will be more challenging when teams have diverse ways of thinking, these teams generally perform better because their differences force people to stretch out of their comfort zones and consider perspectives and ideas they may not have thought about or even agree with. For example, in one study bringing in just one "outsider" to a largely homogenous team actually doubled the team's chances of solving a challenging problem, and this happened precisely because the relationship produced friction. The work may feel harder when diverse teams converge, but the outcomes are also often significantly better.

"As our different perspectives rub against each other,
a burnishing occurs. Together, we make meaning, uncovering
patterns that draw from what each of us brings. Expressing
our differences carries the seeds of what might be. When
conditions enable us all to show up and engage fully, warts and all,
what is most meaningful shines through, over and over. We become
a 'differentiated wholeness' in which our unique gifts weave
together into a coherent tapestry... In the midst of creative
disruption, hearts open and we discover that we are connected."

PEGGY HOLMAN

Tim's team at IDEO also note that the ability to embrace both divergent and convergent thinking often forces people to stretch out of their comfort zones. Be it the incorporation of diverse perspectives and preferences, the need to embrace radical collaboration with strangers, or the requirement of prototyping a concept that will not be perfect and should welcome criticism, design thinking practices push people to let go of knowing the answers as they come together to play, to test, to fail, and to learn. Professor Carol Dweck – one of the world's leading researchers on motivation and performance – describes these as "growth mindset" behaviors.

Carol's research has found that while some people and human systems readily embrace growth mindset beliefs and behaviors by recognizing that the strengths they have can always be built upon provided they are willing to keep learning, practicing and putting in their best efforts, other people and human systems have a fixed mindset – or a naturalness bias – that leaves them fearful of trying things they can't easily master. Her studies suggest that as a result people and systems with a fixed mindset are less likely to embrace new challenges, welcome feedback and criticism or learn from failures and thus eventually fall short of their potential and struggle to flourish.

Michelle found that the design phase of an AI Summit can nudge people into growth mindset behaviors as they move from the divergent thinking process of brainstorming any possible answer to the "How might we?" question, to the convergent thinking process of selecting an idea for prototyping and gaining feedback. It should be noted, however, that if the system in which the AI Summit is being held generally leans more toward fixed mindset than growth mindset beliefs and behaviors we believe that it can be helpful to explicitly introduce the practices and benefits of a growth mindset along with the practices of design thinking so people feel more confident to navigate the messy process of convergence.

She also found that after riding an emotional high during the discovery and dream phase where divergent thinking had been openly encouraged, people sometimes struggled during this phase of an AI Summit if it suddenly became harder and messier to collaborate with people. We believe this shift could be better managed by framing the exercises as an opportunity for people to practice being comfortably uncomfortable if needed, and knowing that any negative emotions experienced during this process are just their body's way of letting them know that something important to them is on the line and to honor what matters most to them in the conversations they are having in their design studios.

Magic Mechanism Tip

When asking the design studio team to vote and select one idea to rapidly prototype it can be helpful to explain that they are moving into convergent thinking practices as they coalesce around the ideas they care enough about to take responsibility for prototyping. Rather than feeling uncomfortable or dismayed about the diverse opinions that may surface during these steps, reassure people that healthy debate is what enables diverse teams to perform better and to engage in these conversations from a place of caring, a willingness to learn together and the desire to make a meaningful difference for others.

Why harness positive urgency to amplify progress?

Peter Senge's widely acclaimed systems thinking book, *The Fifth Discipline*, points out that the juxtaposition of a system's vision (what people want) and a clear picture of its current reality (where people are relative to what they want) results in the natural force of "creative tension" as people try to bring their vision and reality together and seek resolution. As the gap between their vision and their reality dawns, he explains people are often left feeling anxious, stressed or discouraged and this results in "emotional tension," to which people's first response is often to try and lower the vision and thereby lighten their load. However, when people understand the natural force of creative tension and learn to embrace the emotional tension that can accompany it, the gap between a system's vision and current reality can create a positive sense of urgency that generates the energy for designing the new and eclipsing the old.

"The essence of personal mastery is learning how to generate and sustain creative tension in our lives."

PETER SENGE

To be clear, this is not about creating the often recommended "burning platform" that tries to magnify urgency by inciting fear and dissatisfaction – even if it needs to be manufactured – so that staying with the status quo seems more dangerous than launching into the unknown. Rather, it is about drawing on the system's shared sense of purpose to magnify and refract its strengths in the service of others. Once people feel called to be of service to others, researchers have found that they often experience a greater sense of urgency for following the path for which they now feel intended. It is this meaningful beckoning toward activities that are morally, socially and personally significant that liberates and mobilizes the system's courage, commitment and enthusiasm to overcome the constraints of their current reality together.

In his classic paper, *Small Wins: Redefining the Scale of Social Problems,* Karl Weick suggests that in order to harness people's feelings of urgency to make a positive difference for others, the size of challenges need to be shrunk to small wins that ensure emotional tension neither paralyzes nor overwhelms people. By breaking the system's shared dreams down into manageable pieces, he argues that people's levels of emotional tension can be reduced because the potential for creating tangible changes becomes more visible and the sense of control and predictability is increased. He explains: "The deliberate cultivation of a strategy of small wins infuses situations with comprehensible and specific meaning (commitment), reinforces the perception that people can exert some influence over what happens to them (control), and produces changes of manageable size that serve as incentives to expand the repertoire of skills (challenge)."

A small wins approach empowers people to use their strengths to succeed at meaningful work and amplifies their sense of progress. Harvard Business School researchers Professor Teresa Amabile and Steven Kramer have found that of all the things that can boost people's emotions, motivations and perceptions during a day, the single most important is making progress in meaningful work. Furthermore, the more frequently people experience a sense of progress, the more likely they are to be creatively productive and to feel more intrinsically motivated, optimistic, satisfied and connected to others in the long run. By setting clear goals, giving people autonomy, providing sufficient resources and time, connecting people together who can help each other with the work, encouraging a free exchange of ideas and being willing to openly learn from problems and successes, they suggest a system can amplify people's ability to make progress and their power to create meaningful win-win-win outcomes for themselves, the system and the people they serve.

Michelle's research found that the rapid prototyping exercise during the design phase of the AI Summit gave the design studio teams the freedom to move beyond dialogue and into action so they could address the creative tension between their shared dreams and their reality. By encouraging people to play and learn together as they rapidly expanded, integrated and tested their ideas for making a positive difference, these small — and sometimes miraculous as evidenced by Fairmount Santrol's sand filter – wins ignited a "self-reinforcing progress loop" which researchers suggest enables the system and the people in it to more consistently flourish.

Lyell explained of the design phase: "There's concentration, but I would say for the majority of the people there is real joy. People were pulling stuff out of their bags and designing mosquito-head masks right there on the spot as they worked with people they never would have dreamed of working with in the past." Another research participant observed: "It brought enormous human energy to create new possibilities." Another noted: "They're taking their ideas from concept to artifact. They can touch it. They can point to it. It's like seeing is believing." Another explained: "There was an amplification of progress." And another shared: "By the end of the design phase we had mobilized an inspired and empowered cadre of change agents."

David and Lindsey explain that the ability to go beyond words and design rapid prototypes that provide a beacon of hope that people can touch and see creates "waypower" so potent that willpower across a system grows. Building on the research of hope theorists, they argue that as wholepower, plus whypower, plus waypower combine, a system is elevated to an experience of positive change that teaches people that the future is in their hands and gives them valid reasons to hope. As Julie noted: "It created great opportunity in terms of unleashing this amazing innovation and generating energy, and at the same time the challenge by day three was helping the groups to come around to something that they could achieve and hope to really put into action."

Magic Mechanism Tip

When people become aware of the gap between their vision and their reality, the natural force of creative tension generates a positive sense of urgency that can be channeled into the rapid prototyping activity. By encouraging the design studio teams to play and learn together as they rapidly expand, integrate and test their ideas for making a positive difference, these small — and sometimes miraculous – wins can ignite a "self-reinforcing progress loop" that helps people and the system to flourish.

Destiny: Support Self-Organized Generosity

Figure 12: Summary Of Words Used To Describe Destiny Phase By Research Participants

As compassionate coaches of disruption, researchers urge us to embrace nature's process of emergent change by welcoming the disruptions that break apart the status quo, surfacing innovations and distinctions among the system's different parts, and allowing a new, more complex coherence to arise. Originally named "delivery," and sometimes called "deploy," David and Diana explain that: "What we discovered, quite honestly, was that momentum for change and long-term sustainability increased the more we abandoned 'delivery' ideas of action planning, monitoring progress, and building implementation strategies." Instead, they suggest that the goal in this phase is to introduce plans and processes that encourage and nurture ongoing improvised actions by people across the system to ramp up a collective sense of destiny.

"Of all the creatures on earth …
man alone is the architect of his destiny."
WILLIAM JAMES

For example, six of the seven transformational cases in the meta-case analysis of appreciative inquiry applications adopted an "improvisational approach" to the destiny phase where new ideas emerged and were widely accepted and the system sanctioned people to do whatever made sense to them to move toward their shared dreams and designs. Rather than relying on traditional change management tactics to try and implement something as did eleven of the thirteen non-transformational cases, leaders looked for where people were innovating and then helped them along when they could, which enabled change to occur more quickly.

While this may sound like a large leap of faith, remember that when a living system is open, rather than closed to the generative possibilities of its environment, it is capable of self-organizing into new relationships that increase its capacity rather than succumbing to disorder. This order is not created by complex controls, but by the presence of the guiding fields of identity, values and vision for the system that support the exercise of individual freedom and enable its ongoing learning and intelligence. Thus, by replacing rules and procedures designed to control with visions and values that encourage lively, independent action, so that both organizations and individuals benefit, we are able to live in a world where order emerges out of chaos. During this phase therefore, a system has to trust that the previous Ds have created a generative set of images and ideas that are so compelling people will voluntarily and responsibly find ways to transform their work processes in the service of others.

How do AI Summits support self-organized generosity?

Researchers have previously noted that there remains the most confusion and least consensus about what happens in the destiny phase of an AI Summit, and this was true of Michelle's sample also. Typically most of the AI Summits she studied – including Clarke – moved into the destiny phase on the final day of the AI Summit event. Committed to the challenge of ensuring people emerged with clear actions to take their dreams forward, the design studio teams usually reconvened and began by refining and strengthening their prototypes based on the feedback gathered from their presentations or gallery walks.

In the Clarke AI Summit – as is now the case for many AI Summits being designed — the design studio teams were asked to step back and look again at the opportunity area they had chosen, the ideas they had brainstormed, the prototype they had created and the feedback they had been given, and craft an aspiration statement for their chosen opportunity area. Serving as a North Star, the aspiration statement was:

- Something they wanted and desired.

- Stated in the present tense — as if it had happened already.

- A stretch — it took the system beyond the status quo. It was a provocative proposition that left people saying, "I am not sure we can do it... it is bigger, braver, and bolder!"

- Made up of energizing words and provided tangible images: so people could see it.

- Helped to unify long-term focus and provided a sense of direction.

For example, the "Heart of Clarke" aspiration statement read:

> The Chief Communications Officer (CCO) communicates how the Heart of Clarke ignites our passion and imagination to create a more prosperous, flourishing world.

> The story of Clarke includes honoring our past, embracing the present, and building a better future.

> Nourishing the Heart of Clarke requires growing our culture internally.

> Sharing the Heart of Clarke with the world will inspire the world to embrace our mission, vision and values.

> Bringing the Heart of Clarke to the world will make the world more prosperous by encouraging Peace Through Public Health.

See www.thechangelabs.com for more examples of Clarke's aspiration statements.

Each of the Clarke design studio teams were also invited to explore how they might self-organize beyond the AI Summit to realize their aspirations. The teams were encouraged to:

- Assess business/financial logic: Will this have a positive impact on the world, our customers, communities and people? Will it strengthen the bottom-line and payoff in the short-term? Will it make us a bigger, braver, bolder business? What stakeholder groups will see the most value and benefit?

- Name the one to two individuals who will best lead this initiative. And list names of group members who might want to continue with this initiative (include their contact information). Determine whose input or partnership would be most valuable at this stage of development (Are there structures or groups within the organization, external within the industry or with external stakeholders that we should collaborate with?).

- Explore a possible action plan including: early steps (first 3 weeks) including the very first step; moderate term steps (next 3 months); and longer-term steps (up to 3 years).

They were also asked to provide a short written summary of these ideas and to nominate a reporter from the group to share their aspiration statement, what they considered to be most exciting, important or valuable about their opportunity and the very first step they had decided to take to move it forward. It is important to note that in all the AI Summits studied, there was never an expectation that everyone would contribute their names to continue with an initiative. In every case, people were encouraged to only take responsibility for what they cared about and had the capacity to support. As a result, typically 40 to 60 percent of people attending an AI Summit volunteered to help beyond the AI Summit event.

Each Clarke design studio team then provided a two-minute report back to the group. As each statement was shared one after the other, Julie noted that the impact of what had already been generated from the AI Summit began to dawn around the room. Their hard work paid off in this moment as people realized the incredible impact Clarke could have when their strengths were aligned and magnified to realize their shared dreams and make a difference for others, elevating their collective energy and restoring their appreciation for the power of the whole system working together.

To be clear, there is a reason the word "work" features so prominently in Figure 12, which summarizes the research participants' insights from this phase. David describes this step as "nitty gritty, hard work" as people try to figure out how they will go forward together. For example, one research participant noted: "The conversation starts to move from heart to head. There was a real moment of suspense at the beginning of the destiny phase about who was going to do the work." Another observed: "There was a bit of anxiety about how are we going to make all this happen?" Another shared: "There was a tension of ownership and pride and skepticism." And another explained: "We asked people to go back and create aspiration statements for each of their initiatives. This helped to bring excitement and energy back into the Summit so we could end on a high."

The word "role" features prominently in Figure 12. The reality is that self-organization creates new networks, and researchers point out that networks have no hierarchy, just nodes or hubs for which leaders emerge as individuals and groups step forward to take responsibility. As one research participant noted: "Leadership and teamwork were definitely emerging as strong attributes as people started to take responsibility." And another observed: "There's a self-regulation capacity emerging, where leadership shifts and roles move as people get clear on who's good at what. It's not top-down or bottom-up, but it's shared." Other participants repeatedly shared that this process can feel "ambiguous" and "uncertain," particularly in systems that do not typically allow for the freedom for self-organization. It is one of the reasons the words "nervousness," "clueless" and "tumultuous" appear in the research participants' observations of this phase.

Research participants explained that the other reason for these experiences surfacing was due to confusion about "What's next?" How would the aspiration statements and shared purpose become a reality beyond the AI Summit event? In their second AI Summit, the Clarke steering committee used this moment to explain that it would be up to each person in the room to shape what happened next. They made it clear that Clarke was giving them full permission to continue self-organizing and taking action around their aspiration statements, but that other than providing the boundaries of their shared dreams, and some guiding principles and tools, leaders would not be doing this for them. Instead, leaders would help provide regular check-in points for the teams to track, celebrate and amplify their progress and could provide access to resources and offer support if teams had specific requests.

In all of the AI Summits Michelle reviewed, during the final moments of the event people were asked to return to their discovery interview partner and discuss:

- The three most important things that happened at this AI Summit for them including one key area of learning, one high point moment and one of the most important outcomes in their view.

- The one message of innovation or inspiration they will communicate to others to ensure the success of the system.

- Their personal pledges or commitments.

People were then usually given an open microphone opportunity to share their reflections if they felt called to do so. The facilitators and sponsors then thanked everyone for their participation and reminded people of the next steps being taken.

Why prioritize a culture of self-protective giving?

Professors Richard Ryan and Edward Deci note that perhaps the most common, and yet overlooked, attribute of human beings is that people are normatively cooperative, social creatures with robust capacities for kindness, compassion and benevolence. Contrary to the popular view of human nature as inherently selfish and aggressive, they suggest that both evolutionary and cultural developments have instead prepared people to primarily be relationally engaged, norm assimilating, rule following and generous unless conditions thwart the satisfaction of their needs for competence, relatedness and autonomy.

Other researchers echo these observations, noting that when people are given room to take responsibility for their passions, it awakens a sense of abundance and generosity toward others. For example, after Hurricane Katrina the community of Ville Platte — a small town of 11,000 people with an average yearly income of only $5300 — generously self-organized to serve 5,000 displaced and traumatized victims, inviting them to share their homes not as refugees or evacuees but as "company." They rescued people from rooftops, picked up the dead and transported the injured to trauma centers, without any federal or Red Cross aid. All they needed to rely on was human compassion and their inherent ability to self-organize. As one community member explained: "All of us know how to spontaneously cooperate. My God, we're always organizing christenings or family gatherings."

"Effective self-organization in human systems starts with voluntary self-selection in response to a genuine invitation."

HARRISON OWEN

Professor Adam Grant explains that while people are inherently generous, their beliefs about the types of social interactions a system values shapes just how generous they will be with each other. For example, in a system where people are forced to compete for scarce resources against each other, generosity is discouraged in favor of being "takers" who get as much as they can from others, or being "matchers" who constantly try to ensure an even exchange of favors, to ensure their own success. In contrast, in a system where people feel supported and valued for behaving generously and caring about others, they are more likely to behave as "givers" who willingly share their time, energy, knowledge, skills, ideas and connections to benefit others.

Studies have found that when a culture of generosity is prioritized people are more efficient at solving problems, getting their work done and balancing their workloads to ensure consistent performance. They build teams that are cohesive and coordinated and establish environments in which others feel their needs are the system's top priority. As a result, the system and the people in it are more likely to flourish.

Lyell observed of the destiny phase: "There's an out-of-control level of caring and collaboration at this point." Another research participant noted: "There's a strong sense of beyond the self-focus to the other." Another shared: "There was a sense of collaboration and committed partnership around taking action." Another reported: "We've gone to a 'we' consciousness and there is an improvisational capacity emerging because of trust." And another explained: "People were so grateful for the work that had been put in."

While this level of caring and generosity sounds ideal to ensure people continue taking responsibility after the AI Summit, researchers have found that there is a genuine risk of collaboration burnout in systems that rely heavily on self-organization. For example, a study of more than three hundred organizations found that the distribution of collaborative work often becomes extremely lopsided with 20-30 percent of value-added collaborations coming from only 3-5 percent of people who become known for being both capable and willing to help. Thus, the increasing demands placed on givers can turn a virtuous cycle into a vicious cycle that creates system bottlenecks and undermines the givers' effectiveness and ability to flourish.

As a result, Adam and his colleagues caution that although givers are the most valuable people in a system, they're also at the greatest risk of burnout. They explain that while "selfless givers" have a high concern for others, they suffer from having a low concern for themselves and consequently their acts of generosity leave them exhausted and paradoxically helping others less. In contrast, "self-protective givers" are generous, but they know their limits so instead of saying "yes" to every request, they look for high-impact, low-cost ways of giving and consequently offer the most direct support, take the most initiative, make the best suggestions and the most sustainable contributions in a system.

To ensure they can sustain their generosity and flourish as they support others, self-protective givers are thoughtful about:

- How they help (i.e. proactively aligning their giving with their strengths and passions so that giving renews their energy and provides greater value).

- When they help (i.e. chunking their giving into dedicated blocks of time to maintain their focus).

- Whom they help (i.e. prioritizing requests and saying yes when it matters most and referring requests to others when they don't have the time or skills).

Michelle's research found that during the destiny phase, AI Summits can help to build or reinforce a culture of self-protective giving by ensuring that the invitation for continued participation is genuinely offered, rather than being a veiled command. By providing people with different opportunities (i.e. joining an opportunity team or their individual pledges) to shape how, when and whom they help, this phase of the AI Summit enables like-minded and motivated people to find each other across the system and make something happen. Of course, a real invitation carries the risk that people may not choose to give, but we believe it is better before the AI Summit event concludes to honestly confront such a lack of willingness or capacity to take responsibility for realizing the shared purpose than to naively push forward.

Magic Moment Tip

Allow people to prioritize how, when and with whom they might share their strengths to make the system's shared purpose a reality. Offer open and genuine invitations for post-Summit participation to help realize the aspiration statements or make a personal pledge or commitment. Trust that whoever chooses to volunteer are precisely the right people because they cared enough to take responsibility for what happens next.

Why celebrate authentic grit?

Researchers note that the seeds of most great ideas are often misunderstood, dismissed and sometimes actively discouraged by others. As a result, beginnings are often laden with self-doubt, false starts and hard work as the dynamic tension between people's habits and their pioneering spirit enables them to carve a trail of learning, innovation and adaptation toward something they find so compelling they feel they have no choice but to try and make it happen. In a word, it requires what Professor Angela Duckworth describes as "grit."

Angela and her colleagues explain that: "Grit is the passion and perseverance for long-term goals." Their research suggests that the most successful people in any system rarely succumb to thoughts of giving up and instead of interpreting the inevitable obstacles, setbacks, and plateaus in their progress as signals to quit, they see these as signs to intensify their effort and practice and persist because they believe they have the capacity to learn and grow. Strongly intertwined with the practices of Carol's growth mindsets, grit is what enables people to "fall down seven times, stand up eight."

Carol cautions, however, that grit and growth mindset practices can backfire when people and systems become so focused on achieving an outcome, they are no longer attuned to the environment around them. Unable to find the pause or stop button to assess the feedback about why their approach is not working, performance coach and researcher Caroline Adams Miller suggests that moments of "stupid grit" make it difficult for people to step away from a goal that no longer makes sense because of the "sunk costs" of their energy and resources. In order to avoid this risk, she recommends cultivating "authentic grit."

"Authentic grit is the passionate pursuit of hard goals that awe and inspire others to become better people, flourish emotionally, take positive risks, and live their best lives."

CAROLINE ADAMS MILLER

Caroline suggests that people with authentic grit have discovered that setbacks, failures and disappointments are part of how they learn, grow and build resilience. Knowing that they are running a marathon and not a sprint, authentically gritty people practice having a growth-mindset and being a self-protective giver to ensure that their determination is not leading to the harm or neglect of themselves or others and instead provides inspiration and helps a system to flourish. Grounded in purpose and able to fill people with hope, authentic grit gives people the ongoing confidence, humility, and determination to take responsibility for their passions, not to boost themselves up in the eyes of others, but because they want to make a difference.

In his book *Emotional Success,* Professor David DeSteno also recognizes the gritty power of social emotions – such as gratitude, compassion and authentic pride – that are evoked when we help others. Pointing out that self-control has evolved from people's need to co-operate with each other, he notes that the experience of social emotions has been found to help people to be more future-orientated in their choices, to willingly acquire new skills, and to persevere in the face of difficulty, so they can achieve outcomes that benefit themselves and others in the long run.

For example, when Clarke opened the microphone to anyone who wanted to share their reflections of the AI Summit it created a moment for the system to recognize and celebrate the authentic grit of the people present. Lyell noted: "There was a collective feeling that we had done so much and that we had made a difference, as well as a recognition of things we could do straight away and things that were going to be a more long-term effort and what could we do to make sure it all happened." Another research participant observed of this moment: "There was a real sense of satisfaction. We're on our way. We can do it. Whatever it takes we'll get it done." Another explained: "It felt like a launching, not a closing." And another reported: "They were just the most energizing, engaging, uplifting moments to finish a Summit."

Michelle's research found that the open microphone reflection at the end of the destiny phase and the AI Summit event itself, created a moment for authentic grit to be recognized and celebrated in a system. By savoring their newly awakened shared purpose, the difference they had already started to make for others, and the gratitude they felt for the experience they'd just had together, the social emotions of compassion, authentic pride and gratitude were evoked. Given studies have found that people who habitually experience these social emotions have lower levels of anxiety, a greater desire to help others and are more likely to persevere and achieve their goals, the open microphone reflection is a powerful and effective way to close an AI Summit event.

As a result, the research participants repeatedly noted that the open microphone reflection was one of the most important across the entire AI Summit. They often shared that it was during this moment that the most skeptical pre-Summit participants reflected on their renewed sense of hope and determination to move forward together and where people sometimes made incredibly public generous commitments (i.e. the Mayor of Cleveland announced at this point that the city would run an AI Summit every year for the next decade). One participant explained: "It was the icing on the cake as they spoke their truth about their excitement of what they had created together. Everyone left on a very upward spiral." And another shared: "As they left the dominant emotion was still hope. And now there was a sense of determination as well to take the necessary steps to make change happen." Lyell noted that by the end of the open microphone reflection: "No matter what functional area they were from or what they did, people understood that they had value and were valued here."

Magic Mechanism Tip

An open microphone reflection at the end of the AI Summit event gives people a chance to express and savor the social emotions of compassion for the difference they want to make together, authentic pride for what they have already achieved together and gratitude for how they have been supported by each other. Evoking these social emotions as people leave not only ensures a peak-end experience, but buffers people's levels of grit for post-Summit actions.

Drum: Sustain Appreciative Vitality

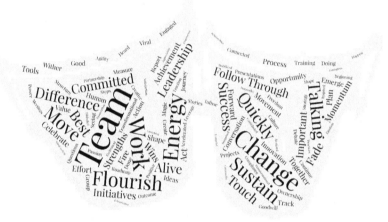

Figure 13: Summary Of Words Used To Describe Drum Phase By Research Participants

Flourishing is not a static state, but an emergent property of change that provides the energy and vitality for new levels of organization and inspires people to act. Human flourishing is enabled by the elusive life-energy that Peggy Holman suggests: enlivens people to be aware of what is happening around them, helps them to prioritize taking responsibility for what matters to them, enables them to be generous and compassionate with themselves and others, and keeps them open to learning and growth as they climb the path to mastery of their environment.

While much is still being learned about how human systems create and maintain collective energy, organizational researcher Michael Cole and his colleagues have added to our understanding by proposing that within a system, productive energy is not simply an individual experience but a collective one that comprises: positive affect (feelings of enthusiasm), cognitive arousal (desire to focus attention and find solutions), and purposeful behavior (willingness to invest effort toward shared goals) among system members to realize its potential. They explain that productive energy fluctuates as a result of context, inputs and outcomes, but can become individually and collectively self-reinforcing when leaders and key influencers recognize and legitimize desired actions.

Other researchers suggest that a mirror energy or contagion effect is created between a system and the people in it when there is an experience of shared meaning, positive relationships, positive agency and positive emotions. Note in this list the presence of many of the PERMA pillars and self-determination nutrients that we discovered enable human flourishing, which suggests that not only are energy and flourishing closely interrelated emergent states, but that they can both be supported through the appreciative inquiry practices we have explored throughout this book.

Thus, once the AI Summit event is complete, the goal of the drum phase is to embed appreciative intelligence within a system so that people's ability to seek out generative information, create generative connections, and continuously self-organize to amplify and magnify their strengths supplies productive energy that enables the system to realize its expanding potential and flourish. This means ensuring that people understand and can use the skills they have acquired during the preceding AI Summit phases, so that the system can continue dancing to the rhythm of emergent change.

How does an AI Summit sustain collective vitality?

Appreciative inquiry researchers and practitioners repeatedly caution that once the AI Summit event concludes, in many ways the real work begins. Julie agreed, noting that: "It's what happened after the Summit that really made the difference." Another research participant shared: "Follow-up is very important." Another urged: "Thinking about how you continue to infuse energy into that team is really important." And another explained: "We had to keep the momentum alive." Yet of all the AI Summit phases, to date there is the least agreement, guidance or support for what happens post the AI Summit event.

Knowing how important it was not to lose momentum after the AI Summit event, Clarke made sure they had a post-Summit team established that included:

- An integration leader (a senior-level leader with broad authority and influence and the capacity to oversee the entire process of the Summit integration work).

- An executive sponsor for each opportunity area (a senior leader who could provide guidance and general direction to their opportunity area team and champion).

- A champion for each opportunity area (a spokesperson who would coordinate team meetings and facilitate the team's post-Summit work – these were great opportunities for emerging leaders).

Michelle's research found that the first daunting task during the drum phase was sorting through the hundreds of research artifacts from the discovery, dream, design and destiny phases and curating and summarizing them in a respectful and meaningful way. For example, Clarke chose to quickly share the "How might we?" questions and aspirations statements throughout their system within fourteen days of the AI Summit event. Schuberg Philis produced detailed documents complete with images and participant experiences to try and preserve the full AI Summit experience (http://www.lead2flourish.com/schuberg-philis). However, while the AI Summit event outputs varied depending on a system's preferred norms and means of communication, all of the research participants agreed that it was important a summary was circulated as quickly as possible to everyone in the system – not just those who attended – and that this communication included a clear outline of the next steps to be taken.

The next challenge faced by each AI Summit during this phase was finding ways to support the champions and the teams who had volunteered to take their aspirations forward, many of whom needed additional information, guidance, training, resources and new members. For the systems that had not previously explicitly taught and/or endorsed self-organization practices, more structure and support was needed to help the opportunity teams understand how to flourish as they continued working together. For the systems that already encouraged self-organization, the primary requirement was connecting the opportunity teams to existing methods of communication, tracking and reporting.

"The intention is not to develop a project with a beginning, a middle, and an end, but to create a new way of thinking, learning, communicating, working, and innovating that becomes so embedded into the organization it changes the culture."

MOLLY MCGUIGAN AND C.J. MURPHY

For example, Lyell shared that he learned the important leadership decision to be made during this phase was to: "Continue to give people ownership of their opportunity areas and provide them with the structure and support they need to integrate it into the organization. Leadership had to provide a framework, and then get out of the way." As a result, Clarke scheduled a number of follow-up checkpoints to guide the opportunity teams, which included:

- 14 days after the AI Summit event: The opportunity team met while the momentum was still fresh to refine their ideas and confirm their first three to five short-, medium- and long-term initiatives.

- 90 days after the AI Summit event: All the opportunity champions came together to present the one to three recommendations they hoped to pursue and a draft of their project plan with a preliminary cost/benefit analysis. The champions and their teams were asked to identify any low-hanging fruit they could knock out with minimal resources and give feedback on the projects and go/no-go decisions when possible.

- 120 days after the AI Summit event: The champions once again gathered to each present a refined and detailed project plan that incorporated their previous feedback. Following this meeting, projects were formally mapped to strategic initiatives and funded through Clarke's company's planning and budgeting process.

Julie noted that as a result of how the opportunity teams were encouraged to self-organize and apply the appreciative practices they had learned: "The methodology of appreciative inquiry has become part of our language and part of our culture and is becoming more and more part of our DNA. It was this systemic culture change where we began to incorporate these ideas of positive thinking and positive orientation toward things, being aspirational, seeing opportunities."

Professor Gervase Bushe urges systems toward an even more generative and self-organized approach for the opportunity teams, by giving permission for strategic, self-generated "probes" based on the aspiration statements and encouraging people to find the resources and support they need from across the system with leaders "tracking and fanning" the initiatives deemed as most valuable. Those that flourish survive, and the rest naturally lose energy and disappear over time but provide important learning opportunities.

Again, there is no right way to execute the drum phase, there is only what is right for the system and the people in it. However, researchers caution that the drum phase often runs the risk of becoming a project with rigid deadlines and return on investments, and while both are important in most systems to maintain appreciative vitality, the system needs to structure the drum phase in a way that will keep the dialogue, energy and momentum alive.

Finally, the research participants all agreed that it was essential throughout the drum phase to track and share how progress was being made toward the shared dreams. For example, one participant shared: "We created a position for someone to follow-up with the teams and to help keep things moving forward and sustain the energy and momentum." Another reported: "The stuff that came out of the Summit caught fire and was acted on pretty fast." And another recommended: "Look for short-term win projects and big game changer projects. Some teams naturally died. Not every idea is great."

Studies suggest that carefully timed announcements and updates can influence people's perception of momentum for the opportunity areas and thus generally "the more news the better." Clarke understood that sharing the progress being made by the opportunity teams was essential to maintaining people's individual and collective energy post-Summit, and in addition to the immediate post-Summit event communication laid out the following milestones:

- 28 days after the AI Summit event: Share the integration plan and outline the formal check-in points scheduled.

- 90 days after the AI Summit event: Share some of the projects that are in the works and the preparation materials for the champions' checkpoint meeting and thank people for their continued work and enthusiasm.

- 120 days after the AI Summit event: Share the progress that has been made on each opportunity area and news of those still in development. Outline the next steps and set the vision for what will be accomplished by the one-year anniversary.

- 365 days after the AI Summit event: Celebrate the one-year anniversary and what has been achieved. Celebrate the failures as well as the clear successes to ensure the system continues learning and growing from the experience.

(An example of Clarke's post-Summit plan and recommendations can be seen at www.thechangelab.com.)

Clarke also established measures for the opportunity areas and integrated this into their existing quarterly review structure to ensure the AI Summit initiatives remained top-of-mind for the leaders. Where possible, as the initiatives matured they were integrated into existing business planning and management processes to embed real ownership and accountability. Julie explains: "We made business as usual unusual and made the unusual business as usual." Following their first AI Summit in 2012, Clarke found that it took three years for the initiatives and ideas from the AI Summit event to either reach their natural conclusion or become embedded in Clarke's ways of working.

Another research participant noted of the drum phase: "There's a lot more energy and action toward where we want to go, versus getting stuck in what's not working. This has become part of our day-to-day culture."

Why fuel diverse feedback loops?

A flourishing system is a learning system and ultimately its ability to notice new forms of information, learn from them and respond to them determines its level of intelligence. Feedback loops – the means by which a system talks to itself – hold the key to ensuring a system continues receiving and connecting information inside and outside, at the top and at the bottom, and across and within the system, to prompt self-organization in ways that enable its resilience and growth. The conscious monitoring of feedback loops enables generative thinking to become an organic behavior in a system, by giving people the opportunity to improve their ability to see the bigger patterns and emergent solutions arising from their interactions. As a result, when groups within a system are truly learning, not only do studies suggest they produce more extraordinary results, but that people grow more rapidly than they could have alone and thus the system becomes increasingly intelligent.

"Amplifying and damping feedback serves like the throttle of a propulsion system; it causes a process of change either to accelerate or to slow down."

RICHARD PASCALE

By drawing attention to new possibilities, "amplifying feedback loops" reinforce whatever general direction of change is being imposed – be it a virtuous cycle of growth or a vicious cycle of collapse – and ensure that small changes quickly build upon themselves to become self-fulfilling prophecies. For example, in a bull market, as share prices rise, the amplifying feedback loop causes people to buy more shares. In a bear market, however, where share prices are falling, the amplifying feedback loop causes people to sell more shares.

Peter Senge reminds us, however, that pure accelerating growth or decline rarely continues unchecked in nature, because amplifying processes rarely occur in isolation. Eventually, limits are encountered in the system's environment in the form of dampening feedback to slow, stop, divert or reverse growth in an effort to restore balance and stop the system from destroying itself. Like a thermostat in a house, dampening feedback continually guards the system against being "too hot" or "too cold." It signals deviations from a goal and provides information to help keep a system stable and on track once its course has been established.

Of course, a system's feedback loops are rarely singular, but are linked together often in fantastically complex patterns that tug against each other so people can learn, create, design, self-organize and evolve. As a result, living systems do much more than explode exponentially, stay steady or approach goals smoothly, instead as we learned throughout this book they dance between order and chaos to ensure their resilience and growth. Fueling the productive energy to maintain this dance are the diverse feedback loops a system chooses to monitor and learn from.

Thus, during the drum phase it is essential that diverse feedback loops are intentionally established and consciously monitored for the opportunity teams. Clarke ensured this occurred by providing the 90- and 120-day check-ins for the teams and establishing a measurement dashboard. Having come to understand the power of an appreciative eye, Julie noted that in reviewing these feedback loops: "We find ourselves articulating questions differently and incorporating into our discussion the concepts of leveraging our strengths."

Other research participants also noted the importance of establishing ongoing opportunities for dialogue across the system, finding ways to capture people's learning and sharing the progress being made. For example, one participant explained: "We shared quick wins after the

Summit." Another shared: "It's the stories that go viral and really start infecting the system." Another reported: "Continuing to connect and shape the debate as we moved forwards has been really important." And another noted: "We track how we're doing. We measure, we report and we celebrate our success."

By intentionally fueling diverse feedback loops for the shared dreams and opportunity areas during the drum phase, the AI Summits were able to ensure that a system's productive energy for change neither burnt out nor became stuck. This is why researchers note that leadership during this phase is essential, not for defining and directing change, but for tracking, recognizing and celebrating small, important opportunities and working to amplify them into big, important changes that are integrated into the system. By helping new information to continue circulating throughout the system at an optimal pace, leaders can shape the balance between chaos and order and ensure that learning and intelligence continue to grow throughout the system.

Magic Mechanism Tip

Encourage leaders to establish, monitor and share feedback loops for the dreams and opportunity areas that emerge from the AI Summit to help people track, recognize, learn from, celebrate and amplify the progress being made. Consciously note if the information being received is amplifying or dampening the desired change and create space for intentionally generative conversations as needed.

Why nurture gratitude and belonging?

The challenge for most human systems is to transform the isolation and disconnection being experienced into connectedness and caring for the whole. Only then will people have the ongoing necessary self-determination nutrients of relatedness, autonomy and competence to support the activation of the PERMA pillars and enable themselves, others and the system to flourish. Thus, we need to find sustainable ways to create structures where people feel like they belong.

Found to be a fundamental drive of human motivation, people's need for belonging is what causes them to seek out and connect with others across a system. Peggy Holman explains: "When people feel like they belong, they show up and bring their gifts. Coupled with shared purpose, a sense of community keeps the fires of commitment burning, fueling ever more creativity and innovation."

Studies have found that people feel like they belong when they:

- Are recognized for their accomplishments.
- Have the opportunity to express their opinions freely.
- Feel like their contributions are valued.
- Feel like they are genuinely cared about.
- Are comfortable enough to be themselves with others.

"True belonging doesn't require you to change who you are; it requires you to be who you are."
BRENÉ BROWN

Studies also suggest a simple, but powerful way, to meet this need for belonging in a system is by nurturing the practice of gratitude inside and outside, at the top and bottom, and across and within the system. Positive psychology researcher and practitioner, Shawn Achor suggests that encouraging people to become "praise prisms" can grow gratitude throughout a system. He recommends that in order for people to truly benefit from gratitude and feel like they belong, praise practices within a system need to:

- Focus on processes, effort and learning, not just outcomes. (i.e. "I really appreciate how hard you worked on that.")

- Celebrate what's working. (i.e. "What's working well?")

- Avoid lifting one person up at the expense of another. (i.e. "You're the smartest person on this team.")

- Emphasizing the collective efforts of people and not just the star performers. As Michael Jordan said: "Talent wins games, but teamwork and intelligence wins championships."

As a result, Shawn's studies have found that by helping people to willing and authentically shine grateful recognition and appreciation on others across the system, and accept gratitude for their own actions, a virtuous cycle of gratitude emerges.

Professor David DeSteno concurs, explaining that people are grateful when they feel others have invested in them, which makes them willing to return the favor in the future. David's studies have found, however, that the feeling of gratitude extends beyond simply helping a previous benefactor and actually ramps up people's willingness to help others for the long-term benefit of the system. He has also discovered that differences in people's daily levels of gratitude are also strongly associated with their levels of self-control (i.e. the more gratitude people experience in their day, the more likely they are to wait for or persevere toward a greater future reward). And best of all he concludes that gratitude doesn't require a lot of effort and the more people experience it, the easier and more rewarding it becomes.

Professor Teresa Amabile and Steven Kramer have found that ultimately progress is nourished by acts of interpersonal support, such as respect and recognition, encouragement, and opportunities for affiliation – all of which can be met through Shawn's praise prisms. They write: "The nourishment factors refer to something that everyone craves at work: human connection... Although nourishers may matter more to some people than others, none of us can truly thrive without them."

Michelle's research found that the drum phase could be used to transfer the respect, appreciation and value shared between people during the

AI Summit event into post-Summit activities. For example, in their post-AI Summit guide (find at www.thechangelabs.com), Clarke noted the importance of thanking and recognizing people for their work throughout their communication milestones. In addition, the regular and inclusive nature of their communications has helped to ensure that over time people have remained connected and felt included in the ongoing work of the opportunity teams.

Lyell noted that as a result during the drum phase: "There's respect and a higher level of caring for people. You've created new friendships." Another research participant shared: "That's the beautiful part to come out of the Summit; just seeing the respect that people have for each other and the respect for allowing everyone to be heard." And another reported: "There is an absolute feeling of connectedness, and of being together."

Magic Mechanism Tip

Belonging is a fundamental drive of human motivation. Transfer the respect, appreciation and affection people gained for each other during the AI Summit event into the system by encouraging gratitude practices for and within the opportunity teams to maintain momentum and connection across the system.

CHAPTER 6

How Can We Continue Improving AI Summits?

"Appreciative inquiry was a gift.
Now every day I wake up and ask:
How can I be my best self so I can really enable
other people to be their best self?"
ENRIQUE TAMES, UNIVERSIDAD TECMILENIO

Before beginning this book we knew from the growing body of evidence and our own experiences that AI Summits can create positive disruptions that support systemic flourishing.

However, while much wonderful work has been written about the guiding principles that enable these outcomes, increasingly we have felt this guidance barely scratched the surface of what practitioners need to effectively design and deliver AI Summits. Psychologically, neurologically, socially and systemically it appeared that more mechanisms were in play, which could help compassionate coaches of disruption deliver more reliable change experiences.

"When you want to build a ship, do not begin by gathering wood, cutting boards, and distributing work, but rather awaken within men the desire for the vast and endless sea."

ANTOINE DE SAINT-EXUPÉRY

We believe this book adds important insights to our shared understanding of what makes an AI Summit work. For example, when we work with systems in the future we will:

- **Ensure they understand how change works in complex, adaptive systems.** That rather than being mechanical and in need of being controlled, living systems flourish when they have opportunities to identify, organize and elevate their strengths in an ongoing dance between chaos and order, stability and growth.

- **Explain that an AI Summit is a strengths-based, positive disruption that creates generative connections and a sense of psychological safety and belonging that supports individual and systemic flourishing.** Therefore the richer the diversity of connections invited, the richer the rewards for the system as unique information and strengths are given the opportunity to dynamically and genuinely connect well beyond the AI Summit event. It is also essential, however, that the AI Summit process enables the system to be supportive of people's needs for competence, relatedness and autonomy and provides opportunities to trigger the PERMA pillars so that flourishing self-organized teams emerge.

- **Help leaders assess if an AI Summit is a good fit for their system right now.** By deciphering the current state of the system and the dynamics driving it, determining leaders' willingness to support self-organization, and discovering the openness for generative practices, a lot can be learned about the suitability of an AI Summit. The questions posed in

Figure 4 provide a helpful guide to ascertain whether leaders are truly aligned with being compassionate and supportive coaches of the disruption.

- **Outline the 6D cycle and level of investment (particularly in the define and drum stages) that an AI Summit requires.** By integrating all the requirements of an AI Summit into one cycle, it is our hope that leaders will realize that these phases are every bit as important and worthy of their attention, resources and planning as the actual AI Summit event. In particular, we need to ensure that the drum phase is never an afterthought if we are to help systems to flourish.

- **Educate a diverse steering committee and give them time to find a bold, generative topic.** If there is not the willingness or resources to define the AI Summit task properly, we believe this is a good sign to call an AI Summit off. From the outset there must be a committed group of champions who understand how complex, dynamic systems and the people within them flourish and why the ultimate goal of an AI Summit is to create a positive disruption that connects people in new ways around their shared hopes and enables them to self-organize and take responsibility for making things happen in ways that are good for them and good for others. There must also be an agreed topic that is so bold and generative that just talking about it with a diverse representation of the system is enough to touch people's hearts and start changing the way people think and act.

- **Create a safe, appreciative space for people to align, amplify and magnify their strengths together.** Every step of the AI Summit event from the duration, location, participants, activities, facilitation and logistics must be designed to maximize the opportunities for people to individually and collectively flourish. It is not enough to simply make this a "positive" experience. In order for transformation to take place it needs to be a generative experience and that means creating a psychologically safe space where people can speak honestly about their hopes and their fears. It's important to recognize and be prepared for the fact that not everyone may feel positive throughout the entire experience, but instead that emotions are likely to ebb and flow and that this is a natural and healthy part of any growth experience. It's also helpful to know that the magic mechanisms that can be baked into an AI Summit design are likely to psychologically, neurologically, socially and systemically draw out the best in the people participating and enable the alignment, amplification and magnification of strengths across the system.

- **Invest in drumming in the change by preparing leaders and champions to be compassionate coaches within the system.** Ensuring that the insights and practices of individual and systemic flourishing are passed to the leaders and champions for the drum phase is essential if vitality and productive energy are to be maintained. We believe there is more we can do to formally train people stepping into these roles – just as we do during the define stage of the steering committee – that would ensure this stage is less tumultuous and more effective. In addition, leaders and champions need to be prepared for the marathon, rather than a sprint, during this phase and be recognized and appreciated not simply for the opportunity areas they are leading, but the ways in which they are changing how the system is working. At the end of an AI Summit process this is perhaps the most transformational outcome any system can hope to achieve.

There is no doubt that as we face the most significant geopolitical, environmental, social, and economic challenges in history, we need more adaptive, creative and resilient ways to enable individual and systemic flourishing. We are not suggesting that AI Summits are the magic pill that can resolve all of these challenges, but we do believe they offer a powerful approach that can enable individual and systemic flourishing when used in the right ways and at the right time.

Limitations And Further Research

This book should be interpreted in light of its potential limitations. For example, the intentional application of the 6D cycle and 12 magic mechanisms needs to be further measured and assessed. Although these themes and best practices clearly surfaced in Michelle's research, none of the AI Summits studied deliberately applied this approach. The next obvious step is to determine if the whole really adds up to the sum of the parts identified.

In addition, little has been done to collect self-report measures on the PERMA pillars or self-determination nutrients pre, during or post an AI Summit. Quantitative measures of these kinds could provide valuable data to help us better understand the 12 magic mechanisms and their psychological and social impact. Similarly, as wearable devices become more affordable and available the collection of biometrical data from a sample of participants may also provide us with more valuable insights.

Finally, as positive psychology researchers and system scientists continue to merge their insights and research, we can't help but feel more could be done to track the system's impact of an AI Summit across the cycle that would help us to better gather and harness the many levels of feedback available. For example, network analysis tools to track the impact on relationships pre, during and post the AI Summit could help leaders understand the real impact of an AI Summit.

Most importantly, as AI Summits continue to grow in popularity we encourage you to embed opportunities for data collection and measurement within their AI Summit designs so together we can become more effective at creating positive disruptions that support individuals and systems to flourish.

Our Invitation To You

It is our hope that this book helps to amplify and build upon your understanding of what makes an AI Summit work well and how it can provide a positive disruption that enables a living system to become more adaptive, creative and resilient. As we gift these insights into the world, we are in no doubt that there is still much to learn. Thus, in the spirit of generativity, we invite you to take these thoughts and ponder them, play with them, pull them apart and share in return what you learned so together we can help build a more flourishing world.

Appendix A

Avon Mexico

Purpose: Avon Mexico had more than 3,000 employees supporting a 250,000-member sales force when their CEO decided it was time to initiate an AI Summit into cross-gender relationships and ensure the organization was living its corporate vision to serve the "wants, needs and aspirations of women around the world."

Format: Over four days, twenty people from across the company gathered to be led through an AI Summit 4-D process by an external facilitator that was focused on the topic: "The nature of exceptional inter-gender working relationships."

Outcomes: From the first interviews the culture began to reshape itself. By the end of the Summit process other changes included: the invitation of the two most senior women in the company to attend all officer meetings; in less than a year, the first woman officer was appointed; new programs and initiatives that included basing salaries on ability and job performance equally for men and women; developing gender awareness training; and requiring all Avon Mexico task forces and managing teams to have male and female membership. As a result, Avon Mexico received the 1997 Catalyst Award.

For More: appreciativeinquiry.champlain.edu/ai-stories/the-case-story-of-avon-mexico/

City of Cleveland

Purpose: While over 973 mayors have signed up to the U.S. Mayors Climate Protection Agreement, most initiatives to date are either within a specific sector or a small area of a city resulting in the absence of systemic approaches to change. Cleveland's Mayor Jackson — who had heard about the power of systemic collaboration – decided to take a different approach and drew together business leaders, grass-roots networks, universities, the faith community, public schools, sustainability leaders and the design field to learn how to create the country's first local sustainable economy.

Format: An unprecedented three-day AI Summit was held on the topic "Creating an Economic Engine to Empower a Green City on a Blue Lake." Attended by over 700 business leaders, civic entrepreneurs and community members of all ages, the AI Summit engaged twenty-five design studio teams to prototype actions that included: working on radical energy efficiency, transforming abandoned land into urban farms, and sustainable mobility systems.

Outcomes: At the end of the first AI Summit, Mayor Jackson announced the city's dedication to a "decade of determination" and his commitment to run an AI Summit every year for the next ten years. As the AI Summits have continued Cleveland continues to create incredible outcomes toward its shared vision – among them a $40 million grant to become the first freshwater offshore wind energy experiment in the world.

For more: www.sustainablecleveland.org/annual-summits

Clarke

Purpose: Transform a mosquito control products and services company, established in 1946, into a sustainability-focused environmental products and services company.

Format: Customers, suppliers, key external stakeholders and sustainability thought leaders from other countries joined the 130 Clarke employees gathered for a three-day AI Summit on the topic: "Accelerating a Sustainable Clarke: Radical Innovation to Secure a Shared Global Future." A second AI Summit followed four years later to build on this work with the topic: "Clarke. Bigger, Braver, Bolder: Igniting our passion and imagination to realize a prosperous and flourishing world."

Outcomes: With renewed vision and purpose after the Summit, Clarke pursued transformational energy initiatives, established a zero waste program, elevated their wellness efforts to extraordinary health and happiness, imagined and then created a new corporate campus of innovation, and pushed themselves to become a bold catalyst for change in their industry and within their communities. As a result, Clarke has an ongoing commitment to run an AI Summit every four years.

For More: www.clarke.com/appreciative-inquiry

Core Change Cincinnati

Purpose: To openly discuss and move to solve some of Cincinnati neighborhoods' greatest dilemmas, including crime rates, urban poverty and unemployment.

Format: More than 500 people including residents, community leaders, reformed convicts and business executives gathered for a three-day AI Summit to "Unleash the possibilities of the urban core."

Outcomes: As an outgrowth of the Summit, twenty working groups were formed to tackle long-standing challenges — employment for those with limited skills, transportation in and out of the urban core, general health knowledge and more. Unfortunately, progress on these initiatives has remained challenging.

For More: http://www.corechangecincinnati.org

Fairmount Santrol

Purpose: To expand the care and concern the mining organization has always exhibited for its employees, to include the environment and the community by establishing a sustainability focus.

Format: Three hundred people came together for three full days, and one goal was to come away with actual prototypes of new products and "green design" business opportunities that would allow the organization to take account of the "entire life cycle from the sourcing of raw materials and energy from the earth to the reuse, remanufacture, or return of materials to the earth."

Outcomes: Two years later they were recognized as the top corporate citizen in the U.S., they also doubled their earnings, with 40 percent per year earnings growth in each of the years following the Summit. Today Fairmount brings the whole system together every three years for advancing new sustainability visions and strategies for their high growth enterprise.

For More: http://www.lead2flourish.com/fairmount-minerals

Fathom

Purpose: A leading digital marketing and analytics firm based in Cleveland, Fathom had been growing by 25 percent year per year for the past eight years when they decided they needed to establish a collective vision for their next phase of growth.

Format: Focused on "Unleashing Our Heroic Spirit," the AI Summit brought together 150 employees with clients, strategic partners and community leaders to design a shared future based on their strengths.

Outcomes: Having previously operated as five different businesses, Fathom came out of the event with one shared aspiration that would require them to start working together as one company. Supported by their existing discipline of 30-day check-ins, following the Summit the company has reorganized its structure, become clearer on their ideal clients and seen a more inclusive and helping culture across the previously separate business units as the company continues to grow.

For More: http://www.fathomdelivers.com/blog

Healthy Kids, Healthy Schools

Purpose: Reframe the issue of fighting obesity and supercharge efforts to enhance wellness within the Houston Independent School District (HISD).

Format: Focused on finding ways to build "Healthy Kids, Healthy Schools," business leaders, dairy farmers, teachers, parents and kids came together for two days to chart a new course leading toward a healthier generation of Houstonians.

Outcomes: Quick wins and working documents for other schools to use were shared with everybody through the website to keep people connected, over time, however, the lack of support for self-organizing teams has relied on more individual efforts in each school than a collaborative systemic response.

For More: http://www.taosinstitute.net/healthy-kids-healthy-schools

Hunter Douglas

Purpose: A leading manufacturer and marketer of custom window coverings in North America, whose products are found in millions of homes and commercial buildings around the globe, their first AI Summit had three goals: foster cooperation, trust, and mutual support across silos and hierarchical boundaries; build current and future leadership; and enhance creativity and commitment.

Format: Branded "Focus 2000" with the tagline "All Voices . . . All Opinions . . . All Ideas," one hundred people representing all positions, functions, and levels in the organization, as well as key external stakeholders - customers, suppliers, and community members - gathered for three days. During this Summit, a series of design statements were conceived, addressing issues of leadership, vision, employee development and quality. These set the course for the planning and operational improvement activities that were to follow.

Outcomes: This AI Summit launched fourteen cross-functional Innovation Teams, which later involved the broader workforce. These teams worked for between three months and two years making significant contributions to the organization in the areas of: leadership and employee training, education and development, strategic planning, and employee engagement. The early results from these first efforts were compelling enough that over the next five years Hunter Douglas held annual AI Summits and from 1998 to 2003: sales increased 30.1 percent; profitability increased 37.1 percent; employee turnover was reduced by 52.2 percent; returned goods were reduced by 55 percent; and on-time delivery of fabric and shades reached 97 and 95 percent respectively.

For More: positivechange.hk/2015/10/01/hunter-douglas-appreciative-inquiry-case-study/

GTE/Verizon

Purpose: To establish partnership at all levels of the company, and a focus on initiatives that benefit employees, customers, the unions, and the company.

Format: A two-day Partnership AI Summit involving 250 people (including the union's training and development staff, the company's labor-relations staff, public affairs staff and organization effectiveness staff and the Federal Mediation Consultants) to chart a new partnership with GTE.

Outcomes: The local support for the union-management partnership was contagious. Local Partnership Councils formed to provide direction and to ensure that, whenever possible, local decisions are made in partnership. Efforts already underway became showcases for how to address essential business issues, such as overtime, the company's use of contractors, and workforce retention in call centers, through real partnership.

For More: Appreciative Inquiry and Organizational Transformation: Reports From The Field – Chapter 8.

John Deere

Purpose: Achieve higher performance through flexible, self-directed teams across their organization.

Format: John Deere Harvester Works engaged 200 employees and stakeholders across their system in a five-day AI Summit. Finally managing to break through years of apathy and distrust, by the end of the week, the group had launched ten cross-functional strategic initiatives to decrease costs, increase quality, improve product cycle time, and enhance working relationships.

Outcomes: As a result, the plant experienced many successes, including a significant reduction in product cycle time which delivered immediate savings of more than $3 million and projected earnings and millions more in new market share. But perhaps the most significant results were the transformed relationships, particularly between labor and management with many participants sharing that this was the first time that they had the opportunity to sit down as equals with management to plan for the future and to appreciate the gifts, strengths, and humanity of their colleagues.

For More: https://appreciativeinquiry.champlain.edu/educational-material/an-appreciative-inquiry-summit-ai-summit-at-john-deere/

Loreto Mandeville Hall Toorak

Purpose: Establish a positive education strategy across all levels of an Australian Catholic girls' school to improve the wellbeing of students from Preparatory to Year 12, teachers, staff and parents.

Format: With limited previous exposure or experience to the emerging science and practices of positive education a half-day training was completed for 200 staff as they concluded the year. Then on the first day back at school a one-day AI Summit was held for teachers, non-teaching staff, parents, and school council members on the top: "Creating a flourishing school community."

Outcomes: Within twelve months positive education theories and practices were taught explicitly as a subject on a weekly basis from Preparatory to Year 10. Students had seized opportunities at a whole school level to practice their growth mindsets on "Have A Go Day," perform random acts of kindness, say "hello" to people they don't know, write letters of gratitude (to each other and even their parents!), and spot the strengths in their teachers and fellow students. In addition, a Positive Education in-house boarding experience was created for Year 9 students. Staff members continued to participate in positive education professional development sessions, shared their best practices at an internal positive education expo and created their own "wellbeing warriors" initiative to improve their physical wellbeing. Parents turned out in record numbers for a positive parenting evening presentation and many attended a strength-based parenting coaching series.

For More: Future Directions In Wellbeing – Chapter 14.

National Grid

Purpose: How does the number one energy efficiency state in the U.S. do its state-wide energy planning with a focus on capturing radical energy efficiencies and "paying it forward" to build a future of renewable and advanced energy?

Format: National Grid and other utilities co-convened an unprecedented macro collaboration entitled "Massachusetts: Leading the Nation in the Energy Savings Revolution—Building a Better Tomorrow through Energy Efficiency Today" that brought together 300 energy institutions, leaders from business, government and civil society for a three-day AI Summit.

Outcomes: Since the Summit was held, the collaboration unveiled a new three-year plan to deliver energy efficiency services that will result in nearly US$9 billion in benefits to residents and businesses across the Commonwealth of Massachusetts. The whole system collaboration has been recognized as a major innovation—receiving the prestigious award of ASEP in 2013.

For More: www.emeraldinsight.com/doi/abs/10.1108/S1475-9152(2013) 0000004010

Neighborhood Centers Inc.

Purpose: Established in 1907 to help marginalized populations to participate more meaningfully in society in ways that nurture self-sufficiency over dependency, Neighborhood Centers is a non-profit human services agency that serves the greater Houston, Texas area. Considered a "poverty agency" in the 1960s and 70s, not just because of the population it served, but because of how it operated, the Center wanted to link neighbor to neighbor and asset to asset by asking, listening and empowering residents.

Format: The Voices to Vision Summit was held with more than 400 staff, residents, educators, business owners, donors, volunteers, students, and elected officials gathering for a three-day collaborative learning and strategic planning journey. By the end of the second day, one donor stood up and pledged $100,000 on the spot to further the organization's work.

Outcomes: The organization went on to raise $25 million to build the Baker-Ripley Neighborhood Center, a five-building, four-acre complex designed by community members for community members, with services ranging from tax preparation to low-cost banking, a clinic, and charter school. Since the Center opened, crime has decreased 11 percent in Gulfton. Perhaps most noteworthy of the many innovations spawned and honors received was the agency's own transformation from the outside-in, from a facilitator of strength-based service delivery for others to an owner of strength-based, possibility-seeking human capital development for itself.

For More: www.youtube.com/watch?v=KSW2MVvIZzs

Nutrimental Foods

Purpose: Nutrimental Foods is a manufacturer of healthy food products, located in Curitiba, State of Parana, in Brazil. A privately held Brazilian corporation who was heavily dependent on government programs, the organization decided it needed to go through a complete transformation and diversify their products and customers.

Format: The company closed down the plant for a full day to bring all 700 employees together to discover the factors and forces that have given life to their system when it had been the most effective, most alive, and most successful as a producer of high-quality health foods. Then with cheers and good wishes, a smaller group of 150 stakeholders — employees from all levels, suppliers, distributors, community leaders, financiers, and customers — went into a four-day strategy session to articulate a new and bold corporate dream. With the stories from the day before in mind, people were asked to dream: "What is the world calling us to become?" Following appreciative analysis, planning, and articulation of three new strategic business directions, the organization launched into its future with focus, solidarity and confidence.

Outcomes: A year after the Summit the company reported a record 300 percent increase in earnings, a 75 percent decrease in absenteeism, and was later recognized as one of the top 100 best places to work in Brazil. Since then, Nutrimental Foods has used appreciative inquiry annually as the process to organize and facilitate whole-system strategic planning, as well as for the founding of an innovative leadership institute to develop appreciative leadership capacity throughout Brazil.

For more: Appreciative Inquiry: A Positive Revolution In Change

Roadway Express

Purpose: In an industry renowned for its razor-thin profit margins, Roadway Express — one of America's leading transporters of industrial, commercial, and retail goods – needed new ways to drive out costs and more rapidly increase business by creating an organization with leadership at every level.

Format: From 2000-2004, Roadway Express implemented more than forty AI Summits for its 28,000 employees. Everyone from dock workers, truck drivers, stackers, and all levels of professionals joined with the senior management team at facilities across the network to conduct annual strategic planning, learn everything about the economics and financials of the business, and create new levels of partnership between the unions and the company as a whole.

Outcomes: As union and non-union workers began to work together toward critical and common goals, the organization experienced a 25.7 percent increase in revenues, significant improvements in operating ratios and employee-driven improvements that translated into an additional $17 million in revenue and $7 million in annual profit, causing shares to rise from $14 to $40 in just two years, before a 2003 merger with Yellow Roadway Corporation.

For More: www.fastcompany.com/43166/leaders-long-haul

Schuberg Philis

Purpose: Schuberg Philis, a leading Dutch IT solutions developer, was already doing well, but the organization wanted to discover what was really possible for an organization when it goes beyond satisfied customers, happy colleagues and good citizenship.

Format: More than 200 employees, customers, partners and other stakeholders came together in a passenger terminal in Amsterdam to explore the topic "Beyond Cupfighting."

Outcomes: The answer they discovered together: "A company based on love." This became their company slogan. Despite sixteen projects emerging from the Summit such as prioritizing open source solutions, automating everything they do, and embracing agile methods of development, the company's leaders note that the main success lay in their 117 employees coming away with the same energy and a level of affection for each other and more meaningful work that has been able to fuel their company to be stronger than ever before.

For More: http://www.lead2flourish.com/schuberg-philis

Steel USA

Purpose: Steel USA employed approximately 1,600 unionized workers and the mill was one of the most productive in tonnage per man hour, but its safety performance record was quite poor.

Format: Around 180 participants representing all functions, shifts, ranges of employment tenure and levels of responsibility at Steel USA, along with external stakeholders (customers, suppliers, community leaders and global parent leadership) came together for a one-day AI Summit titled: "Embracing Our Future." Of the dozen new change initiatives that emerged, one in particular focused on safety and how to make Steel USA injury free by ensuring all employees understand that safety is our number one priority.

After the Summit, this change team gained approval to conduct a similar AI Summit in 2007, and to prepare for the second AI Summit 1,400 (out of 1,600 total employees) participated in a one-on-one appreciative interview.

Outcomes: Several months after the second AI Summit the trends on accidents reported to OSHA were reviewed. Year-to-year comparisons revealed a strong and dramatic improvement with the number of accidents an average of 46 percent lower year on year. In fact, the average number of accidents recorded each month dropped sharply by 58 percent between December 2006 and January 2007 (when the interviews were conducted) and the new, lower averages were then maintained. Follow-up inquiries at Steel USA revealed a major shift in cultural norms around safety that has been sustained since 2007 with Steel USA having risen from the lowest quartile in the parent system's North American sites to the highest in safety performance, while maintaining their top productivity ranking.

For More: "Improving safety in a steel mill: Words create worlds!" by Ronald Fry in the AI Practitioner, May 2012.

Universidad TecMilenio, Mexico

Purpose: Universidad TecMilenio, a private not-for-profit institution serving 52,000 students at twenty-nine campuses across Mexico (high school, college and masters programs), had set themselves the goal of being a positive university that creates a learning community that cultivates the best of each person to allow them to flourish. Three years on they faced the challenge of consolidating the university's culture to consistently deliver on this promise.

Format: Their AI Summit that brought together 400 students, professors, staff, service providers and feeder schools to create an appreciative culture across the institution.

Outcomes: The simple act of listening to all the voices across their system immediately created change for TecMilenio and began moving the organization toward a more appreciative culture. From the Summit twelve projects emerged of which two to three will be prioritized each year for the foreseeable future using the university's well-established strategic planning processes.

For More: http://www.ipositive-education.net/ipens-state-of-positive-education-report/

The U.S. Dairy Industry Sustainable Innovation Summit

Purpose: The board of directors for Dairy Management Inc. wanted to build consensus for a "constitution for sustainable dairy" and to find ways to spark sustainability innovations that would strengthen farm businesses, reduce GHG emissions for fluid milk by 25 percent, and increase business value.

Format: More than 250 stakeholders from farms, academia, governmental and nongovernmental organizations, and food retailers for a three-day AI Summit.

Outcomes: Never in the history of the U.S. dairy industry had such a conversation been held. Consensus was created for action around projects that would increase farm business value on the order of US$238 million by 2009. At the climate summit in Copenhagen, USDA Secretary Vilsack held out the industry's work as a template for innovation in agriculture, and signed a memorandum of understanding with the Innovation Center for U.S. Dairy to work together, promising to provide government funding to support capital investment and research for GHG-related innovation. In April 2013, representatives from the effort met at the White House in recognition of their achievements.

For More: issuu.com/aipractitioner/docs/aip-may-2012

The United Nations Global Compact

Purpose: To unite the strengths of markets with the power of universal ideals, and reconcile the creative forces of private entrepreneurship with the needs of the disadvantaged and the requirements of future generations to fulfill the Millennium Development Goals.

Format: When Secretary-General Kofi Annan convened the Global Compact Leaders Summit at the United Nations Headquarters in New York, nearly 500 leaders, including chief executive officers, government officials and the heads of various labor groups, civil society organizations and UN agencies, came together for a one-day AI Summit on the topic: "Responsible Global Citizenship" to produce strategic designs and action imperatives to grow, become mainstream and scale up the initiative.

Outcomes: Within three years — by the next summit in Geneva, Switzerland — the Global Compact had grown from 1,500 firms to over 8,000 of the world's largest corporations; measures showed a 433 percent growth rate, averaging 144.4 percent per year.

For More: appreciativeinquiry.champlain.edu/educational-material/united-nations-global-compact-leaders-summit/

The United Religions Initiative

Purpose: Establish a "UN among religions" — a place of dialogue to unite the strengths of people of all faiths that could lift up a self-organizing system to promote enduring, daily interfaith cooperation to end religiously motivated violence and to create cultures of peace, justice and healing for the Earth and all living beings.

Format: Over five years, five global Appreciative Inquiry Summits with approximately 700 business leaders, people of faith and government leaders were held at Stanford University to write the charter and design the organization, based on nature's design principles. On 24 June 2000 the charter was signed at Carnegie Hall.

Outcomes: Today there are over 907 collaboration centers in 104 countries around the world and it is estimated more than seven million people have been involved in fourteen action areas that include education, human rights, health and social services, peace building and conflict transformation, and poverty alleviation/economic development.

For More: uri.org/

U.S. Navy

Purpose: To create enlightened leadership at every level of the U.S. Navy.

Format: The U.S. Navy assembled over 250 people ranging from seamen to admiral that represented all the backgrounds of Navy employees for an AI Summit on "Bold and Enlightened Naval Leadership."

Outcomes: During the Summit thirty projects were created to support this vision, including the establishment of a Center for Positive Change at the Naval Postgraduate School to continue nurturing the projects initiated and to build momentum throughout the Navy for this new way of working. In its first six months of operation, the Center provided internal consulting to a variety of sites, facilitated three additional Summits, coordinated development of an internal website through which people could exchange stories of exceptional leadership and best practices, and trained several dozen officers in the appreciative inquiry approach to change.

For More: http://www.youtube.com/watch?v=uPK8psqzHyg

World Vision

Purpose: To create "Big Goals" that would guide World Vision for the next ten years.

Format: World Vision had the capacity to fund a 150-person AI Summit in Bangkok, but they wanted to design a process that would allow all 20,000 of their employees around the world to participate in the process. To facilitate this, an online community portal was created to support a variety of pre-Summits, including areas for sharing replies to discovery questions regarding "What gives life to World Vision when it is at its best." Then when the Summit began in Bangkok, face-to-face participation with the 150 participants "in the room" (who included not only employees but also donors, partners, and even children who represent the recipients of World Vision's work) was interspersed with input from the rest of the organization who were participating virtually. This was done through a coordinated effort of summary reports and presentations to help make the work happening in Bangkok accessible to the entire organization and vice versa. Specifically, at the conclusion of each day of the Summit, the conversations, outputs, and questions generated were summarized and shared online and coupled with an invitation for virtual participants to weigh in, add their opinions, and even vote on priority areas that emerged just as if they were in the room themselves. Overnight, the virtual input that came in from around the globe was synthesized and shared back into the room in Bangkok each day to establish a spirit of collaborative participation far beyond the meeting room walls in Bangkok.

Outcomes: By the conclusion of the four-day AI Summit, there had been more than one hundred regional groups from fifty-two countries who had logged in to view the daily summaries and more than 4,500 additional individuals who had individually participated online in addition to the 150 people in the room. The impact of this process on the organization was tremendous, and World Vision has pointed to their Big Goals Summit as an important success factor in helping them increase their ability to fulfil their mission to help children around the world.

For More: appreciativeinquiry.champlain.edu/educational-material/the-story-of-world-vision-bringing-all-stakeholders-together-through-ai/

Acknowledgements

With our heartfelt thanks...

Our journey to write this book has been as rich as the content in it, and there have been many wonderful people who have contributed with their presence, love, and expertise.

Thank you to all the participants in Michelle's research who so generously shared their time, insights and experiences to further our understanding of how AI Summits work at their best. This book would not exist without the incredible generosity of Lyell Clarke, Julie Reiter, Chuck Fowler, Cindy Stull, Pim Berger, Shannon Polly, Andrew Watterson, Edward Stockton, Sally Mahe, Ada Jo Mann, John Whalen, Molly McGuigan, Rich Hirst, Lindsey Godwin, Cheri Warren, Scot Lowry, Enrique Tamés, Erin Sexson, Hani Boulos and Jon Berghoff.

We are also incredibly grateful for the ongoing research of remarkable leaders in the fields of appreciative inquiry, social constructionism positive psychology, neuroscience and complexity science. Special thanks to Lindsey Godwin, Ronald Fry, Frank Barrett, John Carter, Diana Whitney, James Ludema, Gervase Bushe, Jacqueline Stavros, and Amanda Trosten-Bloom for their tireless efforts to help us better understand the applications, moderators and mechanisms for appreciative inquiry. Our heartfelt thanks also to Kenneth Gergen, Martin Seligman, Barbara Fredrickson, Ed Deci, Richard Ryan, Jane Dutton, Kim Cameron, David Bright, Ilya Prigogine, Isabelle Stengers, Margaret Wheatley, Ralph Stacey, Harrison Owen,

Stuart Kauffman, Mitchell Waldrop, James Gleick, Matthew Liberman, Tim Brown and the many other researchers whose insights have been featured throughout this book. Please keep leading us forward.

David shares a special thanks to Michelle McQuaid for her intellectual capacity to advance theory & practice while inspiring everyone around her by the way she lives and models what she teaches, writes about, and studies. And Michelle shares a special thanks to David Cooperrider who forever changed her life for the better when he opened her eyes to how questions that look for the true, the good, the possible shape the world around us. She couldn't ask for a better advisor, mentor and role model when it comes to living an appreciative life.

Every word of this book was lovingly poured over by Michelle Etheve, Debbie Hindle, Claudia Young and Marian Black, who challenged our thinking every day. The design of this book is a reflection of the creativity and persistence of Caitlin Judd. The printing of this book is a testament to the organizational and loving ass-kicking skills of Rachel Caradine and Nadia Wouters. And the fact that you even found this book is the result of the unwavering passion of Kelsey Lewis, who shares our work with the world. You couldn't hope to find a more appreciative, loving or supportive team of people.

And to our families and friends who constantly look for the best in us – even when we're miles away again - thank you for helping us to be the positive change we dream of in this world.

References

Chapter 1

Twelve months later, for the first time in the history of the firm, an independent study found... McQuaid, M. (2011). What would you like to change and grow? *AI Practitioner, 13*(2).

The long-standing management misunderstanding that people were somehow like machines whose behavior could be controlled... Heath, C., & Heath, D. (2010). *Switch: How to change when change is hard.* New York, NY: Random House; Pink, D. H. (2009). *Drive: The surprising truth about what motivates us.* New York, NY: Penguin; Wheatley, M. J. (2017). *Who do we choose to be? Facing reality, claiming leadership, restoring sanity.* San-Francisco, CA: Berrett-Koehler.

The evidence-based exploration of human flourishing .. Seligman & Csikszentmihalyi, (2000). Special issue on happiness, excellence, and optimal human functioning. *American Psychologist, 55*(1), 5-183.

David agreed to be Michelle's capstone supervisor... McQuaid & Duaman, (2009). *What good is positive business?, Master of Applied Positive Psychology (MAPP) Capstone Projects. 23. Retrieved from:* http://repository.upenn.edu/mapp_capstone/23

His new PERMA theory of wellbeing... Seligman, M. E. (2012). *Flourish: A visionary new understanding of happiness and well-being.* New York, NY: Simon and Schuster.

David noted that in each of the examples he shared... Cooperrider, D. (2014). Afterword. In C. Laszlo, J.S. Brown, J.R. Ehrenfeld, M. Gorham, I.B. Pose, L. Robson, R. Saillant, D. Sherman, & P. Werder (Eds). *Flourishing enterprise: The new spirit of business.* Stanford, CA: Stanford University Press.

As soon as people come together to accomplish 'doing good' out there... Cooperrider, D. (2014). Afterword. In C. Laszlo, J.S. Brown, J.R. Ehrenfeld, M. Gorham, I.B. Pose, L.

Robson, R. Saillant, D. Sherman, & P. Werder (Eds). *Flourishing enterprise: The new spirit of business.* Stanford, CA: Stanford University Press.

David concluded that this mirror-flourishing effect happens when... Cooperrider, D. L. (2017). The quest for a flourishing earth is the most significant OD opportunity of the 21st century: How macro OD can be the most powerful form of micro OD. *The Organization Development Practitioner,* Vol 49, No. 3, p. 42-51.

Researchers define a flourishing state a ... Fredrickson, B. L., & Dutton, J. E. (2008). Unpacking positive organizing: Organizations as sites of individual and group flourishing. *The Journal of Positive Psychology, 3(1): 1–3;* Wheatley, M. J. (2017). *Who do we choose to be? Facing reality, claiming leadership, restoring sanity.* San-Francisco, CA: Berrett-Koehler.

Professor Felicia Huppert's simpler definition... Huppert, F. A., & So, T. T. (2013). Flourishing across Europe: Application of a new conceptual framework for defining Well-being. *Social Indicators Research, 110(3), 837-861.*

Flourishing is not a static state but an emergent property of change... Weick, K. E. (1979). *The social psychology of organizing* (2nd ed.). New York, NY: McGraw-Hill; Pascale, R., Milleman, M., & Gioja, L. (2000). *Surfing the edge of chaos: The new art and science of management.* New York, NY: Crown Business; Van de Ven, A. H., & Poole, M. S. (2005). Alternative approaches for studying organizational change. *Organization Studies,* 26(9): 1377-1404; Carlsen, A. (2006). Organizational becoming as dialogic imagination of practice: The case of the indomitable Gauls. *Organization Science,* 17(1): 132-149.

Just as our individual wellbeing and performance experiences a steady decline... McQuaid, M., & Kern, P. (2017). *Your wellbeing blueprint: Feeling good and doing well at work.* Melbourne, Australia: Michelle McQuaid Pty Ltd.

A system needs to keep identifying, organizing and elevating its strengths... Roberts, L. M. (2006). Shifting the lens on organizational life: The added value of positive scholarship. *Academy of Management Review,* 31(2): 292-305; Pavez, I. (2017). *Enacting the oak: A theoretical and empirical understanding of appreciative organizing,* (unpublished doctoral dissertation), Case Western Reserve University, Ohio.

A rational, ordered, predictable world that flourishes... Kauffman, S. (1995). *At Home in the universe: The search for the laws of self-organization and complexity. New York, NY: Oxford University Press;* Gleick, J. *(1987). Chaos: Making a new science. New York, NY: Penguin;* Wheatley, M. J. (1992). *Leadership and the new science: Discovering order in a chaotic world.* San-Francisco, CA: Berrett-Koehler.

Except that researchers have discovered that we can't unwind or rewind... Prigogine, I., & Stengers, I. (1984). *Order out of chaos: Man's new dialogue with nature.* New York, NY: Bantam Books; Gleick, J. (1987). *Chaos: Making a new science.* New York, NY: Penguin; Stacey, R. (1991). *The chaos frontier: Creative strategic control for business.* Oxford, United Kingdom: Butterworth-Heinemann; Waldrop, M. M. (1992). *Complexity: The emerging science at the edge of order and chaos.* New York, NY: Simon & Schuster; Wheatley, M. J. (1992). *Leadership and the new science: discovering order in a chaotic world.* San-Francisco, CA: Berrett-Koehler; Kauffman, S. (1995). *At home in the universe: The search for the laws of self-organization and complexity.* New York, NY: Oxford University Press; Pascale, R., Milleman, M., & Gioja, L. (2000). *Surfing the edge of chaos: The new art and science of management.* New York, NY: Crown Business. Santa Fe Institute (2013). Annual report. Retrieved from: http://www.santafe.edu/media/annual_report_pdf/SFI_AR_2013_FNL. pdf; Wheatley, M. J. (2017). *Who do we choose to be? Facing reality, claiming leadership, restoring sanity.* San-Francisco, CA: Berrett-Koehler.

For example, Nobel Prize winner Ilya Prigogine found... Prigogine, I. (1998). *The end of certainty: Time, chaos, and the new laws of nature.* New York, NY: The Free Press.

As a result, Margaret Wheatley, author of the widely acclaimed *Leadership and the New Science*, ... Wheatley, M. J. (1992). *Leadership and the new science: discovering order in a chaotic world.* San-Francisco, CA: Berrett-Koehler.

"There are no either/ors. There is no need to decide between two things... Wheatley, M. J. (1992). *Leadership and the new science: discovering order in a chaotic world.* San-Francisco, CA: Berrett-Koehler.

And his colleagues echo this observation... Cameron, K. S., Dutton, J. E., & Quinn, R. E. (2003). Foundations of positive organizational scholarship. In K. Cameron, J. E. Dutton, & R. E. Quinn (Eds.), *Positive organizational scholarship, (pp. 3 - 13). San Francisco, CA: Berrett-Koehler; Bright, D. S., & Cameron, K. (2012). Positive organizational change: What the field of POS offers to OD practitioners. In J. Stavros, W. J. Rothwell, & R. Sullivan (Eds.), Practicing Organization Development: A Guide for Managing and Leading Change, 3rd Ed. (pp, 397*-410). San Francisco, CA: Pfeiffer-Wiley; Cameron, K. S., & Spreitzer, G. M. (2011). *The Oxford handbook of positive organizational scholarship.* New York, NY: Oxford University Press; Dutton, J. E., & Spreitzer, G. M. (2014). *How to be a positive leader: Small actions, big impact.* San-Francisco, CA: Berrett-Koehler Publishers.

Likewise, Dr. Michael Cavanagh... Cavanagh, M.J. (2006). Coaching from a systemic perspective: A complex adaptive conversation. In D.R. Stober & A.M. Grant (Eds.) *Evidence based coaching handbook: Putting best practice to work for your clients, (pp. 313-354). Hoboken, NJ: John Wiley & Sons;* Cavanagh, M. J. (2016). The coaching engagement in the twenty-first century: New paradigms for complex times. *Beyond goals: Effective* *strategies for coaching and mentoring*, 151-184. Cavanagh, M., & Lane, D. (2012). Coaching psychology coming of age: The challenges we face in the messy world of complexity. *International Coaching Psychology Review, 7*(1), 75-90; O'Connor, S., & Cavanagh, M. (2013). The coaching ripple effect: The effects of developmental coaching on wellbeing across organizational networks. *Psychology of Well-Being: Theory, Research and Practice, 3*(1), 2.

The new research field of "systems informed positive psychology"... Kern, M.L. (Guest). (2017). Is positive psychology too focused on the individual? [Audio Podcast]. Retrieved from https://www.michellemcquaid.com/podcast/mppw43-peggy-kern/; Williams, P., Kern, M. L., & Waters, L. (2016). Exploring selective exposure and confirmation bias as processes underlying employee work happiness: An intervention study. *Frontiers in Psychology, 7, 878.*

This growing body of research has led researchers to conclude that for a system to flourish it must... Laszlo, C., Brown, J.S., Ehrenfeld, J.R., Gorham, M., Pose, I.B., Robson, L., Saillant, R., Sherman, D. & Werder, P (2014). *Flourishing enterprise: The new spirit of business.* Stanford, CA: Stanford University Press.

Originally designed as an action research methodology... Cooperrider, D. (1986). *Appreciative inquiry: Toward a methodology for understanding and enhancing organizational innovation.* Ph.D. dissertation, Case Western Reserve University, Cleveland, OH. Ann Arbor Michigan: University Microfilms; Cooperrider, D. (2017) "The gift of new eyes: Personal reflections after 30 years of appreciative inquiry in organizational life." In, Shani, A.B., & Noumair, D.A. (Eds.) *Research in organizational change and development*, Volume 25. Bingley UK: Emerald Publishing.

Appreciative Inquiry has been taught to hundreds of organizations and thousands of people around the world... Bushe, G. R., & Kassam, A. F. (2005). When is appreciative inquiry transformational? A meta-case analysis. *The Journal of Applied Behavioral Science, 41*(2), 161-181.

While it is a non-prescriptive discipline in which experimentation and innovation... Bushe, G. R. (2012). Foundations of appreciative inquiry: History, criticism and potential. *AI Practitioner, 14*(1); Odell, M. (2017). Appreciative planning and action in Nepal and Liberia. *AI Practitioner, 19*(2).

In the late 1990s, a 4-D cycle emerged to guide interventions... Whitney, D., & Cooperrider, D. L. (1998). The appreciative inquiry summit: Overview and applications. *Employment Relations Today, 25*(2), 17-28; Watkins, J. M., & Mohr, B. (2001). Appreciative inquiry: Change at the speed of imagination. *Organization Development Journal, 19*(3), 92-92; Barrett, F. J., & Fry, R. E. (2005). *Appreciative inquiry: A positive approach to building cooperative capacity.* Chagrin Falls, OH: Taos Institute

Publications; Bushe, G.R. (2011). Appreciative Inquiry: Theory and critique. In D. Boje, B. Burnes, & J. Hassard (Eds.), *The Routledge companion to organizational change* (pp. 87-103). Oxford, UK: Routledge.

Questions about the "best of what is and what has been"... Whitney, D., & Cooperrider, D. L. (1998). The appreciative inquiry summit: Overview and applications. *Employment Relations Today, 25*(2), 17-28; Whitney, D., & Cooperrider, D. L. (2000). The appreciative inquiry summit: An emerging methodology for whole system positive change. *OD Practitioner, 32*(1), 13-26.

Enable the mapping of its positive core of strengths to build upon... Carter, J.D., & Johnson, P.D. (1999). The roundtable project. In C. Elliott (Ed.), *Locating the energy for change: An introduction to appreciative inquiry, (pp. 255-279)*. Winnipeg, MB: International Institute for Sustainable Development; Whitney, D. K., & Trosten-Bloom, A. (2003). *The power of appreciative inquiry: A practical guide to positive change*. San Francisco, CA: Berrett-Koehler Publishers.

End results could look like at some pivotal point in the future... Bushe, G.R. (2007). Appreciative inquiry is not (just) about the positive. *OD Practitioner, 39*(4), 33-38.

Higher ground and generative images that unite people across the system... Ludema, J., Whitney, D., Mohr, B., & Griffin, T.J. (2003). *The appreciative inquiry summit: A practitioner's guide for leading large-group change*. San Francisco, CA: Berrett-Koehler Publishers; Bushe, G. R., & Kassam, A. F. (2005). When is appreciative inquiry transformational? A meta-case analysis. *The Journal of Applied Behavioral Science, 41*(2), 161-181.

Strategies, structures, culture, policies, processes, partnerships and offerings... Mohr, B.J., McLean, A., & Silbert, T. (2003). Beyond discovery and dream: Unleashing change through the design phase of an AI intervention. *AI Practitioner, May, 1-3.*; Barrett, F. J., Cooperrider, D. L., & Fry, R. E. (2005). Bringing every mind into the game to realize the positive revolution in strategy. In W.J. Rothwell, W. J & R. Sullivan (Eds.). *Practicing organization development: A guide for consultants, Vol. 27* (pp. 501-549). San-Francisco, CA: John Wiley & Sons.

Shared to realize the collective purpose and "what should be." Bushe, G. R., & Kassam, A. F. (2005). When is appreciative inquiry transformational? A meta-case analysis. *The Journal of Applied Behavioral Science, 41*(2), 161-181; Cooperrider, D. L., & McQuaid, M. (2012). The positive arc of systemic strengths: How appreciative onquiry and sustainable designing can bring out the best in human systems. *The Journal of Corporate Citizenship,* (46), 71.

As a result, new collaborations emerge across the system as knowledge... Whitney, D., & Cooperrider, D. L. (1998). The appreciative inquiry summit: Overview and applications. *Employment Relations Today, 25*(2), 17-28.

To ensure the momentum is sustained and the desired results achieved... Barrett, F. J., & Fry, R. E. (2005). *Appreciative inquiry: A positive approach to building cooperative capacity.* Chagrin Falls, OH: Taos Institute Publications.

To guide effective applications of the 4-D cycle... Cooperrider, D. L., Whitney, D., and Stavros, J., 2008. *Appreciative inquiry handbook: For leaders of change.* Premium 2nd edition San Francisco: Berrett-Koehler Publishers.

Which are now consistently taught to practitioners... Bushe, G. R., & Kassam, A. F. (2005). When is appreciative inquiry transformational? A meta-case analysis. *The Journal of Applied Behavioral Science, 41*(2), 161-181.

Reality as we know it is a subjective, rather than an objective state... Gergen, K. J. (1994). *Realities and relationships: Soundings in social construction. Cambridge, MA: Harvard University Press.*

Shape the way we think, feel and act, and thus determine our future... Gergen, K. J. (1999) *An invitation to social construction. Thousand Oaks, CA: Sage.*

Shared generative images of the future... Whitney, D. K., & Trosten-Bloom, A. (2003). *The power of appreciative inquiry: A practical guide to positive change.* San Francisco, CA: Berrett-Koehler Publishers. Bushe, G. R. (2012). Foundations of appreciative inquiry: History, criticism and potential. *AI Practitioner, 14*(1).

Every action we take is preceded by a question... Cooperrider, D. L., Barrett, F., & Srivastva, S. (1995). Social construction and appreciative inquiry: A journey in organizational theory. In D. Hosking, P. Dachler, & K. Gergen, (Eds.) *Management and organization: Relational alternatives to individualism (pp. 157-200). Aldershot, UK: Avebury.* Cooperrider, D. L., & Whitney, D. K. (1999). *Appreciative inquiry: A positive revolution in change* (pp. 245-261). San Francisco, CA: Berrett-Koehler.

A question to spark and direct our attention, perception, hope, energy, and effort toward growth and action... Goldberg, M.G. (1998). *The art of the question: A guide to short-term question-centered therapy.* New York, NY: John Wiley.

Creates generative possibilities for positive system growth... Ludema, J., Whitney, D., Mohr, B., & Griffin, T.J. (2003). *The appreciative inquiry summit: A practitioner's guide for leading large-group change.* San Francisco, CA: Berrett-Koehler Publishers.

Endless sources of learning, inspiration, and interpretation... Watkins, J. M., & Mohr, B. (2001). Appreciative inquiry: Change at the speed of imagination. *Organization Development Journal, 19*(3), 92-92.

Fatally shapes what follows... Barrett, F. J., & Fry, R. E. (2005). *Appreciative inquiry: A positive approach to building cooperative capacity.* Chagrin Falls, OH: Taos Institute Publications.

The stories it tells and the actions that are taken... Whitney, D. K., & Trosten-Bloom, A. (2003). *The power of appreciative inquiry: A practical guide to positive change.* San Francisco, CA: Berrett-Koehler Publishers. Robson, L. (2015). *Language of life-giving connection: The emotional tone of language that fosters flourishing campus sustainability programs* (unpublished doctoral dissertation), Case Western University, Ohio.

Toward the highest ideals and values of its stakeholders... Ludema, J. D. (2002). Appreciative storytelling: A narrative approach to organization development and change. In R. Fry, F. Barrett, J. Seiling, & D. Whitney, (Eds.), *Appreciative inquiry and organizational transformation: Reports from the field (pp. 239-261).* Westport, CT: Quorum.

It is imagined images of the future that guide our present-day actions... Wheatley, M. J. (1992). *Leadership and the new science: discovering order in a chaotic world.* San-Francisco, CA: Berrett-Koehler; Barrett, F. J., & Fry, R. E. (2002). Appreciative inquiry in action: The unfolding of a provocative invitation. In R. Fry, F. Barrett, J. Seiling, & D. Whitney (Eds.), *Appreciative inquiry and organizational transformation: Reports from the field (pp. 239-261).* Westport, CT: Quorum.

Can mobilize us to surpass all prior achievements... Bergquist, W. (1993). *The postmodern organization: Mastering the art of irreversible change.* San Francisco, CA: Jossey-Bass.

Images of the future have been found to advance us and move us forward... Cooperrider, D. L. (1990). Positive image, positive action: The affirmative basis of organizing. *Appreciative Management and Leadership*, 91-125; Bushe, G.R. (2012). Foundations of appreciative inquiry: History, criticism and potential. *AI Practitioner, 14*(1).

Stretch the system's collective imagination toward vivid, hope-fueled, generative images of its future potential... Whitney, D. K., & Trosten-Bloom, A. (2003). *The power of appreciative inquiry: A practical guide to positive change.* San Francisco, CA: Berrett-Koehler Publishers.

Social bonding if momentum is to be sustained... Bushe, G.R., & Coetzer, G.H. (1995). Appreciative inquiry as a team-development intervention: A controlled experiment. *Journal of Applied Behavioral Science, 31*:13.

People's enthusiasm, motivation and commitment to change can be elicited... (Elliott, 1999). *Locating the energy for change: An introduction to appreciative inquiry.* Winnipeg, Canada: International Institute for Sustainable Development.

Social systems naturally evolve toward the prevailing affirmative image... Bright, D. S., & Cameron, K. (2012). Positive organizational change: What the field of POS offers to OD practitioners. In J. Stavros, W. J. Rothwell, & R. Sullivan (Eds.), *Practicing organization development: A guide for managing and leading change, 3rd Ed. (pp, 397-410).* San Francisco, CA: Pfeiffer-Wiley.

Inspire people to self-organize toward realizing the true, the good, and the possible... Cooperrider, D. L., & McQuaid, M. (2012). The positive arc of systemic strengths: How appreciative onquiry and sustainable designing can bring out the best in human systems. *The Journal of Corporate Citizenship,* (46), 71.

To date, researchers have identified eight known applications of these Appreciative Inquiry practices... Whitney, D. K., & Trosten-Bloom, A. (2003). *The power of appreciative inquiry: A practical guide to positive change.* San Francisco, CA: Berrett-Koehler Publishers.

First proposed by David... Cooperrider, D. L. (1986). *Appreciative inquiry: Toward a methodology for understanding and enhancing organizational innovation, (unpublished doctoral dissertation), Department of Organizational Behavior, Case Western Reserve University, Ohio;* Cooperrider, D. L., & Srivastva, S. (1987). Appreciative inquiry in organizational life. *Research in Organizational Change and Development, 1*(1), 129-169.

Developed by his colleagues around the world... Cooperrider, D., Whitney, D. D., & Stavros, J. M. (2000). *The Appreciative inquiry handbook: For leaders of change.* San-Francisco, CA: Berrett-Koehler Publishers; Ludema, J., Whitney, D., Mohr, B., & Griffin, T. J. (2003). *The appreciative inquiry summit: A practitioner's guide for leading large-group change.* San Francisco, CA: Berrett-Koehler Publishers; Barrett, F. J., & Fry, R. E. (2005). *Appreciative inquiry: A positive approach to building cooperative capacity.* Chagrin Falls, OH: Taos Institute Publications; Whitney, D. K., & Trosten-Bloom, A. (2003). *The power of appreciative inquiry: A practical guide to positive change.* San Francisco, CA: Berrett-Koehler Publishers.

At its most effective, alive, and capable in economic, ecological, and human terms... Cooperrider, D. L., & McQuaid, M. (2012). The positive arc of systemic strengths: How appreciative onquiry and sustainable designing can bring out the best in human systems. *The Journal of Corporate Citizenship,* (46), 71.

Human systems move in the direction of what they most deeply, rigorously and persistently ask questions about... Gergen, K. J. (1978). Toward generative theory.

Journal of Personality and Social Psychology, 36:11, 1344-1360; Gergen, K. J. (1994). *Realities and relationships: Soundings in social construction. Cambridge, MA: Harvard University Press;* Gergen, K. J. *(1999) An invitation to social construction. Thousand Oaks, CA: Sage.*

People learn little about excellence by studying failure... Buckingham, M., & Clifton, D.O. (2001). *Now, discover your strengths. New York, NY: Free Press;* Cameron, K.S, & Lavine, M. (2006). *Making the impossible possible: Leading extraordinary performance: The Rocky Flats story.* Berrett-Koehler Publishers.

To deliver agreed actions with speed, dexterity and collaboration... Cooperrider, D. L., & McQuaid, M. (2012). The positive arc of systemic strengths: How appreciative onquiry and sustainable designing can bring out the best in human systems. *The Journal of Corporate Citizenship*, (46), 71; Bushe, G. R. (2015). Working with emergent change: Applying appreciative inquiry to adaptive challenges. *AI Practitioner, 17*(1), 6-13.

A 433 percent growth rate... Cooperrider, D. L., & N. Zhexembayeva (2012). Embedded sustainability and the innovation-producing potential of the UN Global Compact's environmental principles, in J. Lawrence (Ed.), *Globally responsible leadership (pp 107-127), London, UK: Sage Publications.*

$9 billion worth of benefits for residents and businesses... Cooperrider, D. L., & McQuaid, M. (2012). The positive arc of systemic strengths: How appreciative onquiry and sustainable designing can bring out the best in human systems. *The Journal of Corporate Citizenship*, (46), 71.

7 million people of different faiths to help build a better world... Gibbs, C. C., & S. Mahe (2003). *Birth of a global community: Appreciative inquiry in action. Bedford Heights, OH: Lakeshore Communications.*

Found that of the cases that followed the 4-D cycle and the five principles, over 90 percent were successful change efforts... Bushe, G. R., & Kassam, A. F. (2005). When is appreciative inquiry transformational? A meta-case analysis. *The Journal of Applied Behavioral Science, 41*(2), 161-181.

This is a big number when contrasted with research by Professor John Kotter at Harvard University... Kotter, J.P. (1995). Leading change: Why transformation efforts fail. *Harvard Business Review,* 73 (2), 59 – 67.

Hewlett Packard... Peery, M. (2012). Creating change ahead of the curve: How AI Summits transformed the culture of Hewlett Packard's imaging and printing group. *AI Practitioner, 14*(2).

Fairmont Santrol... Cooperrider, D. L. (2013). The spark, the flame, and the torch: The

Positive arc of systemic strengths. In D.L. Cooperrider, D.P. Zandee, L.N. Godwin. & M. Avital (Eds), *Organizational generativity: The appreciative inquiry summit and a scholarship of transformation,* (pp. 211-248). Bingley, England: Emerald Group Publishing Limited.

British Airways... Whitney, D. K., & Trosten-Bloom, A. (2003). *The power of appreciative inquiry: A practical guide to positive change.* San Francisco, CA: Berrett-Koehler Publishers.

Including the U.S. Navy... Powley, E.H., Fry, R. E., Barrett, F.J., & Bright, D.S. (2004). Dialogic democracy meets command and control: Transformation through the Appreciative Inquiry Summit. *Academy of Management Executive, 18 (3): 67 – 80;* Tripp, P. B., & Zipsie, M. W. (2002). *The introduction of appreciative inquiry to the US Navy: Using appreciative inquiry interviews and the large group intervention with applications to US Marine Corps Logistics Strategic Management* (unpublished doctoral dissertation), Naval Postgraduate School, California.

The Environmental Protection Agency... Cooperrider, D., Whitney, D. D., & Stavros, J. M. (2000). *The Appreciative inquiry handbook: For leaders of change.* San-Francisco, CA: Berrett-Koehler Publishers.

The National Dairy Council... Whalen, J. (2010). 'Big. Change. Fast.' Retrieved from: www.bluskye.com/thinking/big-change-fast.

Including Lovelace Health Care Systems... Whitney, D. K., & Trosten-Bloom, A. (2003). *The power of appreciative inquiry: A practical guide to positive change.* San Francisco, CA: Berrett-Koehler Publishers.

The Alice Peck Day Health Care System... Cooperrider, D., Whitney, D. D., & Stavros, J. M. (2000). *The Appreciative inquiry handbook: For leaders of change.* San-Francisco, CA: Berrett-Koehler Publishers.

The City of Cleveland... Cooperrider, D. L., & McQuaid, M. (2012). The positive arc of systemic strengths: How appreciative onquiry and sustainable designing can bring out the best in human systems. *The Journal of Corporate Citizenship,* (46), 71.

Imagine Chicago... Browne, B. W., & Jain, S. (2002). *Imagine Chicago: Ten years of imagination in action. Chicago, IL: Imagine Chicago.*

The Canadian Metropolitan School District... Bushe, G. R. (2010). A comparative case study of appreciative inquiries in one organization: implications for practice. *Revista de Cercetare si Interventie sociala,* 29, 7.

St. Peter's College in Australia... Waters, L., & White, M. (2015). Case study of a school wellbeing initiative: Using Appreciative Inquiry to support positive change. *International Journal of Wellbeing*, 5(1).

Non-profit organizations including The Red Cross... Cooperrider, D., Whitney, D. D., & Stavros, J. M. (2000). *The Appreciative inquiry handbook: For leaders of change.* San-Francisco, CA: Berrett-Koehler Publishers.

World Vision... Godwin, L.N., Kaplan, P. & Bodiford, K. (2013). AI Summit in a technologically connected world. In D.L. Cooperrider, D.P. Zandee, L.N. Godwin & M. Avital (Eds), *Organizational generativity: The appreciative inquiry summit and a scholarship of transformation,* (pp. 249-274). Bingley, England: Emerald Group Publishing Limited.

Worldwide initiatives including the United Nations... Lacy, P., Cooper, T., Hayward, R., & Nueberger, L. (2010). *A new era of sustainability: UN Global Compact-Accenture CEO study 2010. Retrieved from: www.unglobalcompact.org/docs/news.events/8.1/UNGC_Accenture_CEO_Study_2010.pdf, accessed 1 March 2013.*

United Religions Initiative... Gibbs, C.C., & S. Mahe (2003). *Birth of a global community: Appreciative inquiry in action. Bedford Heights, OH: Lakeshore Communications.*

For example, Gervase's review of the twenty appreciative inquiry cases... Bushe, G. R., & Kassam, A. F. (2005). When is appreciative inquiry transformational? A meta-case analysis. *The Journal of Applied Behavioral Science*, 41(2), 161-181.

Gervase has argued on numerous occasions... Bushe, G. R. (2007). Appreciative inquiry is not (just) about the positive. *OD Practitioner*, 39(4), 33-38; Bushe, G. R. (2012). Foundations of appreciative inquiry: History, criticism and potential. *AI Practitioner,* 14(1); Bushe, G. R. (2015). Working with emergent change: Applying appreciative inquiry to adaptive challenges. *AI Practitioner,* 17(1), 6-13.

AI leads to transformational change when it addresses or creates enough disruption... Bushe, G. R. (2015). Working with emergent change: Applying appreciative inquiry to adaptive challenges. *AI Practitioner,* 17(1), p 6.

In addition, other studies have suggested that transformational AI Summits are able to... Yaeger, T. F., & Sorensen, P. (2001). What matters most in appreciative inquiry: Review and thematic assessment. In D. L. Cooperrider, P. F. Sorenson, T. F. Yaeger, & D. Whitney (Eds.), *Appreciative inquiry: An emerging direction for organization development.* Champaign, IL: Stipes Publishing; Whitney, D. K., & Trosten-Bloom, A. (2003). *The power of appreciative inquiry: A practical guide to positive change.* San Francisco, CA: Berrett-Koehler Publishers; Powley, E. H. (2004). Underlying ritual practices of the appreciative inquiry summit: Toward a theory of sustained appreciative change. In D. L.

Cooperrider & M. Avital, (Eds.), *Constructive discourse and human organization* (pp. 241-261). Boston, MA: Elsevier Ltd; Baker, A., Peacock, G., Cozzolino, S., Norton, A., Joyce, M., Chapman, T., & Dawson, D. (2009). Applications of appreciative inquiry in facilitating culture change in the UK NHS. *Team Performance Management: An International Journal, 15*(5/6), 276-288; Bushe, G. R. (2010). A comparative case study of appreciative inquiries in one organization: implications for practice. *Revista de Cercetare si Interventie sociala, 29*, 7; Schmidt Jr, A. H. (2017). Resistance is overcome in one dialogic OD model (Appreciative Inquiry). *International Journal of Organization Theory & Behavior (Pracademics Press), 20*(1).

David has recently built upon these observations... Cooperrider, D. L. (2013).The spark, the flame, and the torch: The Positive arc of systemic strengths. In D. L. Cooperrider, D.P. Zandee, L. N. Godwin. & M. Avital (Eds), *Organizational generativity: The appreciative inquiry summit and a scholarship of transformation,* (pp. 211-248). Bingley, England: Emerald Group Publishing Limited.

He has proposed that this requires five generativity success factors that include.. Cooperrider, D. (2012). The concentration effect of strengths, *Organizational Dynamics,* Vol. 42, No. 2, April-May 2012, p. 21-32.

AI Summits appear to deliver the most robust returns when... McGuigan, M, & C. J. Murphy. (2013). Ensuring generativity beyond the AI Summit event: A practical guide for designing an AI Summit and advancing post-summit momentum. In D. L. Cooperrider, D. P. Zandee, L. N. Godwin & M. Avital, (Eds.), *Organizational generativity: The appreciative inquiry summit and a scholarship of transformation,* (pp. 311-338). Bingley, England: Emerald Group Publishing Limited.

The current position of the organization along the continuum... Cameron, K. S., Dutton, J. E., & Quinn, R. E. (2003). Foundations of positive organizational scholarship. In K. Cameron, J. E. Dutton, & R. E. Quinn (Eds.), *Positive organizational scholarship, (pp. 3 - 13).* San Francisco, CA: Berrett-Koehler; Bright, D. S. (2005). *Forgiveness and change: Begrudging, pragmatic, and transcendent responses to discomfiture in a unionized trucking company.* (Unpublished doctoral dissertation), Case Western Reserve University, Cleveland, Ohio; Bright, D. S., Cooperrider, D. L., & Galloway, W. B. (2006). Appreciative Inquiry in the office of research and development: Improving the collaborative capacity of organization. *Public Performance and Management Review, 39*(3), 285– 306; *Bright, D. S., & Cameron, K. (2012). Positive organizational change: What the field of POS offers to OD practitioners. In J. Stavros, W. J. Rothwell, & R. Sullivan (Eds.), Practicing organization development: A guide for managing and leading change, 3rd Ed. (pp, 397-410).* San Francisco, CA: Pfeiffer-Wiley; Bright, D. S., & Miller, M. T. (2013). Appreciative inquiry and positive organizational scholarship. In J. Vogelsang, M. Townsend, M. Minahan, D. Jamieson, J. Vogel, A. Viets, C. Royal, & L. Valek. (Eds), *Handbook for strategic HR: Best* *practices in organization development from the OD network,* (pp. 320). New York, NY: AMACON; Bright, D. S., Fry, R. E., & Cooperrider, D. L. (2013). Exploring transformation innovation through a world inquiry. In D. L. Cooperrider, D.P. Zandee, L. N. Godwin & M. Avital (Eds), *Organizational generativity: The appreciative inquiry summit and a scholarship of transformation,* (pp. 341 -360). Bingley, England: Emerald Group Publishing Limited.

The level of support, openness, and commitment of leadership... Vanstone, C., & Dalbiez, B. (2008). Revitalizing corporate values in Nokia. In S. Lewis, J. Passmore, & S. Cantore (Eds.) *Appreciative inquiry for change management* (pp. 183-195). London, UK: Kogan Page; Bushe, G. R. (2010). A comparative case study of appreciative inquiries in one organization: implications for practice. *Revista de Cercetare si Interventie sociala,* 29, 7; McGuigan, M, & C. J. Murphy. (2013). Ensuring generativity beyond the AI Summit event: A practical guide for designing an AI Summit and advancing post-summit momentum. In D.L. Cooperrider, D. P. Zandee, L. N. Godwin & M. Avital, (Eds.), *Organizational generativity: The appreciative inquiry summit and a scholarship of transformation,* (pp. 311-338). Bingley, England: Emerald Group Publishing Limited.

The extent to which appreciation, discussion of ideals, and a focus on strengths... Pratt, C. (2002). Creating unity from competing integrities: A case study in appreciative inquiry methodology. In R. Fry, F. Barrett, J. Seiling & D. Whitney, (Eds.), *Appreciative inquiry and organizational transformation: Reports from the field, (pp 99–120). Westport, CT: Quorum Books; Barge, J. K., & Oliver, C. (2003). Working with appreciation in managerial practice. Academy of Management Review, 28(1), 124-142.; Bright, D.S. (2009). Appreciative inquiry and positive organizational scholarship: A philosophy of practice for turbulent times. OD Practitioner, 41:3, 2-7;* Fitzgerald, S. P., Oliver, C., & Hoxsey, J. C. (2010). Appreciative inquiry as a shadow process. *Journal of Management Inquiry,* 19(3), 220- 233; Johnson, P. (2011). Transcending the polarity of light and shadow in appreciative inquiry: An appreciative exploration of practice. In D. Zandee, D.L. Cooperrider & M. Avital, (Eds), *Generative organization: Advances in appreciative inquiry, Vol.4. Bingley, England: Emerald Publishing.*

Systems in the pre-identity stage... Bushe, G. R. (2001). Meaning making in teams: Appreciative inquiry with pre-identity and post-identity groups. In R. Fry, F. Barrett, J. Seiling, & D. Whitney (Eds.), *Appreciative inquiry and organizational transformation: reports from the field, (pp 39-63). Westport, CT: Quorum.*

There remains the most confusion and least consensus... Bushe, G. R. (2012). Foundations of appreciative inquiry: History, criticism and potential. *AI Practitioner, 14*(1).

It is not an "event" but rather a long-term process... Whitney, D. K., & Trosten-Bloom, A. (2003). *The power of appreciative inquiry: A practical guide to positive change.* San Francisco, CA: Berrett-Koehler Publishers; McGuigan, M. (May 2012). After the wedding: How to plan for and maintain a successful post-summit process. *AI Practitioner, 14*(2), 79- 81.

As our awareness of mixed AI Summit results has increased... Head, T. C. (2005). A contingency approach to appreciative inquiry: A first small step. In D. L. Cooperrider, P. Sorenson, D. Whitney & T. Yeager. (Eds.), *Appreciative inquiry: Foundations in positive organization development (pp. 401-414).* Champaign, IL: Stipes; Messerschmidt, D. (2008). Evaluating appreciative inquiry as an organizational transformation tool: An assessment from Nepal. *Human Organization, 67*(4), 454-468; Bushe, G.R. (2011). Appreciative Inquiry: Theory and critique. In D. Boje, B. Burnes, & J. Hassard (Eds.), *The Routledge companion to organizational change* (pp. 87-103). Oxford, UK: Routledge.

Due to the complex, adaptive and relational nature... Senge, P. M. (1990). *The fifth discipline: The art & practice of the learning organization.* New York, NY: Doubleday; Wheatley, M. J. (2017). *Who do we choose to be? Facing reality, claiming leadership, restoring sanity.* San-Francisco, CA: Berrett-Koehler.

Michelle took a grounded theory approach... Glaser, B., & Strauss, A. (1967). Grounded theory: The discovery of grounded theory. *The Journal Of The British Sociological Association, 12,* 27-49.

Testing if AI Summits did indeed activate Seligman's PERMA mechanisms... Seligman, M. E. (2012). *Flourish: A visionary new understanding of happiness and well-being.* New York, NY: Simon and Schuster.

At a time when the reported rates of loneliness... Block, P. (2008). *Community: The structure of belonging.* San Francisco, CA: Berrett-Koehler.

Social systems are the external manifestations... Meadows, D. (2008). *Thinking in systems.* White River Junction, VT: Chelsea Green.

You see, despite our illusions of control when it comes to trying to change a system... Meadows, D. (2008). *Thinking in systems.* White River Junction, VT: Chelsea Green; Wheatley, M. J. (2017). *Who do we choose to be? Facing reality, claiming leadership, restoring sanity.* San-Francisco, CA: Berrett-Koehler.

Chapter 2

At a time when leading scientists are suggesting that we face... Fenner, F. (2010). "Healthy climate, planet and people opening address," presented at AAS Fenner conference series, Australia, 2010. Retrieved from: http://www.theaustralian.com.au/higher-education/frank-fenner-sees-no-hope-for-humans/news-story/8d77f0806a8a35 91d47013f7d75699b9; Hawking, S. (2016). This is the most dangerous time for our planet. *The Guardian*. Retrieved from: https://www.theguardian.com/commentisfree /2016/dec/01/stephen-hawking-dangerous-time-planet-inequality; Krauss, L. M., & Titley, D. (2017). Thanks to Trump, the doomsday clock advances toward midnight. *New York Times*. Retrieved from: https://www.nytimes.com/2017/01/26/opinion/thanks-to-trump-the-doomsday-clock-advances-toward-midnight.html?_r=0.

Resilient ways to enable systemic flourishing... Wheatley, M. J. (2017). *Who do we choose to be? Facing reality, claiming leadership, restoring sanity.* San-Francisco, CA: Berrett-Koehler.

Combat strategies that have escalated conflicts... Englehardt, T. (2014). America at war: A record of unparalleledfFailure. *The Nation*. Retrieved from: https://www.thenation.com/article/america-war-record-unparalleled-failure/

The near collapse of well-established economies... Krugman, P. (2009). How did economists get it so wrong? *The New York Times Magazine*. Retrieved from: http://www.nytimes.com/2009/09/06/magazine/06Economic-t.html

Leaving their homes with thousands dying in the process... *The Atlantic. Retrieved from:* https://www.theatlantic.com/international/archive/2015/06/refugees-global-peace -index/396122/

And global sustainability efforts that have failed to slow the pace at which our environment is melting... Torres, P. (2017). It's the end of the world and we know it. *Salon.* Retrieved from: https://www.salon.com/2017/04/30/its-the-end-of-the-world-and-we-know-it-scientists-in-many-disciplines-see-apocalypse-soon/

Our costly attempts at organizational and social change... Wheatley, M. J. (2017). *Who do we choose to be? Facing reality, claiming leadership, restoring sanity.* San-Francisco, CA: Berrett-Koehler.

Fluctuation and change are an essential part of the process by which order is created. Jantsch, E. (1920). *The self-organizing universe. Oxford, UK: Pergamon. Gleick, J. (1987). Chaos: Making a new science. New York, NY: Penguin;* Stacey, R. (1991). *The chaos frontier: creative strategic control for business.* Oxford, United Kingdom: Butterworth-Heinemann; Holman, P. (2015). Complexity, self-organization and emergence. In G. R. Bushe & R. J.

Marshak (Eds.) *Dialogic organization development: The theory and practice of transformational change.* San Francisco, CA: Berrett-Koehler.

For example, researchers have found that disorder can actually be an ally... Prigogine, I. (1998). *The end of certainty: Time, chaos, and the new laws of nature.* New York, NY: The Free Press.

Living systems grow as a result of disequilibrium, not balance... Wheatley, M. J. (2017). *Who do we choose to be? Facing reality, claiming leadership, restoring sanity.* San-Francisco, CA: Berrett-Koehler.

Survival factors heighten wariness and experimentation... Pascale, R., Milleman, M., & Gioja, L. (2000). *Surfing the edge of chaos: The new art and science of management.* New York, NY: Crown Business.

... and certainly diminish its opportunities for flourishing. Wheatley, M. J. (1992). *Leadership and the new science: Discovering order in a chaotic world.* San-Francisco, CA: Berrett-Koehler.

But scientists have discovered that what distinguishes a living system... Starbuck, W. H. (1976). Organizations and their environments. In M. D. Dunnette (Ed.) *Handbook of Industrial and Organizational Psychology. (pp. 1069-1123) New York, NY: Rand. Jantsch, E. (1920). The self-organizing universe. Oxford, UK: Pergamon. Kauffman, S. (1995). At home in the universe: The search for the laws of self-organization and complexity. New York, NY: Oxford University Press.* Coveney, P., & Highfield, R. (1990). *The Arrow of Time: A Voyage Through Science to Solve Time's Greatest Mystery.* New York, NY: Fawcett Columbine.

Everything that is alive partners *with* its environment in a continuous exchange of energy... Wheatley, M. J. (1992). *Leadership and the new science: Discovering order in a chaotic world.* San-Francisco, CA: Berrett-Koehler.

In their ground-breaking book, *Surfing The Edge of Chaos*... Pascale, R., Milleman, M., & Gioja, L. (2000). *Surfing the edge of chaos: The new art and science of management.* New York, NY: Crown Business.

While this process may sound threatening... Prigogine, I., & Stengers, I. (1984). *Order out of chaos: Man's new dialogue with nature.* New York, NY: Bantam Books.

As Peggy – an award-winning researcher and practitioner on creating "whole systems" change... Holman, P. (2010). *Engaging emergence: Turning upheaval into opportunity.* San Francisco, CA: Berrett-Koehler.

It turns out that at the edge of chaos, a system's stability... Prahalad, C. K., & Hamel, G. (1990). The core competence of the corporation. *Harvard Business Review, (May – June), pp. 79–91;* Blanchard, K. H., O'Connor, M. J., & Ballard, J. (1997). *Managing by values.* San Franscico, CA: Berrett-Koehler Publishers.

This is why systems scientist Erich Jantsch urges leaders... Jantsch, E. (1920). *The self-organizing universe. Oxford, UK: Pergamon.*

No longer required to be the guards maintaining control... Holman, P. (2010). *Engaging emergence: Turning Upheaval Into Opportunity. San Francisco, CA: Berrett-Koehler;* Wheatley, M. J. (2017). *Who do we choose to be? Facing reality, claiming leadership, restoring sanity.* San-Francisco, CA: Berrett-Koehler.

After all, it is at the edge of chaos... Waldrop, M. M. (1992). *Complexity: The emerging science at the edge of order and chaos.* New York, NY: Simon & Schuster.

Disrupting compassionately is an aikido strategy... Holman, P. (2010). *Engaging emergence: Turning Upheaval Into Opportunity. San Francisco, CA: Berrett-Koehler.*

For example, Harvard Professor Ronald Heifetz urges leaders to distinguish between... Heifetz, R. A. (1998). *Leadership without easy answers. Cambridge, MA: Harvard University Press; Heifetz, R. A., & Linsky, M. (2002). Leadership on the line.* Boston, MA: Harvard Business School Press.

And other researchers caution that much of today's system angst comes from treating... Holman, P. (2010). *Engaging emergence: Turning upheaval into opportunity. San Francisco, CA: Berrett-Koehler.*

Left to self-organize in what looks like a mess... Stacey, R. (1996). *Complexity and creativity in organizations.* San Francisco, CA: Berrett-Koehler.

Thus, researchers suggest that the goal for any system... Meadows, D. (2008). *Thinking in systems.* White River Junction, VT: Chelsea Green.

To be compassionate coaches of disruption... Wheatley, M. J. (1992). *Leadership and the new science: Discovering order in a chaotic world.* San-Francisco, CA: Berrett-Koehler.

Peggy suggests that once a leader is confident... Holman, P. (2010). *Engaging emergence: Turning Upheaval Into Opportunity. San Francisco, CA: Berrett-Koehler.*

A container is an intangible, yet real space... Corrigan, C. (2015). Hosting and holding containers. In G. R. Bushe & R. J. Marshak (Eds.) *Dialogic organization development: The theory and practice of transformational change.* San Francisco, CA: Berrett-Koehler.

Once a system is at the edge of chaos, biologist Stuart Kauffman notes… Kauffman, S. (**1995**). *At home in the universe: The search for the laws of self-organization and complexity.* New York, NY: Oxford University Press.

Harrison Owen, building on his twenty years of experience… Owen, H. (2008). *Wave rider: Leadership for high performance in a self-organizing world.* San-Francisco, CA: Berrett-Koehler Publishers.

Peggy builds on both of these insights when she suggests… Holman, P. (2010). *Engaging emergence: Turning upheaval into opportunity.* San Francisco, CA: Berrett-Koehler.

Researchers have found over the last few decades… Grant, A. (2014). The #1 feature of meaningless work. *Huffington Post. Retrieved from http://www.huffingtonpost.com/ adamgrant/the-1-feature-of-a-meanin_b_4691464.html.*

Just as a magnet operates as a strange attractor… Wheatley, M. J. (1992). *Leadership and the new science: Discovering order in a chaotic world.* San-Francisco, CA: Berrett-Koehler; Wheatley, M. J. (2017). *Who do we choose to be? Facing reality, claiming leadership, restoring sanity.* San-Francisco, CA: Berrett-Koehler.

After all, as Viktor Frankl… Frankl, V. E. (1985). *Man's search for meaning.* New York, NY: Simon and Schuster.

Meaningful work reawakens us to… Wheatley, M. J. (2017). *Who do we choose to be? Facing reality, claiming leadership, restoring sanity.* San-Francisco, CA: Berrett-Koehler.

The truth is that when humans are being human… Wheatley, M. J. (2017). *Who do we choose to be? Facing reality, claiming leadership, restoring sanity.* San-Francisco, CA: Berrett-Koehler.

Self-organization occurs when a living system exchanges information… Prigogine, I., & Stengers, I. (1984). *Order out of chaos: Man's new dialogue with nature. New York, NY: Bantam Books; Kauffman, S. (1995). At home in the universe: The search for the laws of self-organization and complexity. New York, NY: Oxford University Press;* Pascale, R., Milleman, M., & Gioja, L. (2000). *Surfing the edge of chaos: The new art and science of management.* New York, NY: Crown Business.

And perhaps most challenging of all, the ubiquitous presence of technology… Wheatley, M. J. (2017). *Who do we choose to be? Facing reality, claiming leadership, restoring sanity.* San-Francisco, CA: Berrett-Koehler.

Researchers suggest that chaos is the greatest generator… Wheatley, M. J. (1992). *Leadership and the new science: Discovering order in a chaotic world.* San-Francisco, CA: Berrett-Koehler.

The role of information is revealed... Wheatley, M. J. (1992). *Leadership and the new science: Discovering order in a chaotic world.* San-Francisco, CA: Berrett-Koehler.

The good news is that when this diverse interplay is characterized... Owen, H. (2008). *Wave rider: Leadership for high performance in a self-organizing world.* San-Francisco, CA: Berrett-Koehler Publishers.

This is why creative interactions that enable individual expression... Holman, P. (2010). *Engaging emergence: Turning upheaval into opportunity. San Francisco, CA: Berrett-Koehler.*

Order is accessible when diverse people facing intractable challenges uncover... **Holman, P. (2010).** *Engaging emergence: Turning upheaval into opportunity. San Francisco, CA: Berrett-Koehler.*

When people experience themselves as part of a larger system... Holman, P. (2010). *Engaging emergence: Turning upheaval into opportunity. San Francisco, CA: Berrett-Koehler.*

For example, researchers suggest that amplifying or positive feedback... Pascale, R., Milleman, M., & Gioja, L. (2000). *Surfing the edge of chaos: The new art and science of management.* New York, NY: Crown Business.

A system's ability to notice these new forms of information, learn from it, and respond... Wheatley, M. J. (2017). *Who do we choose to be? Facing reality, claiming leadership, restoring sanity.* San-Francisco, CA: Berrett-Koehler.

Larger patterns taking shape among them and enable meaning to coalesce... Holman, P. (2010). *Engaging emergence: Turning upheaval into opportunity. San Francisco, CA: Berrett-Koehler.*

Compassionate coaches of disruption foster emergence as recommended by the researchers... Holman, P. (2010). *Engaging emergence: Turning upheaval into opportunity. San Francisco, CA: Berrett-Koehler.*

As suggested by the research outlined earlier... Prigogine, I., & Stengers, I. (1984). *Order out of chaos: Man's new dialogue with nature. New York, NY: Bantam Books;* Wheatley, M. J. (1992). *Leadership and the new science: Discovering order in a chaotic world.* San-Francisco, CA: Berrett-Koehler; Kauffman, S. (1995). *At home in the universe: The search for the laws of self-organization and complexity. New York, NY: Oxford University Press; Holman, P. (2010). Engaging emergence: Turning upheaval into opportunity. San Francisco, CA: Berrett-Koehler;* Pascale, R., Milleman, M., & Gioja, L. (2000). *Surfing the edge of chaos: The new art and science of management.* New York, NY: Crown Business.

Now, more than ever, we need compassionate leaders of disruption... Holman, P. (2010). *Engaging emergence: Turning upheaval into opportunity. San Francisco, CA: Berrett-Koehler;* Wheatley, M. J. (2017). *Who Do We Choose To Be? Facing Reality, Claiming Leadership, Restoring Sanity.* San-Francisco, CA: Berrett-Koehler.

Chapter 3

Flourishing is the combination of feeling good... Huppert, F. A., & So, T. C. (2013). Flourishing across Europe: Application of a new conceptual framework for defining well-being. *Social Indicators Research, 110(3), 837-861.*

A growing body of evidence demonstrates that high levels of wellbeing... Oades, L. G., & Duglin, A. (2016). Workplace and organization well-being. In Oades, L. G., Steger, M. F., Delle-Fave, A., & Passmore, J. (Eds.) (2016). *The Wiley-Blackwell handbook of the psychology of positivity and strengths-based approaches at work.* London, UK: Wiley-Blackwell.

Positive self-perceptions and judgements of others, higher performance on complex mental tasks, ... Lyubomirsky, S., Sheldon, K. M., & Schkade, D. (2005). Pursuing happiness: The architecture of sustainable change. *Review of General Psychology, 9, 111-131.*

For example, higher levels of wellbeing have been found... Lyubomirsky, S., King, L., & Diener, E. (2005). The benefits of frequent positive affect: Does happiness lead to success? *Psychological bulletin, 131(6), 803.*

Researchers have also found that when organizations institute... Harter, J. K., Schmidt, F. L., & Hayes, T. L. (2002). Business unit level outcomes between employee satisfaction, employee engagement and business outcomes: A meta-analysis. *Journal of Applied Psychology, 87, 26-279;* Cameron, K., Mora, C., Leutscher, T., & Calarco, M. (2011). Effects of positive practices on organizational effectiveness. *The Journal of Applied Behavioral Science, 47(3), 266-308;* Cameron, K. (2012). *Positive leadership: Strategies for extraordinary performance.* San Francisco, CA: Berrett- Berrett-Koehler Publishers.

The New Economics Foundation concluded that not only does focusing on wellbeing at work... New Economic Foundation (2014). *Wellbeing at work: A review of the literature.* Retrieved from: http://neweconomics.org/2014/03/wellbeing-at-work/?sf_action=get_results&_sf_s=wellbeing&_sft_latest=research

For example, sociologist and psychologist Professor Corey Keyes... Keyes, C. L. M. (2002). The Mental health continuum: From languishing to flourishing in life. *Journal of Health and Social Behavior, 43(2), 207-222.*

Professor Ed Diener — renowned for his decades of global research... Diener, E., Wirtz, D., Tov, W., Kim-Prieto, C., Choi, D. W., Oishi, S., & Biswas-Diener, R. (2010). New well-being measures: Short scales to assess flourishing and positive and negative feelings. *Social Indicators Research, 97(2), 143-156.*

Professor Felicia Huppert and her colleagues suggest that feeling good... Huppert, F. A., & So, T. C. (2013). Flourishing across Europe: Application of a new conceptual framework for defining well-being. *Social Indicators Research, 110(3), 837-861.*

Professor Martin Seligman who, as noted in Chapter 1, has suggested that in order to flourish, we need the right balance... Seligman, M. E. (2012). *Flourish: A visionary new understanding of happiness and well-being.* New York, NY: Simon and Schuster.

Researchers have found that the experience of heartfelt positive emotions... Green, S., McQuaid, M., Putell, A., & Dulagil, A. (2016). The psychology of positivity at work. In Oades, L.G., Steger, M., Delle-Fave, A. & Passmore, J. (Eds.). *The Wiley-Blackwell handbook of the psychology of positivity and strengths-based approaches at work. Chichester, UK: Wiley-Blackwell.*

For example, studies conducted by Barbara – one of the world's leading researchers on emotions — and her colleagues... Fredrickson, B. L. (2013a). Positive emotions broaden and build. In E. Ashby Plant & P. G. Devine (Eds.). *Advances in experimental social psychology. (Vol. 47, pp. 1-53). Burlington, VT: Academic Press.*

Expanding their field of peripheral vision so they can see more of what is happening around them; Rowe, G., Hirsh, J. B. & Anderson, A. K. (2007). Positive affect increases the breadth of attentional selection. *Proceedings of the National Academy of Sciences of the United States of America, 104, 383-388; Schmitz, T. W., De Rosa, E., & Anderson, A. K. (2009). opposing influences of affective state valence on visual cortical encoding. The Journal of Neuroscience, 29(22), 7199-7207.*

Flooding their brains with the neurotransmitters dopamine and serotonin, which can help them to make and sustain more neural connections... Fredrickson, B. L., & Branigan, C. (2005). Positive emotions broaden the scope of attention and thought-action repertoires. *Cognition and Emotion, 19(3), 313–332.*

Helping them to feel closer to others, expanding their circles of trust, and overcoming bias... Dovidio, J. F., Isen, A. M., Guerra, P., Gaertner, S. L., & Rust, M. (1998). Positive affect, cognition, and the reduction of intergroup bias. In C. Sedikides (Ed.), *Intergroup cognition and intergroup behavior (pp. 337–366); Mahwah, NJ: Erlbaum. Dunn, J. R., & Schweitzer, M. E. (2005). Feeling and believing: The influence of emotion on trust. Journal of Personality and Social Psychology, 88(5), 736-748; Johnson, K. J., & Fredrickson, B. L. (2005). "We all look the same to me": Positive emotions eliminate the own-race bias in face recognition. Psychological Science, 16(11), 875-881.*

Build their psychological, social, intellectual, and physical resources, placing them on a positive trajectory of growth... Isen, A. M. (1990). The influence of positive and negative affect on cognitive organization: Some implications for development. In N. Stein, B. Leventhal, & T. Trabasso (Eds.), *Psychological and biological approaches to emotion (pp. 75-94). Hillsdale, NJ: Erlbaum; Fredrickson, B. L. (1998). What good are positive emotions? Review of General Psychology, 2, 300–319; Aspinwall, L. G. (2001). Dealing with adversity: Self-regulation, coping, adaptation, and health. In A. Tesser & N. Schwarz (Eds.), The Blackwell handbook of social psychology: Vol. 1. Intraindividual processes (pp. 591–614). Malden, MA: Blackwell; Fredrickson, B. L., & Joiner, T. (2002). Positive emotions trigger upward spirals toward emotional wellbeing. Psychological Science, 13(2), 172-175.*

People who consistently flourish also experience negative emotions... Kashdan, T. B., & Rottenberg, J. (2010). Psychological flexibility as a fundamental aspect of health. *Clinical Psychology Review*, 30(7), 865-878.

Barbara acknowledges that people can't really be connected and grounded... Fredrickson, B.L. (2009). *Positivity: groundbreaking research reveals how to embrace the hidden strength of positive emotions, overcome negativity, and thrive. New York, NY: Random House.*

Take the required actions, and to let the emotions pass... Hayes, S. C., Strosahl, K. D., & Wilson, K. G. (2003). *Acceptance and commitment therapy: An experiential approach to behavior change. New York, NY: Guilford Press.*

Barbara's research has found that people who flourish experience a higher frequency of heartfelt positive emotions... Fredrickson, B. L. (2013b). Updated thinking on positivity ratios. *American Psychologist, 68, 814-822.*

Professor Mihaly Csikszentmihalyi – one of the founding fathers of positive psychology — describes... Csikszentmihalyi, M. (1990). *Flow: The psychology of optimal experience. New York, NY: Harper Perennial.*

As a result, researchers have found that the experience of flow... Lyubomirsky, S. (2008). *The how of happiness: A scientific approach to getting the life you want. New York, NY: Penguin*

"Other people matter." Peterson, C. (2006). *A primer in positive psychology. New York, NY: Oxford University Press. 249.*

At high risk for psychological distress, physical and mental illness, and early mortality... Cacioppo, J. T., & Patrick, W. (2008). *Loneliness: Human nature and the need for social connection. New York, NY: W. W. Norton & Company.*

In contrast, a sense of belonging has been found to correlate with a range of positive outcomes... Rath, T., Harter, J. K. & Harter, J. (2010). *Wellbeing: The five essential pillars. New York, NY: Simon and Schuster.*

Professor Jane Dutton – one of the pioneers of the field of positive organizational scholarship... Dutton, J. E., & Heaphy, E. D. (2003). The power of high-quality connections. In K. Cameron, J. E. Dutton, & R. E. Quinn (Eds.), *Positive organizational scholarship: Foundations of a new discipline (pp 263-278) New York, NY: Oxford University Press.*

In fact, studies suggest that when people experience warm and trusting feelings... Fredrickson, B. (2013c). *Love 2.0: How our supreme emotion affects everything we feel, think, do, and become. New York, NY: Hudson Street Press.*

More than simply a physical response, however, Jane explains that the positive interactions... Dutton, J. E. (2003). *Energize your workplace: How to create and sustain high-quality connections at work. New York, NY: John Wiley & Sons.*

She calls these encounters "high-quality connections"... Dutton, J. E. (2014). Build High Quality Connections. In J.E. Dutton & G.M. Spreitzer (Eds.), *How to be a positive leader: Small actions, big impact. (pp 11-21) San Francisco, CA: Berrett-Koehler.*

For example, Professor Adam Grant – one of the world's leading organizational psychologists and researchers – suggests... Grant, A. (2013). In the company of givers and takers. *Harvard Business Review, 91(4), 90-97.*

For decades, people have ranked having a sense of purpose in their work... Cascio, W.F. (2003). Changes in workers, work, and organizations. In W. C. Borman, D. R. Ilgen, R. J. Klimoski, & I. B. Weiner (Eds.), *Handbook of psychology. Volume 12, Industrial and organizational psychology.* New York, NY:Wiley.

After all, as we saw, Viktor suggests that people have a universal need... Frankl, V. E. (1985). *Man's search for meaning.* New York, NY: Simon and Schuster.

They are likely to be happier, more motivated, more committed, and more satisfied, which enables them to perform better... Steger, M. F., & Dik, B. J. (2010). Work as meaning: Individual and organizational benefits of engaging in meaningful work. In Linley, P.A., Harrington, S. & Page, N. (Eds.). *Oxford handbook of positive psychology and work, (pp 131-142). Oxford, UK: Oxford University Press.*

Professor Adam Grant suggests that the single strongest predictor of meaningfulness... Grant, A. (2014). The #1 feature of meaningless work. *Huffington Post. Retrieved from http://www.huffingtonpost.com/adamgrant/the-1-feature-of-a-meanin_b_4691464.html.*

The good news is that researchers believe that meaning can be found in any job... Smith, E. E. (2017). *The Power of meaning: Crafting a life that matters. New York, NY: Random House.*

How they think about the work they do each day and their ability to have a positive impact on others... Wrzesniewski, A., LoBuglio, N., Dutton, J. E., & Berg, J. M. (2013). Job crafting and cultivating positive meaning and identity in work. In A. B. Bakker (Ed.) *Advances in positive organizational psychology, Volume 1. (pp. 281-302).* Bingley, UK: Emerald Group Publishing Limited.

For example, his studies have found that when people's passion starts taking control of them... Vallerand, R. J., & Houlfort, N. (2003). Passion at work. In Gilliland, S. W., Steiner, D. D., & Skarlicki, D. P. (Eds.). *Emerging perspectives on Values in Organizations.* (pp 175-204) Greenwich, CA: IAP.

In contrast, when people feel in control of what they love... Vallerand, R. J., Houlfort, N., & Forest, J. (2014). Passion for Work: Determinants and Outcomes. In Gagné, M. (Ed.). *The Oxford Handbook of Work Engagement, Motivation, and Self-Determination Theory,* (pp 85-105). Oxford, UK: Oxford Library of Psychology.

Professor Carol Dweck – one of the world's leading researchers in the field of motivation... Dweck, C. (2006). *Mindset: The new psychology of success. New York, NY: Random House.*

What made these performers extraordinary was the fact that they were able to consistently... Chambliss, D. F. (1989). The mundanity of excellence: An ethnographic report on stratification and olympic swimmers. *Sociological theory, 7(1), 70-86.*

Have led researchers to conclude that it is people's willingness to exert effort and learn... Duckworth, A. (2016). *Grit: The power of passion and perseverance. New York, NY: Simon and Schuster.*

Fortunately, Associate Professor Kristen Neff – one of the world's leading researchers on self-compassion... Neff, K. D., & Dahm, K. A. (2015). Self-compassion: What it is, what it does, and how it relates to mindfulness. In B. D., Ostafin, M. D. Robinson, & B. P. Meier (Eds.) *Handbook of mindfulness and self-regulation, (pp. 121-137). New York, NY: Springer.*

As a result, studies have found that self-compassion activates... Neff, K. (2003). Self-compassion: An alternative conceptualization of a healthy attitude toward oneself. *Self and Identity, 2(2), 85-101.*

Far from being self-indulgent or "soft," the deliberate use of self-compassionate talk... Neff, K. D. (2011). Self-compassion, Self-esteem, and well-being. *Social and Personality Psychology Compass, 5(1), 1-12.*

Thus in the end, Professor Angela Duckworth... Eskreis-Winkler, L., Gross, J. J., & Duckworth, A. L. (2017). Grit: Sustained self-regulation in the service of superordinate goals. In K. D. Vohs & R. F. Baumeister (Eds.), *Handbook of self-regulation: Research, theory and applications (3rd ed.). New York, NY: Guilford.*

Carol describes this as "a growth mindset." Dweck, C. (2006). *Mindset: The new psychology of success. New York, NY: Random House.*

Her studies have found that a growth mindset makes it easier... Dweck, C. S. (2002). Beliefs that make smart people dumb. In R. J. Sternberg (Ed.). *Why smart people do stupid things. New Haven, CT: Yale University Press; Mangels, J. A., Butterfield, B., Lamb, J., Good, C. D., & Dweck, C.S. (2006). Why do beliefs about intelligence influence learning success? A social-cognitive-neuroscience model. Social, Cognitive, and Affective Neuroscience, 1, 75-86; Murphy, M. C., & Dweck, C.S. (2010). A culture of genius: How an organization's lay theories shape people's cognition, affect, and behavior. Personality and Social Psychology Bulletin, 36, 283-296.*

Sparking hope by helping people to feel like... Snyder, C. R. (Ed.). (2000). *Handbook of hope: Theory, measures, and applications. Orlando, FL: Academic Press; Lopez, S. J. (2013). Making hope happen: Create the future you want for yourself and others. New York, NY: Simon and Schuster.*

Researchers believe that people's wellbeing — much like their body weight... Diener, E., & Biswas-Diener, R. (**2011**). *Happiness: Unlocking the mysteries of psychological wealth. New York, NY: John Wiley & Sons.*

In order to flourish, Martin suggests that people need to cultivate... Seligman, M. E. (2012). *Flourish: A visionary new understanding of happiness and well-being.* New York, NY: Simon and Schuster.

The PERMA theory of wellbeing provides us with ways to measure... Butler, J., & Kern, M. L. (2016). The PERMA-Profiler: A brief multidimensional measure of flourishing. *International Journal of Wellbeing, 6(3).*

And thus shape how AI Summits are designed and delivered. McQuaid, M., & Kern, P. (2017). *Your wellbeing blueprint: Feeling good and doing well at work. Melbourne, Victoria: Michelle McQuaid Pty Ltd.*

To assume that people can simply activate the PERMA pillars... Wheatley, M. J. (1992). *Leadership and the new science: Discovering order in a chaotic world.*

San-Francisco, CA: Berrett-Koehler; Wheatley, M. J. (2017). *Who do we choose to be? Facing Reality, Claiming Leadership, Restoring Sanity.* San-Francisco, CA: Berrett-Koehler.

In attempting to answer this question we are aided by Professors Richard and Edward... Ryan, R. M., & Deci, E. L. (2017). *Self-determination theory: Basic psychological needs in motivation, development, and wellness.* New York, NY: Guilford Publications.

Clearly, it is in our 'natures'... Ryan, R. M., & Deci, E. L. (2017). *Self-determination theory: Basic psychological needs in motivation, development, and wellness.* New York, NY: Guilford Publications.

They posit that an environment that is effectance supportive... Ryan, R. M., & Deci, E. L. (2017). *Self-determination theory: Basic psychological needs in motivation, development, and wellness.* New York, NY: Guilford Publications.

In the classical view of human development from Aristotle through various philosophical... Rogers, C. R. (1963). The actualizing tendency in relation to "motives" and to consciousness. In M. R. Jones (Ed.), *Nebraska Symposium on Motivation (Vol. 11, pp. 1-24). Lincoln, NE: University of Nebraska Press; Piaget, J. (1971). Biology and knowledge: An essay on the relations between organic regulations and cognitive processes. Chicago: University of Chicago Press.*

In fact, anthropologist Edward Hall has concluded... Hall, E. (1989). *Beyond culture.* New York, NY: Anchor.

Robert White, who gave birth to the modern era of motivation research... White, R. W. (1959). Motivation reconsidered: The concept of competence. *Psychological Review, 66(5), 297-333; White, R. W. (1963). Ego and reality in psychoanalytic theory: A proposal regarding independent ego energies. Madison, CT: International Universities Press.*

For example, researchers point out that when playing children... Ryan, R. M., & Deci, E. L. (2017). *Self-determination theory: Basic psychological needs in motivation, development, and wellness.* New York, NY: Guilford Publications.

Robert labelled this tendency "effectance motivation"... White, R. W. (1959). Motivation reconsidered: The concept of competence. *Psychological Review, 66(5), 297-333.*

In order to develop a true sense of competence... Deci, E. L., & Ryan, R. M. (1985). *Intrinsic motivation and self-determination in human behavior. New York: Plenum Press.*

For example, studies have found that performing well on tasks... Nix, G. A., Ryan, R. M., Manly, J. B., & Deci, E. L. (1999). Revitalization through self-regulation: The effects of autonomous and controlled motivation on happiness and vitality. *Journal of Experimental Social Psychology*, 35(3), 266-284; Ryan, R. M. (1982). Control and information in the intrapersonal sphere: An extension of cognitive evaluation theory. *Journal of Personality and Social Psychology, 43(3), 450-461.*

Researchers agree that it is not possible for people... Bowlby, J. (1979). *The making and breaking of affectional bonds. London, UK: Tavistock; Baumeister, R. F., & Leary, M. R. (1995). The need to belong: Desire for interpersonal attachments as a fundamental human motivation. Psychological Bulletin, 117(3), 497-529; Wilson, E. O. (2012). The social conquest of earth. New York, NY: Norton; Lieberman, M. D. (2013). Social: Why our brains are wired to connect. New York, NY: Crown;* Ryan, R. M., & Deci, E. L. (2017). *Self-determination theory: Basic psychological needs in motivation, development, and wellness.* New York, NY: Guilford Publications; Senge, P. M. (2006). *The fifth discipline: The art & practice of the learning organization.* New York, NY: Doubleday.

As we saw in the PERMA pillars, this need for connection goes beyond... Reis, H. T. (1994). Domains of experience: Investigating relationship processes from three perspectives. In R. Erber & R. Gilmour (Eds.), *Theoretical frameworks for personal relationships (pp. 87-110); Hilsdale, NJ: Erlbaum. de Waal, F. (2009). The Age of Empathy: Nature's Lessons for a Kinder Society. New York, NY: Crown Archetype; Deci, E. L., & Ryan, R. M. (2014). Autonomy and need satisfaction in close relationships: Relationships motivation theory. In N. Weinstein (Ed.), Human motivation and interpersonal relationships: Theory, research and applications (pp. 53-73). Dordrecht, Netherlands: Springer.*

In fact, William James, the father of modern psychology, suggested... James, W. (1920). *The letters of William James*, Vol. 2, (p. 33). London, UK: Little, Brown Publishing.

And other researchers have found that people have a basic need... de Waal, F. (2009). *The age of empathy: Nature's lessons for a kinder society. New York, NY: Crown Archetype.*

For example, many hygiene habits, social rituals... Baumeister, R. F., & Leary, M. R. (1995). The need to belong: Desire for interpersonal attachments as a fundamental human motivation. *Psychological Bulletin, 117(3), 497-529.*

As are people's tendencies, for better or worse... Ryan, R. M., & Deci, E. L. (2011). A self-determination theory perspective on social, institutional, cultural, and economic supports for autonomy and their importance for well-being. In V. I. Chirkov, R. M. Ryan,

& K. M. Sheldon (Eds.), *Human autonomy in cross-cultural context: Perspectives on the psychology of agency, freedom, and well-being (pp. 45-64). New York: Springer.*

Researchers note that it is not merely being admired that counts... Ryan, R. M., & Deci, E. L. (2017). *Self-determination theory: Basic psychological needs in motivation, development, and wellness.* New York, NY: Guilford Publications.

This is why relationally supportive environments allow people to autonomously... Downie, M., Mageau, G. A., & Koestner, R. (2008). What makes for a pleasant social interaction?: Motivational dynamics of interpersonal relations. *Journal of Social Psychology, 148(5), 523-534; Fredrickson, B. (2013c). Love 2.0: How our supreme emotion affects everything we feel, think, do, and become. New York, NY: Hudson Street Press.*

In contrast, when people feel ignored, ostracized or excluded... Williams, K. D. (2009). Ostracism: Effects of being excluded and ignored. In M. P. Zanna (Ed.), *Advances in experimental social psychology (pp. 275-314). New York, NY: Academic Press;* Eisenberger, N. I., Lieberman, M. D., & Williams, K. D. (2003). Does rejection hurt?: An fMRI study of social exclusion. *Science, 302, 290– 292;* Legate, N., DeHaan, C. R., Weinstein, N., & Ryan, R. M. (2013). Hurting you hurts me too: The psychological costs of complying with ostracism. *Psychological Science, 24(4), 583-588.*

The good news is that, contrary to many worldviews, social psychology researchers have found... Welzel, C. (2013). *Freedom rising: Human empowerment and the quest for emancipation.* Cambridge, UK: Cambridge University Press; Deci, E. L., & Ryan, R. M. (2012). Motivation, personality, and development within embedded social contexts: An overview of self-determination theory. In R. M. Ryan (Ed.), *The Oxford handbook of human motivation (pp. 85-107). Oxford, UK: Oxford University Press;* Ryan, R. M., & Deci, E. L. (2017). *Self-determination theory: Basic psychological needs in motivation, development, and wellness.* New York, NY: Guilford Publications.

This gives people the freedom to act authentically... Ryan, R. M., & Lynch, J. H. (1989). Emotional autonomy versus detachment: Revisiting the vicissitudes of adolescence and young adulthood. *Child Development, 60(2), 340-356;* Reeve, J., Jang, H., Carrell, D., Barch, J., & Jeon, S. (2004). Enhancing high school students' engagement by increasing their teachers' autonomy support. *Motivation and Emotion, 28(2), 147-169.*

Although providing people with autonomy can be feared... Murray, H. A. (1938). *Explorations in Personality. New York, NY: Oxford University Press;* Van Petegem, S., Vansteenkiste, M., Soenens, B., Beyers, W., & Aelterman, N. (2015). Examining the longitudinal association between oppositional defiance and autonomy in adolescence. *Developmental Psychology, 51(1), 67-74.*

Autonomy actually relies on people's connections with others... Ryan, R. M., La Guardia, J. G., Solky-Butzel, J., Chirkov, V., & Kim, Y. (2005). On the interpersonal regulation of emotions: Emotional reliance across gender, relationships, and cultures. *Personal Relationships, 12(1), 145-163.*

Thus, rather than autonomy leading people into a descent of destructive disorder... Wheatley, M. J. (1992). *Leadership and the new science: Discovering order in a chaotic world.* San-Francisco, CA: Berrett-Koehler.

This process is evidenced in examples around the world of organizations... (Pink, 2009) Pink, D. H. (2011). *Drive: The surprising truth about what motivates us.* New York, NY: Penguin; Doshi, N., & McGregor, L. (2015). *Primed to perform: How to build the highest performing cultures through the science of total motivation. New York, NY: HarperCollins.*

Gravitate toward, make choices in relation to... Ryan, R. M., & Deci, E. L. (2017). *Self-determination theory: Basic psychological needs in motivation, development, and wellness.* New York, NY: Guilford Publications.

Richard and Edward have found that the dark side of human nature... Ryan, R. M., & Deci, E. L. (2017). *Self-determination theory: Basic psychological needs in motivation, development, and wellness.* York, NY: Guilford Publications.

Although references from emerging researchers... McQuaid, M., & Dauman, B. (2009). *What good is positive business? Master of Applied Positive Psychology (MAPP) Capstone Projects. 23. Retrieved from: http://repository.upenn.edu/mapp_capstone/23*

Unfortunately, most people lack the knowledge, tools and support... Seligman, M. E. (2012). *Flourish: A visionary new understanding of happiness and well-being.* New York, NY: Simon and Schuster.

As Richard and Edward's research has repeatedly demonstrated, a system directly impacts... Ryan, R. M., & Deci, E. L. (2017). *Self-determination theory: Basic psychological needs in motivation, development, and wellness.* New York, NY: Guilford Publications.

Chapter 4

Fairmount Santrol's customers were taken by surprise... Fowler, C. (2018). Sustainability as a good investment for business. In R. Sisodia, T. Henry, & T. Eckschmidt (Eds.) *Conscious capitalism field guide: Tools for transforming your organization.* Boston, MA: Harvard Business School Publishing Corporation.

You can never direct a living system... Maturana, H., & Varela, F. (1992). *Autopoiesis and cognition: The realization of the living.* London, UK: Reidl.

Researchers caution, however, that while living systems can be... Pascale, R., Milleman, M., & Gioja, L. (2000). *Surfing the edge of chaos: The new art and science of management.* New York, NY: Crown Business.

Describing how the theoretical example of a butterfly flapping its wings... Gleick, J. (1987). *Chaos: Making a new science.* New York, NY: Penguin.

Appreciative inquiry researcher and practitioner, Frank Barrett suggests... Barrett. F. (2015). Social constructionist challenge to representational knowledge: Implications for understanding organization change. In G.R. Bushe & R.J. Marshak (Eds.) *Dialogic organization development: The theory and practice of transformational change.* San Francisco, CA: Berrett-Koehler.

What happens in living systems is a dynamic dance between... Wheatley, M. J. (1992). *Leadership and the new science: Discovering order in a chaotic world.* San-Francisco, CA: Berrett-Koehler.

Positive organizational researcher David Bright proposes... Bright, D. S. (2005). *Forgiveness and change: Begrudging, pragmatic, and transcendent responses to discomfiture in a unionized trucking company.* (Unpublished doctoral dissertation), Case Western Reserve University, Cleveland, Ohio; Bright, D.S. (2009). Appreciative inquiry and positive organizational scholarship: A philosophy of practice for turbulent times. *OD Practitioner, 41:3, 2-7*; Bright, D. S., Cooperrider, D. L., & Galloway, W. B. (2006). Appreciative inquiry in the office of research and development: Improving the collaborative capacity of organization. *Public Performance and Management Review, 39(3), 285-306*; Bright, D. S., & Cameron, K. (2012). *Positive organizational change: What the field of POS offers to OD practitioners. In J. Stavros, W. J. Rothwell, & R. Sullivan (Eds.), Practicing organization development: A guide for managing and leading change, 3rd Ed. (pp, 397-410).* San Francisco, CA: Pfeiffer-Wiley; Bright, D. S., Fry, R. E., & Cooperrider, D. L. (2013). Exploring transformation innovation through a world inquiry. In D. L. Cooperrider, D. P. Zandee, L. N. Godwin & M. Avital (Eds), *Organizational generativity: The appreciative inquiry summit and* *a scholarship of transformation* (pp. 341-360). Bingley, England: Emerald Group Publishing Limited.

While researchers have suggested that a living system can be lured... Kauffman, S. (1995). *At home in the universe: The search for the laws of self-organization and complexity.* New York, NY: Oxford University Press.

It can redesign itself into a new and more sophisticated form... Bright, D. S., & Miller, M. T. (2013). Appreciative inquiry and positive organizational scholarship. In J. Vogelsang, M. Townsend, M. Minahan, D. Jamieson, J. Vogel, A. Viets, C. Royal, & L. Valek. (Eds), *Handbook for strategic HR: Best practices in organization development from the OD network,* (pp. 320). New York, NY: AMACON.

For example, in a system struggling with the forces of depreciating dynamics... Edmondson, A. C. (2012). *Teaming: How organizations learn, innovate, and compete in the knowledge economy.* San Francisco, CA: John Wiley & Sons; Cameron, K. (2013). *Practicing positive leadership: Tools and techniques that create extraordinary results.* San Francisco, CA:Berrett-Koehler Publishers.

At the far end of this continuum, introducing an AI Summit... Pratt, C. (2002). Creating unity from competing integrities. A case study in appreciative inquiry methodology. In R. Fry, F. Barrett, J. Seiling, & D. Whitney (Eds.*), Appreciative inquiry and organizational transformation: reports from the field.* (pp. 99-120). Westport, CT: Quorum Books.

Without context for the introduction of a positive disruption... Bright, D. S., & Miller, M. T. (2013). Appreciative inquiry and positive organizational scholarship. In J. Vogelsang, M. Townsend, M. Minahan, D. Jamieson, J. Vogel, A. Viets, C. Royal, & L. Valek. (Eds), *Handbook for strategic HR: Best practices in organization development from the OD network,* (pp. 320). New York, NY: AMACON.

The use of an AI Summit risks creating a negative disruption... Fitzgerald, S. P., Oliver, C., & Hoxsey, J. C. (2010). Appreciative inquiry as a shadow process. *Journal of Management Inquiry,* 19(3), 220-233; Bushe, G. R. (2013). Generative process, generative outcome: The Transformational potential of appreciative inquiry. In D. L. Cooperrider, D. P. Zandee, L. N. Godwin & M. Avital (Eds), *Organizational generativity: The appreciative inquiry summit and a scholarship of transformation* (pp. 341-360). Bingley, England: Emerald Group Publishing Limited.

By creating a safe container for the system to explore everything people... Fitzgerald, S. P., Oliver, C., & Hoxsey, J. C. (2010). Appreciative inquiry as a shadow process. *Journal of Management Inquiry,* 19(3), 220-233.

An AI Summit can unleash renewed energy and creativity... Bright, D. S., & Miller, M. T. (2013). Appreciative inquiry and positive organizational scholarship. In J. Vogelsang, M. Townsend, M. Minahan, D. Jamieson, J. Vogel, A. Viets, C. Royal, & L. Valek. (Eds), *Handbook for strategic HR: Best practices in organization development from the OD network*, (pp. 320). New York, NY: AMACON.

For example, when British Airways was struggling... Whitney, D. K., & Trosten-Bloom, A. (2003). *Power of appreciative inquiry: A practical guide to positive change.* San Francisco, CA: Berrett-Koehler Publishers.

Stimulating this kind of generative change doesn't simply harness... Bright, D. S. (2009). Appreciative inquiry and positive organizational scholarship: A philosophy of practice for turbulent times. *OD Practitioner, 41:3, 2-7.*

Thus, researchers suggest that the goal of an AI Summit for a system... Bright, D. S., & Miller, M. T. (2013). Appreciative inquiry and positive organizational scholarship. In J. Vogelsang, M. Townsend, M. Minahan, D. Jamieson, J. Vogel, A. Viets, C. Royal, & L. Valek. (Eds), *Handbook for strategic HR: Best practices in organization development from the OD network*, (pp. 320). New York, NY: AMACON.

For example, the affirming and nonjudgmental approach... Johnson, P. (2007). Transcending the polarity of light and shadow in appreciative inquiry: An appreciative exploration of practice. In D. Zandee, D. Cooperrider, & M. Avital (Eds.), *Advances in appreciative inquiry: Organizational generativity (p. 15); Amsterdam: Elsevier B. V.* Fitzgerald, S. P., Oliver, C., & Hoxsey, J. C. (2010). Appreciative inquiry as a shadow process. *Journal of Management Inquiry*, 19(3), 220-233; Bushe, G.R. (2011). Appreciative inquiry: Theory and critique. In D. Boje, B. Burnes, & J. Hassard (Eds.), *The Routledge companion to organizational change* (pp. 87-103). Oxford, UK: Routledge.

By choosing to recognize and honor a system's capacities... Kolodziejski, K. (2004). *The organization shadow: Exploring the untapped, trapped potential in organizational setting. Dissertation Abstracts International, 66, DAI-B. (UMI No. AAT-3166383)*

An AI Summit can allow people to reclaim... Kolodziejski, K. (2004). *The organization shadow: Exploring the untapped, trapped potential in organizational setting. Dissertation Abstracts International, 66, DAI-B. (UMI No. AAT-3166383)*

Researchers note that any process that promotes transformation... Bushe, G. R. (2011). Appreciative inquiry: Theory and critique. In D. Boje, B. Burnes, & J. Hassard (Eds.), *The Routledge companion to organizational change* (pp. 87-103). Oxford, UK: Routledge.

In Chapter 2 we also learned that new and novel information that disturbs... Wheatley, M. J. (1992). *Leadership and the new science: Discovering order in a chaotic world.* San-Francisco, CA: Berrett-Koehler.

Consequently, Professor Gervase Bushe suggests three ways the generative potential... Bushe, G. R. (2013). Generative process, generative outcome: The transformational potential of Appreciative Inquiry. In D. L. Cooperrider, D. P. Zandee, L. N. Godwin & M. Avital (Eds), *Organizational generativity: The appreciative inquiry summit and a scholarship of transformation* (pp. 341 -360). Bingley, England: Emerald Group Publishing Limited.

The most generative images influence people's feelings... Bushe, G. R. (2013). Generative process, generative outcome: The transformational potential of Appreciative Inquiry. In D. L. Cooperrider, D. P. Zandee, L. N. Godwin & M. Avital (Eds), *Organizational generativity: The appreciative inquiry summit and a scholarship of transformation* (pp. 341 -360). Bingley, England: Emerald Group Publishing Limited.

Gervase notes that these images don't have to be new to the world... Bushe, G. R. (2013). Generative process, generative outcome: The transformational potential of Appreciative Inquiry. In D. L. Cooperrider, D. P. Zandee, L. N. Godwin & M. Avital (Eds), *Organizational generativity: The appreciative inquiry summit and a scholarship of transformation* (pp. 341 -360). Bingley, England: Emerald Group Publishing Limited.

They put life back into a system that has become conceptually frozen... Barrett, F. J., & Cooperrider, D. L. (1990). Generative metaphor intervention: A new approach for working with systems divided by conflict and caught in defensive perception. *Journal of Applied Behavioral Science, 26, 219-239.*

Gervase suggests that for a topic to be generative... Bushe, G. R. (2013). Generative process, generative outcome: The transformational potential of Appreciative Inquiry. In D. L. Cooperrider, D. P. Zandee, L. N. Godwin & M. Avital (Eds), *Organizational generativity: The appreciative inquiry summit and a scholarship of transformation* (pp. 341 -360). Bingley, England: Emerald Group Publishing Limited.

Gervase suggests that while most people planning an AI Summit begin... Bushe, G. R. (2007). Appreciative inquiry is not (just) about the positive. *OD Practitioner,* 39(4), 33-38.

Gervase has found that generative questions have four qualities... Bushe, G. R. & Storch, J. (2015). Generative image: Sourcing novelty. In G. R. Bushe & R. J. Marshak (Eds.), *Dialogic organization development: The theory and practice of transformational change.* San Francisco, CA: Berrett-Koehler.

He also recommends that for pre-identity groups... Bushe, G. R. (2013). Generative process, generative outcome: The transformational potential of appreciative inquiry. In D. L. Cooperrider, D. P. Zandee, L. N. Godwin & M. Avital (Eds), *Organizational generativity: The appreciative inquiry summit and a scholarship of transformation* (pp. 341 -360). Bingley, England: Emerald Group Publishing Limited.

Gervase notes that who, when, where and how people... Bushe, G. R. (2007). Appreciative inquiry is not (just) about the positive. *OD Practitioner*, 39(4), 33-38.

If this is the conversation a system needs to have... Fry, R. (2007). Generative inquiry vs. positivity in appreciative inquiry. Paper submitted as part of the symposium, *20 years of appreciative inquiry: The best of the past, present, and future, Academy of Management conference, Philadelphia, PA.*

Finally, Gervase urges systems not to shy away from opportunities... Bushe, G. R. (2013). Generative process, generative outcome: The transformational potential of appreciative inquiry. In D. L. Cooperrider, D. P. Zandee, L. N. Godwin & M. Avital (Eds), *Organizational generativity: The appreciative inquiry summit and a scholarship of transformation* (pp. 341 -360). Bingley, England: Emerald Group Publishing Limited.

AI Summits help to enable transformational change when they create a positive disruption... Bushe, G. R. (2007). Appreciative inquiry is not (juts) about the positive. *OD Practitioner*, 39(4), 33-38.

Being open to generativity requires a system to get comfortably uncomfortable... Wheatley, M. J. (1992). *Leadership and the new science: Discovering order in a chaotic world.* San-Francisco, CA: Berrett-Koehler.

For example, Gervase's analysis of twenty appreciative inquiry cases... Bushe, G. R., & Kassam, A. F. (2005). When is appreciative inquiry transformational? A meta-case analysis. *The Journal of Applied Behavioral Science, 41*(2), 161-181.

Recall that research suggests that unlike a clockwork machine... Prigogine, I., & Stengers, I. (1984). *Order out of chaos: Man's new dialogue with nature. New York, NY:* Bantam Books.

Wired for preservation, when a system is faced with increasing levels of disturbance... Coveney, P., & Highfield, R. (1990). The arrow of time: A voyage through science to solve time's greatest mystery. New York, NY: Fawcett Columbine.

This innate ability for order and form are made possible not by complex controls... Wheatley, M. J. (1992). *Leadership and the new science: Discovering order in a chaotic world.* San-Francisco, CA: Berrett-Koehler.

Rather than autonomy leading a system into a descent of self-centered disorder... Holman, P. (2015). Complexity, self-organization and emergence. In G. R. Bushe & R. J. Marshak (Eds.) *Dialogic organization development: The theory and practice of transformational change.* San Francisco, CA: Berrett-Koehler; Ryan, R. M., & Deci, E. L. (2017). *Self-determination theory: Basic psychological needs in motivation, development, and wellness.* New York, NY: Guilford Publications.

Instead, Harrison Owen suggests that the power of authentic leadership occurs... Owen, H. (2008). *Wave rider: Leadership for high performance in a self-organizing world.* San-Francisco, CA: Berrett-Koehler Publishers.

Gervase suggests that from the outset a system needs to accept... Bushe, G. R. (2015). Working with emergent change: Applying appreciative inquiry to adaptive challenges. *AI Practitioner, 17*(1), 6-13.

David Snowden and Mary Boone's award-winning paper on... Snowden, D. J., and Boone, M. E. (2007) A leader's framework for decision making. *Harvard Business Review,* 85(11), 68-76.

For example, studies of organizations that thrived in complexity found... Collins, J. and Hansen, M. (2011) *Great by choice: Uncertainty, chaos and luck why some thrive despite them all.* New York, NY: Harper Business.

Thus, Gervase recommends that... Bushe, G. R. (2013). Generative process, generative outcome: The transformational potential of Appreciative Inquiry. In D. L. Cooperrider, D. P. Zandee, L. N. Godwin & M. Avital (Eds), *Organizational generativity: The appreciative inquiry summit and a scholarship of transformation* (pp. 341 -360). Bingley, England: Emerald Group Publishing Limited.

This is why Peggy Holman urges us as compassionate coaches... Holman, P. (2010). *Engaging emergence: Turning upheaval into opportunity. San Francisco, CA: Berrett-Koehler.*

After all, as Erich Jantsch observed... Jantsch, E. (1920). *The self-organizing universe. Oxford, UK: Pergamon.*

Fueling these networks with generative information... Pascale, R., Milleman, M., & Gioja, L. (2000). *Surfing the edge of chaos: The new art and science of management.* New York, NY: Crown Business.

For example, Gervase notes that encouraging self-organization in a system... Bushe, G. R. (2015). Working with emergent change: Applying Appreciative Inquiry to adaptive challenges. *AI Practitioner, 17*(1), 6-13.

When assessed against David Bright's continuum of organizational states... Bright, D. S. (2005). *Forgiveness and change: Begrudging, pragmatic, and transcendent responses to discomfiture in a unionized trucking company.* (Unpublished doctoral dissertation), Case Western Reserve University, Cleveland, Ohio; Bright, D. S. (2009). Appreciative inquiry and positive organizational scholarship: A philosophy of practice for turbulent times. *OD Practitioner, 41:3, 2-7;* Bright, D. S., Cooperrider, D. L., & Galloway, W. B. (2006). Appreciative inquiry in the office of research and development: Improving the collaborative capacity of organization. *Public Performance and Management Review, 39(3), 285-306; Bright, D. S., & Cameron, K. (2012). Positive organizational change: What the field of POS offers to OD practitioners. In J. Stavros, W. J. Rothwell, & R. Sullivan (Eds.), Practicing organization development: A guide for managing and leading change, 3rd Ed. (pp, 397-410).* San Francisco, CA: Pfeiffer-Wiley; Bright, D. S., Fry, R. E., & Cooperrider, D. L. (2013). Exploring transformation innovation through a world inquiry. In D. L. Cooperrider, D. P. Zandee, L. N. Godwin & M. Avital (Eds), *Organizational generativity: The appreciative inquiry summit and a scholarship of transformation* (pp. 341-360). Bingley, England: Emerald Group Publishing Limited; Bright, D. S., & Miller, M. T. (2013). Appreciative inquiry and positive organizational scholarship. In J. Vogelsang, M. Townsend, M. Minahan, D. Jamieson, J. Vogel, A. Viets, C. Royal, & L. Valek. (Eds), *Handbook for strategic HR: Best practices in organization development from the OD network*, (pp. 320). New York, NY: AMACON.

Gervase notes that AI Summits lead to transformational change... Bushe, G. R. (2010). A comparative case study of Appreciative Inquiries in one organization: implications for practice. *Revista de Cercetare si Interventie sociala, 29, 7;* Bushe, G. R. (2015). Working with emergent change: Applying appreciative inquiry to adaptive challenges. *AI Practitioner, 17*(1), 6-13.

As noted earlier, Gervase has also argued that opportunities... Bushe, G. R. (2007). Appreciative inquiry is not (just) about the positive. *OD Practitioner,* 39(4), 33-38; Bushe, G. R. (2011). Appreciative inquiry: Theory and critique. In D. Boje, B. Burnes, & J. Hassard (Eds.), *The Routledge companion to organizational change* (pp. 87-103). Oxford, UK: Routledge; Bushe, G. R. (2013). Generative process, generative outcome: The transformational potential of appreciative inquiry. In D. L. Cooperrider, D. P. Zandee, L.N. Godwin & M. Avital (Eds), *Organizational generativity: The appreciative inquiry summit and a scholarship of transformation* (pp. 341-360). Bingley, England: Emerald Group Publishing Limited; Bushe, G. R. (2015). Working with emergent change: Applying appreciative inquiry to adaptive challenges. *AI Practitioner, 17*(1), 6-13.

And in his five generativity success factors for AI Summits mentioned in Chapter 1... Cooperrider, D. L. (2013). The spark, the flame, and the torch: The positive arc of systemic strengths. In D. L. Cooperrider, D. P. Zandee, L. N. Godwin & M. Avital

(Eds), *Organizational generativity: The appreciative inquiry summit and a scholarship of transformation* (pp. 211-248). Bingley, England: Emerald Group Publishing Limited.

Chapter 5

It was scary. It was a risk. It was also the right thing to do... L. Clarke, personal communication, 15 September, 2013.

I have no idea. But I'm going to figure it out... J. Reiter, personal communication, 22 December, 2016.

As noted since the late 1990s, a 4-D cycle... Whitney, D. & Cooperrider, D. L. (1998). The appreciative inquiry summit: Overview and applications. *Employment Relations Today, 25*(2), 17-28; Cooperrider, D., Whitney, D. D., & Stavros, J. M. (2000). *The appreciative inquiry handbook: For leaders of change*. San-Francisco, CA: Berrett-Koehler Publishers; Watkins, J. M., & Mohr, B. (2001). Appreciative inquiry: Change at the speed of imagination. *Organization Development Journal, 19*(3), 92-92; Whitney, D. K., & Trosten-Bloom, A. (2003). *The power of appreciative inquiry: A practical guide to positive change*. San Francisco, CA: Berrett-Koehler Publishers; Barrett, F. J., & Fry, R. E. (2005). *Appreciative inquiry: A positive approach to building cooperative capacity*. Chagrin Falls, OH: Taos Institute Publications; Bushe, G. R. (2011). Appreciative inquiry: Theory and critique. In D. Boje, B. Burnes, & J. Hassard (Eds.), *The Routledge companion to organizational change* (pp. 87-103). Oxford, UK: Routledge.

An AI Summit is no exception... Ludema, J., Whitney, D., Mohr, B., & Griffin, T. J. (2003). *The appreciative inquiry summit: A practitioner's guide for leading large-group change*. San Francisco, CA: Berrett-Koehler Publishers.

The Clergy Leadership Institute in the U.S... Bushe, G. R. (2012). Foundations of appreciative inquiry: History, criticism and potential. *AI Practitioner, 14*(1).

Widely used AI Summit practitioner guides have also emphasized... Ludema, J., Whitney, D., Mohr, B., & Griffin, T.J. (2003). *The appreciative inquiry summit: A practitioner's guide for leading large-group change*. San Francisco, CA: Berrett-Koehler Publishers. Whitney, D. K., & Trosten-Bloom, A. (2003). *The power of appreciative inquiry: A practical guide to positive change*. San Francisco, CA: Berrett-Koehler Publishers; McGuigan, M, & C. J. Murphy. (2013). Ensuring generativity beyond the AI Summit event: A practical guide for designing an AI Summit and advancing post-summit momentum. In D. L. Cooperrider, D. P. Zandee, L. N. Godwin & M. Avital, (Eds.), *Organizational generativity: The appreciative inquiry summit and a scholarship of transformation*, (pp. 311-338). Bingley, England: Emerald Group Publishing Limited.

Given the diversity, variability, experimentation and self-organization... Prigogine, I., & Stengers, I. (1984). *Order out of chaos: Man's new dialogue with nature.* New York, NY: Bantam Books; Gleick, J. (1987). *Chaos: Making a new science.* New York, NY: Penguin; Stacey, R. (1991). *The chaos frontier: Creative strategic control for business.* Oxford, United Kingdom: Butterworth-Heinemann; Waldrop, M. M. (1992). *Complexity: The emerging science at the edge of order and chaos.* New York, NY: Simon & Schuster; Wheatley, M. J. (1992). *Leadership and the new science: Discovering order in a chaotic world.* San-Francisco, CA: Berrett-Koehler; Kauffman, S. (1995). *At home In the universe: The search for the laws of self-organization and complexity.* New York, NY: Oxford University Press; Pascale, R., Milleman, M., & Gioja, L. (2000). *Surfing the edge of chaos: The new art and science of management.* New York, NY: Crown Business.

Researchers suggest that in order to relinquish control... Holman, P. (2010). *Engaging emergence: Turning upheaval into opportunity.* San Francisco, CA: Berrett-Koehler.

David and his colleagues have explained in the past that to appreciate... Cooperrider, D., Whitney, D. D., & Stavros, J. M. (2000). *The appreciative inquiry handbook: For leaders of change.* San-Francisco, CA: Berrett-Koehler Publishers.

Appreciative spaces disrupt, but they do so by... Holman, P. (2010). *Engaging emergence: Turning upheaval into opportunity.* San Francisco, CA: Berrett-Koehler.

The sobering question that has to be asked... J. Reiter, personal communication, 22 December, 2016.

It gets a little scary when you're opening up... L. Clarke, personal communication, 15 September, 2013.

Quantum physicist David Bohm suggests that wholeness... Bohm, D. (1980). *Wholeness and the implicate order.* New York, NY: Routledge.

Diana Whitney and Amanda Trosten-Bloom, in their acclaimed book... Whitney, D. K., & Trosten-Bloom, A. (2003). *The power of appreciative inquiry: A practical guide to positive change.* San Francisco, CA: Berrett-Koehler Publishers.

In life, the issue is not control, but dynamic connectedness... Jantsch, E. (1980). *The self-organizing universe.* Oxford, UK: Pergamon.

Researchers have found that similar ideas surface over and over... Rock, D., Grant, H., & Grey, J. (2016). Diverse teams feel less comfortable—and that's why they perform better. *Harvard Business Review, 22.*

When people have the opportunity to discover they are the system... Holman, P. (2010). *Engaging emergence: Turning upheaval into opportunity. San Francisco, CA: Berrett-Koehler.* **While David has previously pointed out that several decades of research...** Cooperrider, D. L. (1990). Positive image, positive action: The affirmative basis of organizing. *Appreciative Management and Leadership*, 91-125.

Researchers caution that it is not simply the positive nature of these images... Bushe, G. R. (2015). Working with emergent change: Applying appreciative inquiry to adaptive challenges. *AI Practitioner*, *17*(1), 6-13.

As we learned in Chapter 4, defining a generative Summit topic is central... Bushe, G. R. (1995). Advances in appreciative inquiry as an organization development intervention. *Organization Development Journal, 13, 14-22*; Bushe, G. R. (2010). A comparative case study of appreciative inquiries in one organization: implications for practice. *Revista de Cercetare si Interventie Sociala*, 29, 7; Bushe, G. R. (2013). Generative process, generative outcome: The transformational potential of appreciative inquiry. In D. L. Cooperrider, D. P. Zandee, L. N. Godwin, & M. Avital (Eds.), *Organizational generativity: The appreciative inquiry summit and a scholarship of transformation*, (pp. 341-360). Bingley, England: Emerald Group Publishing Limited; Bushe, G. R., & Kassam, A. F. (2005). When is appreciative inquiry transformational? A meta-case analysis. *The Journal of Applied Behavioral Science*, *41*(2), 161-181.

Researchers suggest that strange attractors... Pascale, R., Milleman, M., & Gioja, L. (2000). *Surfing the edge of chaos: The new art and science of management.* New York, NY: Crown Business.

For example, in one study where a municipal healthcare... Bushe, G. R. & Storch, J. (2015). Generative image: Sourcing novelty. In G. R. Bushe & R. J. Marshak (Eds.), *Dialogic organization development: The theory and practice of transformational change.* San Francisco, CA: Berrett-Koehler.

People do not resist change, per se. People resist loss... Heifetz, R. A., & Linsky, M. (2002). *Leadership on the line. Boston, MA: Harvard Business School Press.*

To guarantee the best lift-off for an AI Summit, David and his colleague Lindsey Godwin... Cooperrider, D., & Godwin, L. (2015). Elevation-and-change: An eight-step platform for leading POSITIVE change. *AI Practitioner*, *17*(3), 7-14.

As Donald Schön – one of the key contributors to the theory of organizational learning... Schön, D. A. (1979). Generative metaphor: A perspective on problem-setting in social policy. In A. Ortony (Ed.), *Metaphor and Thought* (pp. 137-163). Cambridge, United Kingdom: Cambridge University Press.

New and novel information that is freely generated... Wheatley, M. J. (1992). *Leadership and the new science: Discovering order in a chaotic world.* San-Francisco, CA: Berrett-Koehler.

Stories — the written or verbal accounts that link a set of ideas... Bushe, G. R. (2001). Meaning making in teams: Appreciative inquiry with pre-identity and post-identity groups. In R. Fry, F. Barrett, J. Seiling, & D. Whitney (Eds.), *Appreciative inquiry and organizational transformation: Reports from the field,* (pp 39-63). *Westport, CT: Quorum;* Richley, B., & Cooperrider, D. L. (2013). The generative diffusion of innovation. In D. L. Cooperrider, D. P. Zandee, L. N. Godwin & M. Avital (Eds.), *Organizational generativity: The appreciative inquiry summit and a scholarship of transformation,* (pp. 361-376). Bingley, England: Emerald Group Publishing Limited; Marshak, R. J., Grant, D. S., & Floris. M. (2015). Discourse and dialogic organization development. In G. R. Bushe, & R. J. Marshak (Eds.), *Dialogic organization development: The theory and practice of transformational change,* (pp. 77-100). San Francisco, CA: Berrett-Koehler.

They are at the heart of a human system's identity... Whitney, D. K., & Trosten-Bloom, A. (2003). *The power of appreciative inquiry: A practical guide to positive change.* San Francisco, CA: Berrett-Koehler Publishers.

Thus, creating a positive disruption in a system that will support its ability to flourish... Ludema, J. D. (2002). Appreciative storytelling: A narrative approach to organization development and change. In R. Fry, F. Barrett, J. Seiling, & D. Whitney, (Eds.), *Appreciative inquiry and organizational transformation: Reports from the field, (pp. 239-261). Westport, CT: Quorum;* Barrett, F. J., & Fry, R. E. (2005). *Appreciative inquiry: A positive approach to building cooperative capacity.* Chagrin Falls, OH: Taos Institute Publications; Bushe, G. R. (2011). Appreciative inquiry: Theory and critique. In D. Boje, B. Burnes, & J. Hassard (Eds.), *The Routledge companion to organizational change* (pp. 87-103). Oxford, UK: Routledge.

As noted in Chapter 1, researchers have found that a system learns little... Buckingham, M., & Clifton, D. O. (2001). *Now, discover your strengths. New York, NY: Free Press;* Cameron, K.S, & Lavine, M. (2006). *Making the impossible possible: Leading extraordinary performance: the Rocky Flats story.* Berrett-Koehler Publishers.

Rather than allowing the past to be romanticized... Cooperrider, D., Whitney, D. D., & Stavros, J. M. (2000). *The appreciative inquiry handbook: For leaders of change.* San-Francisco, CA: Berrett-Koehler Publishers.

David and Lindsey describe this experience of discovering the resources... Cooperrider, D., & Godwin, L. (2015). Elevation-and-change: An eight-step platform for leading POSITIVE change. *AI Practitioner, 17*(3), 7-14.

Intended to be a holographic beginning... Ludema, J., Whitney, D., Mohr, B., & Griffin, T.J. (2003). *The appreciative inquiry summit: A practitioner's guide for leading large-group change.* San Francisco, CA: Berrett-Koehler Publishers.

Although researchers have noted that the more people involved in interviewing... Bushe, G. R. (2007). Appreciative inquiry is not (just) about the positive. *OD Practitioner*, 39(4), 33-38.

For example, Hunter Douglas Windows Fashion Division conducted interviews... Whitney, D. K., & Trosten-Bloom, A. (2003). *The power of appreciative inquiry: A practical guide to positive change.* San Francisco, CA: Berrett-Koehler Publishers.

The questions were generally written with a positive preface... Cooperrider, D., Whitney, D. D., & Stavros, J. M. (2000). *The appreciative inquiry handbook: For leaders of change.* San-Francisco, CA: Berrett-Koehler Publishers; Whitney, D. K., & Trosten-Bloom, A. (2003). *The power of appreciative inquiry: A practical guide to positive change.* San Francisco, CA: Berrett-Koehler Publishers.

Researchers suggest that the best generative questions... Bushe, G. R. (2013). Generative process, generative outcome: The transformational potential of appreciative inquiry. In D. L. Cooperrider, D. P. Zandee, L. N. Godwin, & M. Avital (Eds.), *Organizational generativity: The appreciative inquiry summit and a scholarship of transformation*, (pp. 341-360). Bingley, England: Emerald Group Publishing Limited.

It's incredible how quickly they get engaged in talking about something... L. Clarke, personal communication, 15 September, 2013.

This reflection not only helps the system to unite... Ludema, J., Whitney, D., Mohr, B., & Griffin, T.J. (2003). *The appreciative inquiry summit: A practitioner's guide for leading large-group change.* San Francisco, CA: Berrett-Koehler Publishers.

Instead, researchers suggest thinking of it as a journey... Cooperrider, D. L., & Avital, M. (2004). *Constructive discourse and human organization (Vol. 1). Advances in appreciative inquiry.* Oxford: Elsevier Science.

It was an opportunity for shared meaning making, or sense making... Weick, K. E. (1995). *Sensemaking in organizations (Foundations for organizational science).* Thousand Oaks, CA: Sage Publications Inc.

In the earlier chapters, we learned that people have a deep drive to belong... James, W. (1920). *The letters of William James*, Vol. 2, (p. 33). London, UK: Little, Brown Publishing.; Senge, P. M. (1990). *The fifth discipline: The art & practice of the learning organization.* New York, NY: Doubleday; Reis, H. T. (1994). Domains of experience: Investigating relationship processes from three perspectives. In R. Erber, & R. Gilmour (Eds.), *Theoretical frameworks for personal relationships (pp. 87-110). Hilsdale, NJ: Erlbaum*; De Waal, F. (2009). *The age of empathy: Nature's lessons for a kinder society. New York, NY: Crown Archetype*; Lieberman, M. D. (2013). *Social: Why our brains are wired to connect. New York, NY: Crown*.

It is clear from Michelle's research, and it has been argued elsewhere... Bushe, G. R. (2001). Meaning making in teams: Appreciative inquiry with pre-identity and post-identity groups. In R. Fry, F. Barrett, J. Seiling, & D. Whitney (Eds.), *Appreciative inquiry and organizational transformation: Reports from the field, (pp 39-63). Westport, CT: Quorum*; Cooperrider, D. L., & Whitney, D. D. (2001). A positive revolution in change: Appreciative inquiry. *Public Administration and Public Policy, 87*, 611-630.

The sense of vulnerability that arises from these conversations... Bushe, G. R. (2013). Generative process, generative outcome: The transformational potential of appreciative inquiry. In D. L. Cooperrider, D. P. Zandee, L. N. Godwin, & M. Avital (Eds.), *Organizational generativity: The appreciative inquiry summit and a scholarship of transformation*, (pp. 341-360). Bingley, England: Emerald Group Publishing Limited.

Building on the emerging work of neuroscientists... Hasson, U. (2010). I can make your brain look like mine. *Harvard Business Review, 88*(12), 32-33.

Professor Barbara Fredrickson suggests that when people share the kind of heartfelt positive... Fredrickson, B. (2013). *Love 2.0: How our supreme emotion affects everything we feel, think, do, and become. New York, NY: Hudson Street Press*.

Consequently, as people discovered kindred spirits... Holman, P. (2010). *Engaging emergence: Turning upheaval into opportunity. San Francisco, CA: Berrett-Koehler*.

These small, but important, design choices build psychological safety... Edmondson, A. C. (2012). *Teaming: How organizations learn, innovate, and compete in the knowledge economy. New York, NY: John Wiley & Sons*.

Generative stories are powerful because... Richley, B., & Cooperrider, D. L. (2013). The generative diffusion of innovation. In D. L. Cooperrider, D. P. Zandee, L. N. Godwin & M. Avital (Eds.), *Organizational generativity: The appreciative inquiry summit and a scholarship of transformation*, (pp. 361-376). Bingley, England: Emerald Group Publishing Limited.

Researchers suggest that when people listen with sincerity... Holman, P. (2010). *Engaging emergence: Turning upheaval into opportunity. San Francisco, CA: Berrett-Koehler*.

It opens unexpected doors to elevation... Holman, P. (2010). *Engaging emergence: Turning upheaval into opportunity. San Francisco, CA: Berrett-Koehler; DeSteno, D. (2018). Emotional success: The power of gratitude, compassion and pride. New York, NY: Houghton Mifflin Harcourt Publishing.*

Left feeling surprised, stunned, and emotionally moved... Haidt, J. (2000). The positive emotion of elevation. *Prevention & Treatment*, Vol 3(1); Haidt, J. (2003). Elevation and the positive psychology of morality. In Keyes, C. L. M., & Haidt, J. (Eds.), *Flourishing: Positive psychology and the life well-lived*, (pp. 275-289). Washington, DC: American Psychological Association.

Johnathan has found that elevation is a calming... Algoe, S. B., & Haidt, J. (2009). Witnessing excellence in action: The 'other-praising' emotions of elevation, gratitude, and admiration. *The Journal of Positive Psychology*, 4(2), 105-127.

Previously, researchers have proposed that by engaging in appreciative reflections... Cooperrider, D. L., & Sekerka, L. E. (2006). Toward a theory of positive organizational change. In J.V. Gallos (Ed.), *Organization development: A Jossey-Bass reader*, (pp 223-238). San Franscico, CA: Josey Bass.

As we learned in Chapter 3, Barbara's research has found that... Fredrickson, B. L. (2009). *Positivity: Groundbreaking research reveals how to embrace the hidden strength of positive emotions, overcome negativity, and thrive. New York, NY: Random House.*

Studies suggest that it is not simply the presence of positive emotions... Kaufman, S. B. (2015). The emotions that make us more creative. *Harvard Business Review.* Retrieved from: https://hbr.org/2015/08/the-emotions-that-make-us-more-creative

For example, the experiences of positive emotions that occur after... Gable, P. A., & Harmon-Jones, E. (2008). Approach-motivated positive affect reduces breadth of attention. *Psychological Science*, 19(5), 476-482.

Which narrows their cognitive scope so they can focus on... Harmon-Jones, E., Gable, P. A., & Price, T. F. (2013). Does negative affect always narrow and positive affect always broaden the mind? Considering the influence of motivational intensity on cognitive scope. *Current Directions in Psychological Science*, 22(4), 301-307.

Researchers believe that creativity requires both of these states... Kaufman, S. B. (2015). The emotions that make us more creative. *Harvard Business Review.* Retrieved from: https://hbr.org/2015/08/the-emotions-that-make-us-more-creative

In an interesting neurological twist, Scott Barry Kaufman... Kaufman, S. B. (2013). Opening up openness to experience: A four-factor model and relations to creative achievement in the arts and sciences. *The Journal of Creative Behavior*, 47(4), 233-255.

Finally, it is worth remembering that researchers have found that people rarely... Vince, R., & Broussine, M. (1996). Paradox, defense and attachment: Accessing and working with emotions and relations underlying organizational change. *Organization Studies, 17*(1), 1-21; Fong, C. T. (2006). The effects of emotional ambivalence on creativity. *Academy of Management Journal, 49, 1016-1030.*

A growing body of research suggests that the experience of ambivalence... Rothman, N., Pratt, M., Rees, L., & Vogus, T. (2016). Understanding the dual nature of ambivalence: Why and when ambivalence leads to good and bad outcomes. *Academy of Management Annals,* annals-2014.

For example, leading organizational theorist Karl Weick posits... Weick, K. E. (1998). Introductory essay—Improvisation as a mindset for organizational analysis. *Organization Science, 9*(5), 543-555; Weick, K. E. (2004). Vita contemplativa: Mundane poetics: Searching for wisdom in organization studies. *Organization Studies, 25*(4), 653-668.

Researchers have also found that ambivalence... Pratt, M. G., & Doucet, L. (2000). Ambivalent feelings in organizational relationships. In S. Fineman, (Ed.), *Emotion in organizations,* (pp 204-226). Thousand Oaks, CA: Sage Publications.

However, as most of us have experienced emotional ambivalence... Edmondson, A. C. 1999. Psychological safety and learning behavior in work teams. *Administrative Science Quarterly.* 44(2):350-83; Ingram, P., & Roberts, P. W. (2000). Friendships among competitors in the Sydney hotel industry. *American Journal of Sociology, 106*(2), 387-423.

Reaches across the barriers that exist... Pratt, M. G., & Barnett, C. K. (1997). Emotions and unlearning in Amway recruiting techniques: Promoting change through 'safe' ambivalence. *Management Learning, 28*(1), 65-88.

And is autonomy supportive. Bright, D. S., Powley, E. H., Fry, R. E., & Barrett, F. (2013). The generative potential of cynical conversations. In D. L. Cooperrider, D. P. Zandee, L. N. Godwin & M. Avital (Eds.), *Organizational generativity: The Appreciative Inquiry Summit and a scholarship of transformation* (pp. 341 - 360). Bingley, England: Emerald Group Publishing Limited.

As a result, people's experience of mutual appreciation and surprise... Cooperrider, D. L., & Sekerka, L. E. (2006). Toward a theory of positive organizational change. In J. V. Gallos (Ed.), *Organization development: A Jossey-Bass reader,* (pp 223-238). San Franscico, CA: Josey Bass.

It is here, in this synergistic moment of empowering continuity and novelty... Cooperrider, D. L., & Sekerka, L. E. (2006). Toward a theory of positive organizational change. In J. V. Gallos (Ed.), *Organization development: A Jossey-Bass reader*, (pp 223-238). San Franscico, CA: Josey Bass.

In order to enable emergence from a disruption... Holman, P. (2010). *Engaging emergence: Turning upheaval into opportunity. San Francisco, CA: Berrett-Koehler.* **It is an invitation to align and amplify its positive core...** Cooperrider, D., Whitney, D. D., & Stavros, J. M. (2000). *The appreciative inquiry handbook: For leaders of change.* San-Francisco, CA: Berrett-Koehler Publishers.

Researchers suggest that to maximize generativity... Bushe, G. R. (2013). Generative process, generative outcome: The transformational potential of appreciative inquiry. In D. L. Cooperrider, D. P. Zandee, L. N. Godwin, & M. Avital (Eds.), *Organizational generativity: The appreciative inquiry summit and a scholarship of transformation*, (pp. 341-360). Bingley, England: Emerald Group Publishing Limited.

Encouraging people to pay attention to what they truly care... Owen, H. (2008). *Wave rider: Leadership for high performance in a self-organizing world.* San-Francisco, CA: Berrett-Koehler Publishers.

The reality is that the most creative, energized, committed results... Holman, P. (2010). *Engaging emergence: Turning upheaval into opportunity. San Francisco, CA: Berrett-Koehler.*

After all, people excel and learn not because... Senge, P. M. (1990). *The fifth discipline: The art & practice of the learning organization.* New York, NY: Doubleday.

For example, Fred Polak, who launched a sweeping study... Polak, F. (1973). *The image of the Future.* New York, NY: Elsevier.

David and Lindsey suggest that this is because magnetic images... Cooperrider, D. L., & Godwin, L. N. (2011). Positive organization development: Innovation-inspired change in an economy and ecology of strengths. In K.S. Cameron, & G.M. Spreitzer (Eds.), *The Oxford handbook of positive organizational scholarship, (pp. 737 – 750). New York, NY: Oxford University Press.*

Finally, people were encouraged to think like artists... Ludema, J., Whitney, D., Mohr, B., & Griffin, T. J. (2003). *The appreciative inquiry summit: A practitioner's guide for leading large-group change.* San Francisco, CA: Berrett-Koehler Publishers.

The creation of these presentations was typically one of the most fondly... Ludema, J., Whitney, D., Mohr, B., & Griffin, T. J. (2003). *The appreciative inquiry summit: A* *practitioner's guide for leading large-group change.* San Francisco, CA: Berrett-Koehler Publishers.

By the time eight to ten groups had presented... Ludema, J., Whitney, D., Mohr, B., & Griffin, T. J. (2003). *The appreciative inquiry summit: A practitioner's guide for leading large-group change.* San Francisco, CA: Berrett-Koehler Publishers.

The freedom to dream just sets them free... L. Clarke, personal communication, 15 September, 2013.

Peter Drucker – one of the greatest scholars of leadership and management over the last century... Drucker, P. F. (1966). *The effective executive* (1st ed.). New York, NY: HarperBusiness.

David agrees, arguing that the strengths... Cooperrider, D., Whitney, D. D., & Stavros, J. M. (2000). *The appreciative inquiry handbook: For leaders of change.* San-Francisco, CA: Berrett-Koehler Publishers.

While this sounds simple enough, researchers have found that the human brain is wired with a negativity bias... Baumeister, R. F., Bratslavsky, E., Finkenauer, C., & Vohs, K. D. (2001). Bad is stronger than good. *Review of General Psychology, 5*(4), 323.

As a result, David has pointed out that deficit-based thinking... Cooperrider, D. L., & Godwin, L. N. (2011). Positive organization development: Innovation-inspired change in an economy and ecology of strengths. In K.S. Cameron, & G.M. Spreitzer (Eds.), *The Oxford handbook of positive organizational scholarship, (pp. 737 – 750). New York, NY: Oxford University Press.*

In fact, a system cannot excel by simply trying to fix its weaknesses and limiting its failures... Cooperrider, D. L., & McQuaid, M. (2012). The positive arc of systemic strengths: How appreciative inquiry and sustainable designing can bring out the best in human systems. *The Journal of Corporate Citizenship,* (46), 71.

This is why David has repeatedly urged us to see human systems... Cooperrider, D. L., & Srivastva, S. (1987). Appreciative inquiry in organizational life. *Research in Organizational Change and Development, 1*(1), 129-169.

David and Lindsey suggest that in order for a human system to flourish... Cooperrider, D. L., & Godwin, L. N. (2011). Positive organization development: Innovation-inspired change in an economy and ecology of strengths. In K.S. Cameron, & G.M. Spreitzer (Eds.), *The Oxford handbook of positive organizational scholarship, (pp. 737 – 750). New York, NY: Oxford University Press.*

As Clarke brought their dreams to life and the real possibilities... Cooperrider, D. L., & Godwin, L. N. (2011). Positive organization development: Innovation-inspired change in an economy and ecology of strengths. In K.S. Cameron, & G.M. Spreitzer (Eds.), *The Oxford handbook of positive organizational scholarship, (pp. 737 – 750). New York, NY: Oxford University Press.*

There was a real sense of respecting each other's dreams... L. Clarke, personal communication, 15 September, 2013.

Nurtured by the appreciative and caring eyes through which people... Vygotsky, L.S. (1978). *Mind in society: The development of higher psychological processes.* Cambridge, MA: Harvard University Press.

Nurtured by the appreciative and caring eyes... D. Cooperrider, personal communication, 1 June, 2016.

It turned out that only by surrounding themselves... Achor. S. (2018). *Big potential: How transforming the pursuit of success raises our achievement, happiness, and well-being.* New York, NY: The Crown Publishing Group.

David believes that the creation of positive images... Cooperrider, D. L. (1990). Positive image, positive action: The affirmative basis of organizing. *Appreciative Management and Leadership,* 91-125.

Studies suggest that the very idea of having the rewards... Kashdan, T. (2009). *Curious? Discover the missing ingredient to a fulfilling life.* New York, NY: Harper-Collins.

What had changed was people's ability to imagine... Wind, Y., Crook, C., & Gunther, R. (2005). The power of impossible thinking. *SCMS Journal of Indian Management,* 108.

Charles Snyder – one of the world's leading researchers on hope... Snyder, C. R. (Ed.). (2000). *Handbook of hope: Theory, measures, and applications.* San Diego, CA: Academic press.

Powered by people's imagination, it is a life sustaining force... Ludema, J. D. (2001). From Deficit discourse to vocabularies of hope: The power of appreciation. In D. L. Cooperrider, Sorensen, P. F., Yaeger, T. F., & Whitney, D. (Eds.), *Appreciative inquiry: An emerging direction for organization development,* (pp 443-465). Champaign, IL: Stipes Publishing; Lopez, S. J. (2013). *Making hope happen: Create the future you want for yourself and others.* New York, NY: Simon and Schuster.

By hoping, we walk toward a light... Kast. V. (1991). *Joy, inspiration and hope. College Station, TX; Texas A & M University Press.*

Researchers explain that hope is generated and sustained... Ludema, J. D. (2001). From Deficit discourse to vocabularies of hope: The power of appreciation. In D. L. Cooperrider, Sorensen, P. F., Yaeger, T. F., & Whitney, D. (Eds.), *Appreciative inquiry: An emerging direction for organization development,* (pp 443-465). Champaign, IL: Stipes Publishing.

That which Plato calls the good, the true, and the beautiful... Tillich, P. (1957). *Dynamics of faith.* New York, NY: Harper and Row.

Thus, hope prospers when people reach beyond the self... Snyder, C. R. (Ed.). (2000). *Handbook of hope: Theory, measures, and applications.* San Diego, CA: Academic press; Ludema, J. D. (2001). Deficit discourse to vocabularies of hope: The power of appreciation. In D. L. Cooperrider, Sorensen, P. F., Yaeger, T. F., & Whitney, D. (Eds.), *Appreciative inquiry: An emerging direction for organization development,* (pp 443-465). Champaign, IL: Stipes Publishing; Lopez, S. J. (2013). *Making hope happen: Create the future you want for yourself and others.* New York, NY: Simon and Schuster.

Hope has also been found to be an essential ingredient in systemic flourishing... (Kast. V. (1991). *Joy, inspiration and hope. College Station, TX; Texas A & M University Press.*

After all, as influential philosopher Ludwig Wittgenstein once explained... Wittgenstein, L. (1922). *Tractatus logico-philosophicus. London, UK: Kegan Paul.*

Researchers suggest that a meaningful language of hope... Ludema, J. D. (2001). Deficit discourse to vocabularies of hope: The power of appreciation. In D. L. Cooperrider, Sorensen, P. F., Yaeger, T. F., & Whitney, D. (Eds.), *Appreciative inquiry: An emerging direction for organization development,* (pp 443-465). Champaign, IL: Stipes Publishing.

Lyell also noted however, that for some people there was a sense of fear... L. Clarke, personal communication, 15 September, 2013.

Hope researcher Shane Lopez explains that hope walks... Lopez, S. J. (2013). *Making hope happen: Create the future you want for yourself and others.* New York, NY: Simon and Schuster.

Hope is created moment by moment... Lopez, S. J. (2013). *Making hope happen: Create the future you want for yourself and others.* New York, NY: Simon and Schuster.

Linda Robson, who coded more than 52,000 words... Robson, L. (2015). *Language of life-giving connection: The emotional tone of language that fosters flourishing campus Sustainability Programs* (unpublished doctoral dissertation), Case Western University, Ohio.

David calls this the Robson Ratio... Cooperrider, D. L., & Godwin, L. N. (2011). Positive organization development: Innovation-inspired change in an economy and ecology of strengths. In K.S. Cameron, & G.M. Spreitzer (Eds.), *The Oxford handbook of positive organizational scholarship, (pp. 737 – 750). New York, NY: Oxford University Press.*

The possibilities of approaching something not as a problem... J. Reiter, personal communication, 22 December, 2016.

We are built to play and built through play... Brown, T. (2009). *Change by design.* New York, NY: Harper Collins.

Then by embracing a generative design thinking process that is open... Avital, M., & Te'Eni, D. (2009). From generative fit to generative capacity: Exploring an emerging dimension of information systems design and task performance. *Information Systems Journal, 19*(4), 345-367. Bushe, G. R. (2013). Generative process, generative outcome: The transformational potential of appreciative inquiry. In D. L. Cooperrider, D. P. Zandee, L. N. Godwin, & M. Avital (Eds.), *Organizational generativity: The appreciative inquiry summit and a scholarship of transformation, (pp. 341-360).* Bingley, England: Emerald Group Publishing Limited.

Without the use of an exhausting or paralyzing search for consensus... Holman, P. (2010). *Engaging emergence: Turning upheaval into opportunity. Francisco, CA: Berrett-Koehler.*

It is the essence of freedom and safety because it is free... Brown, S. (2009). *Play: How it shapes the brain, opens the imagination and invigorates the soul. New York, NY: Avery Group.*

For example, play theorist, Brian Sutton-Smith has found that lifelong play... Sutton-Smith, B. (1997). *The ambiguity of play.* Cambridge, MA: Harvard University Press.

The opposite of play... is not work... Sutton-Smith, B. (1997). *The Ambiguity of Play.* Cambridge, MA: Harvard University Press.

In recent years the design phase of AI Summits has undergone significant change... Cooperrider, D. (2008). Sustainable innovation. *BizEd, 7*(4), 32-38.

This has been aided by the fact that in an increasingly uncertain... Cooperrider, D. L., & Godwin, L. N. (2011). Positive organization development: Innovation-inspired change in an economy and ecology of strengths. In K.S. Cameron, & G.M. Spreitzer (Eds.), *The Oxford handbook of positive organizational scholarship, (pp. 737 – 750). New York, NY: Oxford University Press.*

Neither too broad, nor too narrow, these questions create a launchpad... IDEO (2015). *The field guide to human-centered design.* Retrieved from: http://www. designkit.org/resources/1

Intended to convey an idea – not to be perfect... IDEO (2015). *The field guide to human-centered design.* Retrieved from: http://www.designkit.org/resources/1

By testing sometimes competing ideas against each other... Brown, T. (2009). *Change by design.* New York, NY: Harper Collins.

Researchers caution however, that inviting people to take responsibility... Holman, P. (2010). *Engaging emergence: Turning upheaval into opportunity. San Francisco, CA: Berrett-Koehler.*

Researchers have found that while people often fear that collaboration... Achor. S. (2018). *Big potential: How transforming the pursuit of success raises our achievement, happiness, and well-Being.* New York, NY: The Crown Publishing Group.

The work may feel harder when diverse teams converge... Rock, D., Grant, H., & Grey, J. (2016). Diverse teams feel less comfortable—and that's why they perform better. *Harvard Business Review, 22.*

As our different perspectives rub against each other... Holman, P. (2010). *Engaging emergence: Turning upheaval into opportunity. San Francisco, CA: Berrett-Koehler.*

Tim's team at IDEO also note that the ability to embrace... IDEO (2015). *The field guide to human-centered design..* Retrieved from: http://www.designkit.org/resources/1

Professor Carol Dweck – one of the world's leading researchers on motivation and performance... Dweck, C. (2006). *Mindset: The new psychology of success. New York, NY: Random House.*

Her studies suggest that as a result people and systems with a fixed mindset... Dweck, C. (2006). *Mindset: The new psychology of success. New York, NY: Random House*; Dweck, C. (2014). Talent: How companies can profit from a" growth mindset". *Harvard Business Review, 92*(11), 7; Dweck, C. (2016a). What having a "growth mindset" actually means. *Harvard Business Review.* Retrieved from: https://hbr.org/2016/01/what-having-a-growth-mindset-actually-means; Dweck, C. (2016b).

How Microsoft uses a growth mindset to develop leaders. *Harvard Business Review.* Retrieved from: https://hbr.org/2016/10/how-microsoft-uses-a-growth-mindset-to-develop-leaders

Peter Senge's widely acclaimed systems thinking book... Senge, P. M. (1990). *The fifth discipline: The art & practice of the learning organization.* New York, NY: Doubleday.

To be clear, this is not about creating the often recommended burning platform ... Kotter, J. P. (1995). Leading Change: Why Transformation Efforts Fail. *Harvard Business Review,* 73 (2), 59-67.

Once people feel called to be of service... Baumeister, R.F. (1991). *Meanings of life. New York, NY: The Guilford Press;* Wrzesniewski, A. (2003). *Finding positive meaning in work. In K. S. Cameron, J. E. Dutton, & R. E. Quinn (Eds.), Positive organizational scholarship: Foundations of a new discipline (pp. 296-308) San Francisco, CA: Berrett-Koehler;* Dobrow, S. R. (2006). *Having a calling: A longitudinal study of young musicians.* Doctoral dissertation, Harvard University, Cambridge, MA; Bunderson, J. S., & Thompson, J. A. (2009). The call of the wild: Zookeepers, callings, and the double-edged sword of deeply meaningful work. *Administrative Science Quarterly, 54, 32-57.*

It is this meaningful beckoning toward activities that are morally... Cooperrider, D. L., & Sekerka, L. E. (2006). Toward a theory of positive organizational change. In J. V. Gallos (Ed.), *Organization development: A Jossey-Bass reader,* (pp 223-238). San Franscico, CA: Josey Bass; Wrzesniewski, A., Dekas, K., & Rosso, B. (2009). Calling. In S. J. Lopez & A. Beauchamp (Eds.), *The encyclopedia of positivePsychology* (pp. 115-118). Oxford, UK: Blackwell Publishing.

In his classic paper, Small wins: Redefining the scale of social problems, Karl Weick suggests... Weick, K. E. (1981). Small wins: Redefining the scale of social problems, *American Psychologist,* 39: 40-49.

Deliberate cultivation of a strategy of small wins infuses situations... Weick, K. E. (1981). Small wins: Redefining the scale of social problems, *American Psychologist,* 39: 40-49.

Harvard Business School researchers Professor Teresa Amabile and Steven Kramer... Amabile, T., & Kramer, S. (2011). *The progress principle: Using small wins to ignite joy, engagement, and creativity at work.* Boston, MA: Harvard Business Press.

They suggest a system can amplify people's ability to make progress... Amabile, T., & Kramer, S. (2011). *The progress principle: Using small wins to ignite joy, engagement, and creativity at work.* Boston, MA: Harvard Business Press.

David and Lindsey explain that the ability to go beyond words... Cooperrider, D. L., & Godwin, L. N. (2011). Positive organization development: Innovation-inspired change in an economy and ecology of strengths. In K. S. Cameron, & G. M. Spreitzer (Eds.), *The Oxford handbook of positive organizational scholarship, (pp. 737-750). New York, NY: Oxford University Press.*

Building on the research of hope theorists, they argue... Snyder, C. R. (Ed.). (2000). *Handbook of hope: Theory, measures, and applications.* San Diego, CA: Academic press; Lopez, S. J. (2013). *Making hope happen: Create the future you want for yourself and others.* New York, NY: Simon and Schuster.

It created great opportunity in terms of unleashing this amazing innovation... J. Reiter, personal communication, 22 December, 2016.

As compassionate coaches of disruption, researchers urge us to embrace... Wheatley, M. J. (1992). *Leadership and the new science: Discovering order in a chaotic world.* San-Francisco, CA: Berrett-Koehler. Holman, P. (2010). *Engaging emergence: Turning upheaval into opportunity. San Francisco, CA: Berrett-Koehler.*

What we discovered, quite honestly, was that momentum for change... Cooperrider, D. L., & Whitney, D. D. (2001). A positive revolution in change: Appreciative inquiry. *Public Administration and Public Policy, 87,* 611-630.

For example, six of the seven transformational cases in the meta-case analysis... Bushe, G. R., & Kassam, A. F. (2005). When is appreciative inquiry transformational? A meta-case analysis. *The Journal of Applied Behavioral Science, 41*(2), 161-181.

While this may sound like a large leap of faith, remember that... Holman, P. (2010). *Engaging emergence: Turning upheaval into opportunity. San Francisco, CA: Berrett-Koehler.*

This order is not created by complex controls, but by the presence of the guiding fields of identity... Pascale, R., Milleman, M., & Gioja, L. (2000). *Surfing the edge of chaos: The new art and science of management.* New York, NY: Crown Business.

Researchers have previously noted that there remains the most confusion... Bushe, G.R. (2012). Foundations of Appreciative Inquiry: History, criticism and potential. *AI Practitioner, 14*(1).

David describes this step as "nitty gritty, hard work"... D. Cooperrider, personal communication, 1 June, 2016.

The reality is that self-organization creates new networks... Wheatley, M. J. (2017). *Who do we choose to be? Facing reality, claiming leadership, restoring sanity.* San-Francisco, CA: Berrett-Koehler.

Professors Richard Ryan and Edward Deci note that perhaps the most common... Ryan, R. M., & Deci, E. L. (2017). *Self-determination theory: Basic psychological needs in motivation, development, and wellness.* New York, NY: Guilford Publications.

Other researchers echo this observation, noting that when people are given room... Holman, P. (2010). *Engaging emergence: Turning upheaval into opportunity.* San Francisco, CA: Berrett-Koehler.

For example, after Hurricane Katrina the community of Ville Platte... Wheatley, M. J. (1992). *Leadership and the new science: Discovering order in a chaotic world.* San-Francisco, CA: Berrett-Koehler.

Effective self-organization in human systems starts with... Owen, H. (2008). *Wave rider: Leadership for high performance in a self-organizing world.* San-Francisco, CA: Berrett-Koehler Publishers.

All of us know how to spontaneously cooperate... Wheatley, M. J. (1992). *Leadership and the new science: Discovering order in a chaotic world.* San-Francisco, CA: Berrett-Koehler.

Professor Adam Grant explains that while people are inherently... Grant, A. (2013). *Give and take: A revolutionary approach to success.* New York NY: Penguin.

As a result, the system and the people in it are more likely to flourish... MacKenzie, S. B., Paine, J. B., & Bachrach, D. G. (2000). Organizational citizenship behaviors: A critical review of the theoretical and empirical literature and suggestions for future research. *Journal of Management, 26, 513-563;* Podsakoff, N. P., Whiting, S. W., Podsakoff, P. M., & Blume, B. D. (2009). Individual- and organizational-level consequences of organizational citizenship behaviors: A meta-analysis. *Journal of Applied Psychology, 94*(1), 122. Grant, A. (2013). *Give and take: A revolutionary approach to success. New York NY: Penguin.*

There's an out-of-control level of caring and collaboration at this point... L. Clarke, personal communication, 15 September, 2013.

For example, a study of more than three hundred organizations... Cross, R., Rebele, R., & Grant, A. (2016). Collaborative overload. *Harvard Business Review, 94*(1), 16.

As a result, Adam and his colleagues caution that although givers... Grant, A., & Rebele, R. (2017). Beat generosity burnout. *Harvard Business Review, January, 2-24.*

By providing people with different opportunities... Bushe, G. R. (2015). Working with emergent change: Applying appreciative inquiry to adaptive challenges. *AI Practitioner, 17*(1), 6-13.

Researchers note that the seeds of most great ideas are misunderstood... Holman, P. (2010). *Engaging emergence: Turning upheaval into opportunity. San Francisco, CA: Berrett-Koehler.*

In a word, it requires what Professor Angela Duckworth – one of the world's leading researchers on self-control... Duckworth, A. (2016). *Grit: The power of passion and perseverance. New York, NY: Simon and Schuster.*

Grit is the passion and perseverance for long-term goals... Duckworth, A. L., Peterson, C., Matthews, M. D., & Kelly, D. R. (2007). Grit: Perseverance and passion for long-term goals. *Journal of Personality and Social Psychology, 92*(6), 1087.

Strongly intertwined with the practices of Carol's growth mindsets... Duckworth, A. (2016). *Grit: The power of passion and perseverance. New York, NY: Simon and Schuster.*

Carol (2017) cautions, however, that grit and growth mindset practices can backfire... Dweck, C. (Guest). (2017). *Does your workplace have a growth mindset* [Audio podcast]. Retrieved from: https://www.michellemcquaid.com/podcast/mppw42-carol-dweck/

Unable to find the pause or stop button to assess the feedback... Miller, C. A. (2017). *Getting grit: The evidence-based approach to cultivating passion, perseverance, and purpose. Boulder, CO: Sounds True.*

In his book *Emotional Success*, Professor David DeSteno... DeSteno, D. (2018). *Emotional success: The power of gratitude, compassion and pride. New York, NY: Houghton Mifflin Harcourt Publishing.*

There was a collective feeling that we had done so much... L. Clarke, personal communication, 15 September, 2013.

Given studies have found that people who habitually experience... DeSteno, D. (2018). *Emotional success: The power of gratitude, compassion and pride. New York, NY: Houghton Mifflin Harcourt Publishing.*

No matter what functional area they were from or what they did... L. Clarke, personal communication, 15 September, 2013.

Human flourishing is enabled by the elusive life-energy... Holman, P. (2010). *Engaging emergence: Turning upheaval into opportunity. San Francisco, CA: Berrett-Koehler.*

Michael Cole and his colleagues have added to our understanding by proposing that within a system, productive energy... Cole, M. S., Bruch, H., & Vogel, B. (2012). Energy at work: A measurement validation and linkage to unit effectiveness. *Journal of Organizational Behavior, 33*(4), 445-467.

They explain that productive energy fluctuates as a result of context, inputs and outcomes... Kozlowski, S. W. J., & Klein, K. J. (2000). A multilevel approach to theory and research in organizations: Contextual, temporal, and emergent processes. In K. J. Klein, & S. W. J. Kozlowski (Eds.), *Multilevel theory, research, and methods in organizations: Foundations, extensions, and new directions* (pp. 3-90). San Francisco, CA: Jossey-Bass; Cameron, K. S., Dutton, J. E., & Quinn, R. E. (2003). Foundations of positive organizational scholarship. In K. Cameron, J. E. Dutton, & R. E. Quinn (Eds.), *Positive organizational scholarship, (pp. 3-13). San Francisco, CA: Berrett-Koehler;* Jansen, K. J. (2004). From persistence to pursuit: A longitudinal examination of momentum during the early stages of strategic change. *Organization Science,* 15, 276-294; Luthans, F., & Avolio, B. J. (2009). The "point" of positive organizational behavior. *Journal of Organizational Behavior, 30, 291-307.*

Other researchers suggest that a mirror energy or contagion effect is created... (Rosenquist, J. N., Fowler, J. H., & Christakis, N. A. (2011). Social network determinants of depression. *Molecular Psychiatry, 16*(3), 273; Levine, J. M., Resnick, L. B., & Higgins, E. T. (1993). Social foundations of cognition. *Annual Review of Psychology, 44*(1), 585-612; Barsade, S. G. (2002). The ripple effect: Emotional contagion and its influence on group behavior. *Administrative Science Quarterly, 47*(4), 644-675; Spreitzer, G., Sutcliffe, K., Dutton, J., Sonenshein, S., & Grant, A. M. (2005). A socially embedded model of thriving at work. *Organization Science, 16*(5), 537-549.

Thus, once the AI Summit event is complete, the goal of the drum phase... Cooperrider, D. L. (2013). The spark, the flame, and the torch: The positive arc of systemic strengths. In D. L. Cooperrider, D. P. Zandee, L. N. Godwin, & M. Avital (Eds.), *Organizational generativity: The appreciative inquiry summit and a scholarship of transformation,* (pp. 211-248). Bingley, England: Emerald Group Publishing Limited.

Appreciative inquiry researchers and practitioners repeatedly caution that once the Summit... Ludema, J., Whitney, D., Mohr, B., & Griffin, T.J. (2003). *The appreciative inquiry summit: A practitioner's guide for leading large-group change.* San Francisco, CA: Berrett-Koehler Publishers; McGuigan, M. & Murphy, C.J. (20130. Ensuring generativity beyond the AI Summit event: A practical guide for designing an AI Summit and advancing post-summit momentum. In D. L. Cooperrider, D. P. Zandee, L. N. Godwin & M. Avital, (Eds.), *Organizational generativity: The appreciative inquiry summit and a scholarship of transformation,* (pp. 311-338). Bingley, England: Emerald Group Publishing Limited.

It's what happened after the Summit that really made the difference... J. Reiter, personal communication, 22 December, 2016.

Michelle's research found that the first daunting task during the drum phase... McGuigan, M, & C. J. Murphy. (2013). Ensuring generativity beyond the AI Summit event: A practical guide for designing an AI Summit and advancing post-summit momentum. In D. L. Cooperrider, D. P. Zandee, L. N. Godwin & M. Avital, (Eds.), *Organizational generativity: The appreciative inquiry summit and a scholarship of transformation*, (pp. 311-338). Bingley, England: Emerald Group Publishing Limited.

The intention is not to develop a project with a beginning, a middle... McGuigan, M, & C. J. Murphy. (2013). Ensuring generativity beyond the AI Summit event: A practical guide for designing an AI Summit and advancing post-summit momentum. In D. L. Cooperrider, D. P. Zandee, L. N. Godwin & M. Avital, (Eds.), *Organizational generativity: The appreciative inquiry summit and a scholarship of transformation*, (pp. 311-338). Bingley, England: Emerald Group Publishing Limited.

Continue to give people ownership of their opportunity areas... L. Clarke, personal communication, 15 September, 2013.

Professor Gervase Bushe urges systems toward an even more generative... Bushe, G. R. (2013). Generative process, generative outcome: The transformational potential of appreciative inquiry. In D. L. Cooperrider, D. P. Zandee, L. N. Godwin, & M. Avital (Eds.), *Organizational generativity: The appreciative inquiry summit and a scholarship of transformation*, (pp. 341-360). Bingley, England: Emerald Group Publishing Limited.

However, researchers caution that the drum phase often runs the risk... McGuigan, M, & C. J. Murphy. (2013). Ensuring generativity beyond the AI Summit event: A practical guide for designing an AI Summit and advancing post-summit momentum. In D. L. Cooperrider, D. P. Zandee, L. N. Godwin & M. Avital, (Eds.), *Organizational generativity: The appreciative inquiry summit and a scholarship of transformation*, (pp. 311-338). Bingley, England: Emerald Group Publishing Limited.

Studies suggest that carefully timed announcements and updates... Jansen, K. J. (2004). From persistence to pursuit: A longitudinal examination of momentum during the early stages of strategic change. *Organization Science, 15*, 276-294.

We made business as usual unusual and made the unusual business as usual... J. Reiter, personal communication, 22 December, 2016.

Feedback loops – the means by which a system talks to itself... Pascale, R., Milleman, M., & Gioja, L. (2000). *Surfing the edge of chaos: The new art and science of management.* New York, NY: Crown Business; Meadows, D. (2008). *Thinking in systems.* White River Junction, VT: Chelsea Green.

The conscious monitoring of feedback loops enables generative thinking... Corrigan, C. (2015). Hosting and holding containers. In G. R. Bushe & R. J. Marshak (Eds.), *Dialogic organization development: The theory and practice of transformational change. San Francisco, CA: Berrett-Koehler.*

As a result, when groups within a system are truly learning... Senge, P. M. (1990). *The fifth discipline: The art & practice of the learning organization.* New York, NY: Doubleday.

Peter reminds us, however, that pure accelerating growth... Pascale, R., Milleman, M., & Gioja, L. (2000). *Surfing the edge of chaos: The new art and science of management.* New York, NY: Crown Business.

Fueling the productive energy to maintain this dance are the diverse feedback loops. Meadows, D. (2008). *Thinking in systems.* White River Junction, VT: Chelsea Green.

We find ourselves articulating questions differently... J. Reiter, personal communication, 22 December, 2016.

This is why researchers note that leadership during this phase... Bushe, G. R. (2015). Working with emergent change: Applying appreciative inquiry to adaptive challenges. *AI Practitioner, 17*(1), 6-13.

As we learned in Chapter 1, the challenge for most social systems... Block, P. (2008). *Community: The structure of belonging.* San Francisco, CA: Berrett-Koehler.

Found to be a fundamental drive of human motivation... Maslow, A. (1968). Some educational implications of the humanistic psychologies. *Harvard Educational Review, 38*(4), 685-696; Bowlby, J. (1973). Self-reliance and some conditions that promote it. In R. Gosling (Eds.), *Support, Innovation, and Autonomy (pp. 23-48). London: Tavistock;* Baumeister, R. F., & Leary, M. R. (1995). The need to belong: Desire for interpersonal attachments as a fundamental human motivation. *Psychological Bulletin,* 117(3), 497-529.

When people feel like they belong, they show up and bring their gifts... Holman, P. (2010). *Engaging emergence: Turning upheaval into opportunity. San Francisco, CA: Berrett-Koehler.*

Coupled with shared purpose, a sense of community keeps the fires... McQueen, N. (2016, August, 16). *Diversity, inclusion and belonging: Measuring how employees experience our culture at LinkedIn.* Retrieved from: https://www.linkedin.com/pulse/diversity-inclusion-belonging-measuring-how-employees-nina-mcqueen/

Studies also suggest a simple, but powerful way, to meet this need... Emmons, R. (2003). Acts of gratitude in organizations. In K. S. Cameron, J. E. Dutton, & R. E. Quinn (Eds.), *Positive organizational scholarship* (pp. 81-93). San Francisco, CA: Berrett-

Koehler; Spreitzer, G.M., & Porath, C. (2012). Creating sustainable performance. *Harvard Business Review,* January-February, 92-99; Cameron, K. S. (2015) Activate virtuousness. In J. E. Dutton, & G. M. Spreitzer (Eds.), *How to be a positive leader: Small actions, big impact. San Francisco, CA: Berrett-Koehler;* Emmons, R. (2017, October 11). *Three surprising ways that gratitude works at work . Retrieved from:* https://greatergood.berkeley.edu/article/item/three_surprising_ways_that_gratitude_works_at_work

Positive psychology researcher and practitioner, Shawn Achor, suggests... Achor. S. (2018). *Big potential: How transforming the pursuit of success raises our achievement, happiness, and well-being.* New York, NY: The Crown Publishing Group.

Professor David DeSteno concurs, explaining that people are grateful... DeSteno, D. (2018). *Emotional success: The power of gratitude, compassion and pride. New York, NY: Houghton Mifflin Harcourt Publishing.*

Professor Teresa Amabile and Steven Kramer have found that ultimately progress is nourished by... Amabile, T., & Kramer, S. (2011). *The progress principle: Using small wins to ignite joy, engagement, and creativity at work.* Boston, MA: Harvard Business Press.

There's respect and a higher level of caring for people. You've created new friendships... L. Clarke, personal communication, 15 September, 2013.

Chapter 6

Before beginning this book we knew from the growing body of evidence... Cooperrider, D. L., & McQuaid, M. (2012). The positive arc of systemic strengths: How appreciative inquiry and sustainable designing can bring out the best in human systems. *The Journal of Corporate Citizenship,* (46), 71.

About The Authors

About Michelle McQuaid

Michelle McQuaid is a best-selling author, workplace wellbeing teacher and playful change activator. With more than a decade of senior leadership experience in large organizations around the world, she's passionate about translating cutting-edge research from positive psychology and neuroscience, into practical strategies for health, happiness, and business success.

An honorary fellow at Melbourne University's Graduate School of Education, she blogs for Psychology Today, Huffington Post and Live Happy and her work has been featured in Forbes, the Harvard Business Review, the Wall Street Journal, Boss Magazine, The Age and more.

She holds a Masters in Applied Positive Psychology from the University of Pennsylvania and is currently completing her PhD in Appreciative Inquiry under the supervision of David Cooperrider.

Michelle lives to help people discover their strengths, move beyond their fears, and finally discover what it truly takes to flourish with confidence. You can find more of Michelle's work at www.michellemcquaid.com.

About David Cooperrider

David is the Chair and Chuck Fowler Professor of Business as an Agent of World Benefit and the Fairmount Santrol David L. Cooperrider Professor of Appreciative Inquiry at the Weatherhead School of Management, Case Western Reserve University. David is also the Faculty Director of the Fowler Center for Business as an Agent of World Benefit. Cooperrider is best known for his pioneering theory on Appreciative Inquiry and has served as adviser to senior executives in business and societal leadership roles, including projects with five Presidents and Nobel Laureates such as William Jefferson Clinton, His Holiness the Dalai Lama, and Kofi Annan.

David has brought appreciative inquiry to a wide variety of organizations including Apple, Verizon, Johnson & Johnson, National Grid, Fairmount Minerals, Keurig Green Mountain Coffee, and Walmart as well as the UN Global Compact, Cleveland Clinic, and the US Navy.

David has published over 20 books and authored over 100 articles and book chapters. He has served as editor of the *Journal of Corporate Citizenship* with Ron Fry and the current research series for *Advances in Appreciative Inquiry* with Michel Avital. David's books include Appreciative Inquiry: A Positive Revolution in Change (with Diana Whitney), The Organization Dimensions of Global Change (with Jane Dutton), Organizational Courage and Executive Wisdom (with Suresh Srivastva), and the four-volume research series Advances in Appreciative Inquiry.

David was named Visionary of the Year by Training magazine and was awarded the Peter F. Drucker Distinguished Fellow by the Drucker School of Management, a designation recognizing his contribution to management thought. Most recently, Champlain College's Stiller School of Business honored David with an academic center in his name. It is called the David L. Cooperrider for Appreciative Inquiry. For the center's dedication ceremony, Marty Seligman wrote: "David Cooperrider is a giant: a giant of discovery, a giant of dissemination, and a giant of generosity" and Harvard's Jane Nelson at the Kennedy School of Leadership said: "David Cooperrider is one of the outstanding scholar-practitioners of our generation."